Myths & Hitches

3

MISCONCEPTIONS, FALLACIES

& FALSE BELIEFS

about

Icons & Symbols
Institutions
Beliefs & Traditions
Sports & Diversions
Pop Images

Don M. Ferry

DEDICATION

To my wife Olivia, our children Gia, Rica and Dondi, our sons-in-law Bill and Manley, and all our grandchildren, and to those friends and associates who have supported us in this endeavor.

ACKNOWLEDGMENT

The author is highly indebted to his wife Olivia for editing the greater portion of this work, and to his son Dondi for his contributions to the cover design of the book.

TABLE OF CONTENTS

PREFACE

This is the third volume in the series entitled *Myths & Hitches*, a comprehensive collection of misconceptions and fallacies culled from popular lore. Arrayed in its pages are more than 300 items of information in several genres, from *icons and symbols* to *institutions* to *beliefs and traditions*, and from *sports and diversions* to *pop images*. What they convey may seem ordinary, but only in the sense that most everything in this world is ordinary. In fact, they are a cut above common trivia, owing to a feature that makes them uniquely engaging: each is a pseudo-fact, a lie dressed up as a truth (or vice versa), a belief that's flawed to the gills. People love trivia because they entertain, and trivia debunked can do no less—like a pratfall, which signifies nothing except that it's amusing. A pratfall deflates the pompousness of human behavior, while a fallacy exposed deflates the pomposity of human knowledge.

Many profess to debunk for a higher purpose: to enhance education and promote general literacy by eliminating errors and fallacies from the vast reservoir of popular information. It's an ideal, of course, but in raising the bar, it turns what should be a fun-filled exercise into something truly demanding and, at times, hardly feasible. Very often, the lie to be excised may have already become entrenched as myth, a myth even more wholesome and beguiling than the truth. Should it matter were we to learn, for instance, that the Egyptian sphinxes had been sitting on the desert sands thousands of years before the pharaohs even thought of building the first pyramid? Would our long-held image of American Indians in the Old West change for better or for worse if we were told that they never said "how" to mean "hello," or added "um" to every English verb they spoke, or used smoke signals the way their people are using email today? What if we could actually deduce from the Bible that Seth is the common ancestor of man in the second generation, that there were thousands of people inhabiting the earth at the time of Cain and Abel, and that the ancient Israelites were dark-skinned and shorthaired? And—here comes the apple pun once more—would the apple look or feel any different if we suddenly realized it might not be the forbidden fruit from that certain mysterious tree in the garden of Eden?

We share in the ideal, too, but only where, by exposing the

untruth, we are able to ferret out the corresponding truth. When we fail, as we often do, we can only take comfort in Von Goethe's words: "It is easier to perceive error than to find truth, for the former lies on the surface and is easily seen, while the latter lies in the depth, where few are willing to search for it." Sadly, even the few who do decide to search 'in the depth' find out soon enough that truth has many faces, that "what is true by lamplight is not always true by sunlight." For truth may vary as to place: the ancient Roman writer Suetonius often failed to agree with his Greek counterpart Plutarch on significant details, making the study of Greco-Roman history thoroughly confusing to one who is not a pupil of either. Truth may also vary as to time, a phenomenon that that archetype of reference books, the Encyclopedia Britannica, makes evident whenever it launches a new edition to update or revise an earlier one. In a sense, the 'untruths' presented in this book are just versions of the truth, which means that, unless we are sure of our grounds, we should not impose the ideal by banishing them from popular lore as falsehoods.

Still, while we aim primarily to entertain, we hope to leave the message that the inability or difficulty of finding the truth is no license to falsify it. Information, essential or not, deserves to be reported accurately or not at all, and the historian, journalist, screenwriter, artist and blogger who care enough for what they do must keep that trust. The way information is handled in a society impacts ultimately on that society's respect for truth as a value on which all other values must rest.

Don M. Ferry

N.B.: The above has been lifted essentially from the preface of a similarly themed book, *Untruths and Nothing But* (Infinity Publishing, 2009), by the author. The contents of that book have been greatly expanded, reorganized and carried over into this volume of *Myths & Hitches* as well as into three other volumes of the series (*Myths & Hitches 1, 2* and *4),* all available in eBook format. Please refer to the end of each volume for a detailed list of the topics covered. —DMF

Icons
&
Symbols

I

Wheeling And Dealing

On the Wheel

"Perfect numbers like perfect men are very rare."

•

Rene Descartes

1. Where There's a Wheel

Myth! **The wheelbarrow was Blaise Pascal's brainchild, the roulette was Rene Descartes'.**

The French seem to have a way with wheels, and we don't just mean Michelin. According to an oft-repeated story, source unknown, the French classical genius Blaise Pascal invented two of the most popular wheel-based devices in use today—the simple wheelbarrow and the more complex roulette. Historians deny Pascal the honor for the wheelbarrow, tracing the contraption to China, where the earliest depictions of the single-wheel type can be seen in 2nd century Han Dynasty tomb murals and brick tomb relief. Why Pascal, a multi-faceted physicist, mathematician and philosopher in the Age of Reason, would even dream of making the lowly wheelbarrow is beyond understanding. Perhaps, as one Internet source says (hopefully with tongue in cheek), "Pascal was disturbed by what he felt to be the emptiness, the silence and immensity of the universe, and it would have been nice if he could have invented the wheelbarrow as a kind of antidote to emptiness. A wheelbarrow is (such antidote); it contains things. It pierces the immense silence with a hoarse creaking of its wheels."

Pascal worked on conic sections and with Fermat laid the foundation for the theory of probability. In his less intense moments, he invented numerous wheeled objects, like the digital calculator, the wristwatch and the hydraulic wheel—all these before dying at the young age of 39. Not surprisingly, Pascal is also tagged as the creator of the roulette. One admirer claims the roulette wheel came about as a byproduct in the Frenchman's attempts to create a perpetual motion machine. The more sedate Britannica slams this effort as well as the claim that the roulette was invented by the ubiquitous Chinese, from whom Dominican monks supposedly transmitted it to France. "In reality," says the Britannica, "roulette was derived in France in the early 18th century from the older games *hoca* and *portique*, and it is first mentioned under its current name in 1716 in Bordeaux. Following several modifications, roulette achieved its present layout and wheel structure about 1790, after which it rapidly gained status as the leading game in the casinos and gambling houses of Europe."

9

Francophiles insist that if it wasn't Pascal who invented the roulette, then it must have been Rene Descartes, another French icon of science and philosophy, who died in 1650 at the age of 54. They say a precursor of the contraption called the Descartes/Poisson Machine was constructed "after a discussion between Rene Descartes and another Frenchman, Poisson." Descartes had written in his letters about using the roulette to illustrate his so-called 'target' theory, but whatever this means, the Britannica makes no mention of it in its entry on the mathematician-philosopher. On the contrary, the encyclopedia suggests in a separate section on the device that Descartes had already been dead for some decades before the game came on its own. The Descartes/Poisson Machine, if it truly existed, was probably a crude set-up, not unlike a primitive roulette, which Descartes used to test his geometric and probability theories.

The Frenchmen who rightfully deserve the gratitude of the casinos of Las Vegas and Monte Carlo are François and Louis Blanc, who in 1842 added the "0" to the roulette wheel in order to create a house advantage. A legend that has attached to François Blanc—that he bargained with the devil to obtain the secrets of the device—is based on the coincidence that the sum of all the numbers on the roulette wheel (from 1 to 36) is 666, the 'Number of the Beast'

2. Have Wheels, can't Travel

Myth! The wheel was a requisite tool of ancient civilizations.

The Sumerians simply can't hold a torch to the Mesoamericans, whose accomplishments during their prime were almost beyond belief. The Aztecs had the Great Pyramid of Tenochtitlan, not to mention the urban wonder that is now Mexico City, while the Incas must have had a superbly efficient system of transportation and communication to be able to hold sway over the largest empire in pre-Columbian America. The Mayans, those unwitting subjects of Mel Gibson's controversial and violent film epic, were not just praying to their great god Quetzalcoatl for salvation from the Apocalypto, they were busy devising the only fully developed written language in the Americas and a calendar of remarkable accuracy and complexity to boot.

The pre-Columbian civilizations of North and South America had all sorts of tools, including those for whole cities. But as sophisticated as they were, they lacked the most essential tool to catapult them to a higher state of development—the wheel. The Incas, for one, were obviously aware of the principle of rotary movement—no doubt from seeing all those heads roll down the stone steps of their sacrificial biers. But it never occurred to them to attach wooden wheels to sleds and crates as a facile means of transportation. According to historians, these ancient Mexicans were familiar with the wheel—so familiar, in fact, that they seem to have invented their version independently of the Sumerians. Unfortunately, their use of it was confined to little clay gadgets that appear to be either toys or cult objects. More than 70 terracotta wheeled figures have been found in Mesoamerica, the earliest dating to c. 100 BC, many of them in burial sites of both adults and children.

3. The Cart before the Horse

Myth! **The Mesoamericans lacked a system of transportation because they knew nothing about the wheel.**

If you think a people's inability to apply the wheel to the cause of productivity is a sure sign of backwardness or cultural inferiority, that's not what we're telling you. The apparent ineptitude of the Mesoamericans did not stem from ignorance of the wheel but from lack of an important auxiliary resource—draft animals. Without horses and domesticated cattle, Indians could not do anything with wheeled carts even if they had them. The only beast of burden then prevalent in the Americas was the llama, and this was restricted to certain parts of the Andes. Moreover, the llama was better suited as a pack animal in rugged terrain than as a puller of wheels. When the Incas had to transport heavy objects, they fell back on a combination of manpower and wheel power—men pulling or pushing sledges that moved on logs functioning as rollers. These methods of transportation served the natives well until they encountered the colonizing Europeans, who brought their own beasts of burden and proved that wheels offered all sorts of advantages.

4. Walking for a Camel

Myth! Civilized as they were, the Arabs were almost totally unaware of the wheel until the second millennium.

Like the Mesoamerican (but also unlike it in some respects), another great civilization hundreds of years earlier went without the wheel for a considerable time and yet survived and even prospered. Which just about breaks the wheel as a vaunted civilizer of peoples!

After its invention in Mesopotamia, the wheel as a mode of transportation was put to intensive use for centuries throughout Asia, Europe and the Mediterranean area. Almost without notice, it disappeared from Persia and the Arab world sometime between AD 200 and 700, and wasn't seen again until the eighteenth century. The reason, historians say, is oddly the opposite of what gave rise to the same situation in the Americas—there were enough draft animals, mostly camels, but no wheeled vehicles to pull. Actually, when there had been such vehicles, the nomads began to gain a monopoly on camels, using them exclusively as pack animals. Camel caravans that carried rather than pulled carts exploited long-distance trading routes. A saddle useful in combat was invented to give the camel a military advantage as a carrier. Eventually, even urban Arabs learned to rely on unhitched camels for transportation within their cities. The camel-breeding nomads encouraged this trend because it increased the market for their livestock. This, plus the relative scarcity of wood in desert countries, accelerated the move away from wheeled vehicles.

The foregoing, notes a commentator (with tongue in cheek), could have been the reason for the untimely death of Lawrence of Arabia, who was invincible on a camel but utterly vulnerable on wheels.

5. Spin Story

Myth! **The wheel was a natural for transportation.**

To most people, the wheel was destined by nature for transportation, and all other uses are mere spin-offs from that original design. The wheel's own history debunks this misconception. Some relics, like vases and paintings showing Mesopotamian chariots in 3200 BC and Egyptian chariots around 2000 BC, would suggest that the first extensive use of the wheel was in transportation. But others, such as diagrams on ancient clay tablets and fragments, indicate that the earliest known use was in pottery. Though it is not known precisely when the potter's wheel came about, there is evidence of its early development in Mesopotamia, or alternatively in Egypt or China. A stone potter's wheel found at the Mesopotamian city of Ur in modern-day Iraq has been dated to at least 3200 BC, about the same time that wheeled vehicles began to be used there. Antiquities discovered during the mid-1960s established an even older source, the Kura-Araxes culture, in the region between the Black and Caspian seas of the USSR. By the time of the early Stone Age civilizations the availability of the potter's wheel had become widespread.

In the modern age, the wheel is vaunted to be the single most important component of transportation, but that is not true either. By itself, the wheel can function adequately as a potter's tool; it is a different picture altogether in transportation, where much of the work is done not by the wheel but by the axle and where most of the credit for making the wheel assembly go belong to the latter. Man, it is said, knew the wheel long before he learned how to use it for his benefit. He had already been on earth for centuries when necessity caused him to apply the strange circular shape to the task of moving heavy loads over long distances. But he could not have done it without the axle, which is the crossbar, shaft or spindle supporting the vehicle or other mechanism, and by which the wheel or wheels turn. As one writer puts it: "Enshrined in popular mythology are the forever-to-be-anonymous geniuses who first gave their fellow humanoids the wheel and fire. But the wheel could scarcely have been invented; round shapes are common enough in nature. It was the axle that made the wheel useful." Which is just a way of saying that the wheel was discovered whereas the axle that enabled its use was invented.

Incidentally, the ancient Egyptians were among the last of the early civilizations in the Near East to devote the wheel to transportation. And when they did, it was for transportation on water rather than land. They invented the waterwheel apparently for two reasons: first, transportation on the Nile was cheaper and more convenient, and second, wheeled transport was not adaptable because of the deep mud along the banks of the Nile.

II

Pyramid Schemes

On the Ancient Pyramids

"It was a sight surpassing all precedent,
and one we never dreamed of seeing."

•

Howard Carter

1. Battle of the Pyramids

Myth! **The Great Pyramid is the largest man-made structure in the world.**

Giza's monument to ancient greatness (or extravagance, if you want) does seem to be the biggest there is, if you're not looking at it sideways but upwards. Viewed through panoramic lenses, however, the largest structure ever built by man is the Great Wall of China, which has enough stone to build thirty Great Pyramids. Only recently, China's pride was voted one of the 'New Seven Wonders of the World' in a controversial poll competition that the Swiss-based New7Wonders Foundation held worldwide. Chichén Itzá, the famous Mayan temple city in Mexico that features a pyramid much smaller than Giza's, also made it to the 'New Seven' list, proving that size was farthest from the minds of the almost one hundred millions who were polled. Egypt's monolith at Giza, sometimes called the pyramid of Cheops, was deemed in the running until it was taken out for being already one of the original Seven Wonders of the Ancient World, in fact the only one that has remained standing to the present day.

Cheops', of course, is not even the largest pyramid in the world, although it has merited space in Guinness as the tallest at 481 feet. The second crowd pleaser at Giza, the pyramid of Khafre, looks taller at 471 feet only because it stands on higher ground. No pyramid on earth is bigger than the Quetzalcoatl at Cholula de Rivadabia 63 miles southeast of Mexico City; though a mere 177 feet tall, it has a 45-acre base compared to Cheop's 13.1, surpassing the latter in volume by a little under a million cubic yards. Another Mexican pyramid, Teotihuacan, or the Pyramid of the Sun, looks 210 feet up from a base that is 2,000 feet wider around the girth than the Great Pyramid.

The pre-Columbian pyramids of Mexico, which archaeologists say were constructed for the Aztec and Toltec gods between the sixth and second centuries BC, are generally larger than those of Egypt and just as impressive. But they have not received the same kind of respect or attention, for a number of reasons. First, they are stepped or layered in shape, and hence are not true pyramids. Second, because they are made of adobe, earth and rubble, they cannot match the precision of the stones that went into the construction of their Egyptian counterparts. Finally, having been designed simply as a base for temples of worship, they lack the mystery, treasures and popular appeal of the fabulous pharaonic monuments. Nevertheless, the step pyramid would probably have evolved into a true pyramid in Mexico as it did in Egypt had not the Spanish ventured into North American territory during that period.

2. Shape of Things Past

Myth! The shape of the pyramid is scientifically relevant.

One school of thought holds that the pyramid shape has a mathematical significance that relates to certain measurements of the earth. Another maintains that it is designed to obtain astronomical information or serve as a chronological guide to the principal events of past and future history. A third believes that the shape "concentrates the mystic powers of the universe, and it was this cosmic force that preserved the mummies" (and presumably also sharpens razor blades overnight).

These views are traceable mostly to the theory originating in 1859 that the pyramid shape is the product of the ancient Egyptians' profound mathematical knowledge of the universe. Often cited, for example, is the height of the pyramid in inches, which, when multiplied by one billion, equals the distance between the earth and the sun. Or the volume of the pyramid in cubic pyramid inches, which is supposed to give an idea of how many people have lived on the earth since Creation. Similar beliefs are sometimes expressed about Stonehenge, Mayan and Inca temples, the stones at Carnac, and almost any structure with pretensions to antiquity. However, sober-minded scientists shrug off these conclusions as crackpot efforts that do no more than justify Winifred Needler's observation that 'a formula constructed with sufficient complexity may fit a given phenomenon and yet prove nothing' (*Popular Archaeology*, October 1972). It has been argued, and rightly so, that if any of the pseudo-scientific reasons advanced were true, the pyramid shape would have been featured everywhere in the culture of the ancient Egyptians.

Archaeologist Richard Lepsius opines that the real reason for the pyramid shape is more practical than is generally believed. A pharaoh built his pyramid starting on a small scale so that it could be finished quickly. If the gods granted him a longer life, he continued gradually to enlarge the edifice by adding layers. If he died before the work was finished, it was then given its final form. The resulting dimensions indicated thus the measure of the pharaoh's reign. Sir Flinders Petrie takes exception to this view, however, noting that the pyramid of Pepi II, a pharaoh for 94 years, is smaller than that of Mykerinos, who reigned for only 18 years.

It seems the only agreement so far is on a religious explanation, which holds that the pyramid shape was a dual symbol. It signified, first, the staircase that the pharaoh needed to climb after his death to reunite with the Sun God, and, second, the sun's rays as they shone down over his tomb.

---

3. Old, Cold and Balled

Myth! Cheops' pyramid is the oldest of its kind on earth.

The Great Pyramid of Cheops, built between the 26th and the 25th century BC, is not the oldest pyramid in the world. The structure we call a pyramid evolved through several forms before finally assuming the one now seen at Giza.

The first royal tomb or mausoleum of the pharaohs, called the *mastaba*, was rectangular, not pyramidal, but it anticipated the base of the pyramid. Next came the step pyramid, which first appeared in the period of the third dynasty with the tomb built for the Pharaoh Zoser (or Djoser) at Saqqâra facing Memphis on the other bank of the Nile. This monument is generally regarded by antiquarians as the oldest pyramid, and its architect, Imhotep, as the inventor of the pyramid-shaped building. However, it was less than a true pyramid because its sides were not smooth. The first true pyramid emerged when the structure at Meidum, originally a step pyramid, was covered with a uniform slope from base to top by filling in the steps. The earliest known to have been designed and executed throughout as a true pyramid is the North Stone Pyramid at Dahshur, which was completed at about the time the

Giza group began building in the 4th dynasty.

Incidentally, the ziggurat marking the center of the city of Ur in Mesopotamia is also considered a pyramid, and is believed to be as old as, if not older than, Cheops. Also, while the Great Pyramid is the oldest existing stone-built structure in Egypt, the oldest such structure in the world is one of the megalithic chamber tombs of Western Europe predating the oldest pyramid by several hundred years.

4. Mister Sandman

Myth! **The Egyptian pyramids were used as burial places for the pharaohs.**

Most archaeologists agree that the pyramids served primarily as burial sites for the royal houses of Egypt. This is evident from the dozens of such structures sheltering the mummified remains of Egyptian VIPs and their animals.

Oddly, the greatest of them all, Cheops' pyramid at Giza, does not contain any corpse despite the presence of carefully designed and secured burial chambers deep within its brooding frame. Another six of Egypt's outstanding pyramids have so far not yielded any deceased royalty.

Egyptologists say there was a very practical reason for this apparent anomaly. Egyptians were deeply religious and believed the body must be preserved, along with its treasures, in order to enjoy a second life. But because of the constant threat of grave robbers in search of treasure, some of the Pharaohs decided the pyramids should only be 'decoys' and they themselves should be secretly buried at an inconspicuous site in the desert. In many cases, these robbers were still able to gain access and rob the vaults despite the precautions.

The Arabs who first entered Cheops' supposed tomb in the ninth century found no body or tools, only a box of red granite. This raised the question whether marauders had been able to penetrate the chambers earlier. However, the fact that the entrance was found plugged with a piece of granite larger than the corridor led to the conclusion that the spot had not been defiled and that Cheops simply opted to be buried elsewhere.

5. Time Sentinel

Myth! **The guardian sphinxes were built soon after the Great Pyramid was completed**

Conventional wisdom dictates that the pyramid was already completed when the decision to build a guardian sphinx beside it came as an afterthought. Until recently, Egyptologists have confidently dated the sphinx to 2500 BC, circa the time its equally famous desert companion, the pyramid of Khafre, was being built. The sphinx sat in the Valley of the Kings beside a building that was connected to Khafre's pyramid by a causeway. Its disposition was such that there was probably another sphinx on the other side of the building, and this was destroyed over time. It was apparent that Pharaoh Khafre (or Chephren) commissioned all these structures shortly after the pyramid of his own brother Cheops had been completed.

Contrary to these findings, however, recent lab tests indicate that the sphinx is much older, in fact thousands of years older, than any of the structures at Giza. Most of what it is today was built in 5000 BC, and only certain parts, such as the head, were added while Khafre's pyramid was forming. Experts believe the body of the statue was originally the Egyptian god Harmakis, symbol of the life-giving sun. When the head, a likeness of Khafre, was superimposed, the result was a half-man half-lion configuration 66 feet high and 240 feet long. As the oldest of all the sphinxes built in ancient Egypt, it precedes the concept of the man-eating monster of Greek mythology by at least a millennium.

6. Forever Amber?

Myth! **The Great Pyramid has maintained its brown color over the centuries.**

The Great Pyramid is an earth brown structure rising 450 feet above its leveled bedrock. It has been so since its beginning. Or so we are told.

When it was first built, it was actually a gleaming white structure, its faces dressed with about 115,000 smooth limestone slabs long since lost or stolen. The limestone were taken from the quarries of Tura, while the granite for the temples in the complex, the doors of the pyramid, and certain interior details came from Aswan in the Nile valley. The quarried stones were placed on sledges and brought to Giza in flat-bottomed boats or barges, then dragged to the place of work, the total distance sometimes covering 500 miles.

Cheops is now truncated in shape, whereas originally it had a summit consisting of a small square platform on which rested the final block, known as the *pyramidion*. Cut into the shape of a tiny pyramid, the *pyramidion* not only formed the architectural crown of the work but also represented the *benben*, the sacred stone of the temples of Heliopolis. This magnificent apex, which disappeared long ago, was covered with gold leaf, symbolizing even more strongly the brightness of the Sun God.

7. A Belabored Point

Myth! Slave labor was used extensively in the building of the pyramids.

The wide screen shows teeming hordes of half-naked slaves prodded by whips to move huge stone blocks under the blazing sun. This is Cecil B. De Mille's cinematic vision of how the greatest of ancient engineering marvels, the Egyptian pyramids, were built.

De Mille's vision is spectacular, as it has always been, but it's not consistent with the historical scenario laid out by scientific researchers. According to the latter, paid workers, not slaves, built the pyramids. These were mostly farmers working a second job for food and clothing during the rainy months when farming was not possible. And there were not as many of them as originally thought. Herodotus greatly exaggerated when he wrote 2,000 years after the fact that 100,000 men labored on the pyramid, with fresh crews thrown into the project every three months. British archaeologists estimated that, in order to handle over a period of 20 years about 2,300,000 stones weighing on the average 2 1/2 tons, a gang of eight men would only have to move ten blocks every twelve weeks.

Social historians also err in claiming that the pharaohs, particularly Cheops, were arrogant and heartless kings who abused the peons and made them toil under forced and inhuman conditions. Egyptian iconography includes no scenes showing savage treatment of workers. An inscription from the time of Sesostris III, eight centuries after the building of the pyramids, revealed just the contrary. The laborers worked freely and conscientiously in the belief they were performing an act of faith by building not just a tomb but also a temple for their King-god.

III

Japanned In Usa

On Things Asian

"Don't be afraid to make a mistake.
But make sure you don't make the same mistake twice."

•

Akio Morita

1. Lacquered up and Ready to Go

Myth! **Some postwar export products branded 'Made in USA' actually came from a Japanese city named Usa.**

It had once been rumored that the Japanese renamed an industrial city 'Usa' just after World War II so that its products could be exported with the imprint 'Made in USA'. Later, Usa was revealed to be a legitimate Japanese name given long before World War II to a place that had neither the size nor the shape of an industrial city. Uncle John of *Bathroom Reader* fame tells us Usa is small enough that it doesn't appear on all maps, and some of the Usas that do appear are in Russia, Mozambique and Tanzania. Goods from any of the Usas cannot get into the US with a 'Made in USA' label because US Customs requires all imported stuff to bear the name of their country of origin and not the name of the city or region in which they were made.

2. Low-breed Hybrid

Myth! **The rickshaw was a Chinese creation.**

The movies, particularly the classics that have a Chinese setting, are largely to blame for the fallacy that the rickshaw is a traditional Oriental method of transportation invented by the Chinese. Although it debuted in Japan as the *jinrikisha* around 1870, this human-powered, two-wheeled carriage is not a brainchild of the Orient, but was invented earlier in 1869 by an American Baptist missionary named at times as W. Gobel or Goble and at other times as Jonathan Scobie. While living in Yokohama, Gobel/Scobie needed a means of transport for his invalid wife, so he devised a hand-drawn passenger cart based on the 18th century French *brouette*, a sedan chair with wheels. When the contraption became an immediate success, Gobel/Scobie built many more to provide employment for his Christian converts. The rickshaws have faded with the modernization of Asia in the latter half of the 20th century, and one won't see them anymore except perhaps in the less developed urban areas of Vietnam and Cambodia and as tourist rides elsewhere.

3. Chopsticks in four Hands

Myth! **Chopsticks, named after sticks used to pick up chopped food, were fashioned by a legendary Chinese boy who could not eat as fast as his brothers.**

Several fallacies attend these small even-length tapered eating utensils that we call chopsticks. First is the origin of the word, which on first impression combines 'sticks', from their appearance, and chops', for their use in conveying food to the mouth (chops) or for cutting or shredding (chopping) food into small pieces. Actually, 'chopsticks' is the phonetic equivalent in English of the Chinese word *kwai-tze*, meaning 'quick ones'. It is believed the phrase arose from the legend of Keai (Quick), the youngest of three boys, who, when "all Chinese people ate with their hands…was never fast enough to grab some nourishment before his brothers. In desperation born of hunger, he pulled two sticks from the kindling pile and used them to spear chunks of hot food. His family members immediately copied the tools and named them Keai zi (quick ones) after him." However, according to recent findings, while the story has some basis in Chinese tradition, its documentary source is a Chinese American cookbook of ultramodern vintage. Historically, chopsticks date to as far back as 5,000 years ago in China, when people cooked their food in large pots that retained heat well, and hasty eaters then broke twigs off trees to retrieve the food.

Another fallacy is the belief that, because of their origin, chopsticks are used extensively in all countries that have a strong Chinese influence. Chopsticks are indeed the traditional eating utensils of China, Japan, Korea and Vietnam, but surprisingly, you won't see chopsticks in Thai restaurants unless you ask for them. The preferred eating implements particularly in Bangkok and its sister cities are spoon and fork, and chopsticks have been restricted to just soup and noodles since the introduction of Western utensils by King Rama V in the 19th century.

Finally, if most Westerners believe chopsticks are an inferior way to eat food, it's entirely different in the Eastern hemisphere. As one writer notes, "Orientals used to eat with metal utensils, specifically the knife. Chopsticks, in their way of thinking, elevated man to a more civilized plane. One of the scourges of old age in the Orient is being forced by infirmity to eat with a fork or spoon."

Just as they use karate and taekwondo differently, the Chinese and the Koreans have their unique ways of applying chopsticks at the dinner table. The Chinese raise the rice bowl and with the chopsticks push rice directly into the mouth. Koreans consider it rude to pick the rice bowl off the table and eat from it. Unlike other chopstick cultures, Koreans use a spoon (similar to the Western kind) for their rice and soup, and chopsticks for most other foodstuff. In China and in most of East Asia, rice is often prepared to be sticky, as this is conducive to eating with chopsticks, while rice cooked according to Western methods tend to be fluffy and is particularly difficult to eat with chopsticks.

---

4. Does Karate Rate as Art?

Myth! **Karate originated in Japan.**

Contrary to what the 1984 film *The Karate Kid* and its sequels may imply, karate is not one of the martial arts that have their roots in Japan. And neither did it catch on with the public the first time it was demonstrated there. Karate is believed to have had its primitive beginnings in India, from where, according to legend, the Indian monk Bodhidharma brought it to China in the sixth century. More than a millennium later, in the 17th century, we see it developing into an art as a weaponless form of defense in the once-independent island of Okinawa. Ironically, it had been adapted for use against the Japanese themselves after their administrators of the tributary state prohibited the population from bearing arms.

However karate might have began in Okinawa, what is certain is that Okinawan exchange students coming back from China brought over strong influences in style from that country. From

Okinawa, the art was introduced in Japan at the start of the 20th century mainly through the efforts of Gichin Funakoshi, father of Shotokan karate, and was embraced by dedicated practitioners who developed it further. It finally reached American shores in the version that carried the modern refinements of the Japanese, brought there principally by members of the military who learned it in Okinawa or Japan and opened schools upon their return to the US.

A martial art that originated but did not flourish in Japan is the Korean taekwondo. Although it tells its own story, taekwondo has some similarities with, if not influences from, karate. The notable difference between the two is in the way each dedicates the upper and lower limbs to offense and defense: karate uses the arms and fists for punching and striking with feet firmly balanced on the ground, whereas taekwondo uses the legs and feet for kicking and other offensive maneuvers and the arms and hands for protection. Taekwondo became a demonstration sport at the Olympics in 1988, and in 2000 made its debut as an official Olympic sport along with Japanese judo. For reasons aficionados don't readily understand, the equally popular karate has failed to achieve the same recognition and will continue to be excluded from the Olympic list until after 2012.

5. On the Papyrus Trail

Myth! **The Egyptians invented paper and the Chinese brought it to the rest of the world.**

There is a controversy on who invented paper, with one side claiming it was the Egyptians, based solely on the etymological fact that the English word 'paper' (along with its equivalents in other languages) comes from the Egyptian 'papyrus'. The first in recorded history to be used *like* paper, papyrus was made c. 3500 BC from the papyrus reeds thriving along the riverbanks of the Nile. The process, if there was one at all, involved cutting from each plant several strips, which were then dampened, made into a crisscross pattern and pressed into sheets.

Another side insists real paper appeared much later than the papyrus, when a courtier or scholar named Ts'ai-Lun, from Leiyang, China, invented a primitive form in the 1st century. Legend has it that one day, Ts'ai-Lun watched a wasp chew up pieces of bamboo, mix them with its own saliva and, with its feet, work the resultant ball into a flat sheet that it then used to build a wall in its nest. Emulating the wasp, the Chinese ancient made a paste of bamboo and water and spread the flat sheet to dry in the sun.

Neutral observers believe the difference between the two claims is only semantic and can be resolved by redefining concepts. The Egyptian papyrus is paper if by 'paper' is meant any flat, dry, and soft but cohesive material that provides a writing surface. Nonetheless, papyrus would not be the only known paper of this type; in ancient days, others (the ones generically referred to, along with papyrus, as 'tapa') produced similar results using the inner bark of mulberry, fig and daphne. Thus, even on the basis of a broad definition for paper, there is no certainty that the Egyptians were the earliest pioneers in papermaking, although, as previously noted, they were the first in recorded history.

On the other hand, going by its traditional connotation as 'a pulpy mixture of grasses, wood, rags, fibers, and pulp and water', paper is something manufactured, using a *technical* process much more sophisticated and cost-effective than the *agricultural* one applied to papyrus. The first attempt at papermaking by this method was undoubtedly Ts'ai-Lun's, a clear breakthrough after more than three centuries that 'tapa' products had been the only known facility for writing. The invention saw paper graduating from a rudimentary agricultural product the utility of which was obtained from the intrinsic quality of the materials used, to an industrial one that derived its worth from the processing and the know-how employed on it. Obviously, the only conclusion from this is that, while the Egyptians might have created the concept of paper with papyrus as the prototype, it was the Chinese who realized the product and made it commercial.

As a final word, it is not quite true that the Chinese brought paper to Europe and eventually to its colonies and the rest of the world. According to a Time-Life source (*Golden Ages of Man: Islam*), it was the Arabs who "learned the technique of making paper from Chinese warriors they had captured in a battle near Samarkand in the 8th century, and from there relayed the process to Europe in the late 14th century."

6. Chowhound's Delight

Myth! **The US imported the recipe for chop suey from China.**

'A sort of Oriental mulligan stew' is what most Westerners think of chop suey. This typically Chinese American dish is a mishmash of various things, mainly bits of fried or stewed chicken or pork, rice, noodles, and sesame seeds or oil.

The origin of chop suey is usually presented in two versions. According to the first, a personal cook of the Chinese Ambassador to the US prepared the dish for the great Chinese statesman, Li Hung-Chang, on August 29, 1896, while he was on a state visit in New York on his way around the world. When asked what the concoction was, the cook replied, 'chop suey'. This was assumed to be the Chinese phrase for a mixture or hash, although somebody explained that 'chop' is really English, in the sense of 'chipped' or 'cut', while 'suey' is Chinese *sui*, or 'bits'. (In another variation, the word used is *shap sui*, which purportedly translates into 'miscellaneous bits'.)

According to the second version, the dish first appeared in the Chinese labor camps of the railroads, mines and other projects on the US West Coast. A coolie laborer, desperate to make ends meet with his measly pay, mixed together bits of comestibles and came up with a mish-mash that he called 'chop suey'. This was believed to be a phonetic transliteration of the Mandarin *tsa sui*, meaning 'various things'.

When the folklore was updated to the 20th century, the Chinese cook became a restaurant operator-cum-chef somewhere in Brooklyn. A character in the film *Gangs of New York* (1928) offers a variant—the inventor was a dishwasher in Chinatown San Francisco circa 1860. What all these stories imply, of course, is that the dish is both American and Chinese: American, because it made its debut in the United States, and Chinese, for having been invented by Chinese essentially for Chinese and given its name by Chinese. The Chinese connection loses its clout somewhat when it is revealed that all the ways of making chop suey in the US are practically unknown in China, except probably in the south. In places like Beijing, where Chinese cuisine is high art, efforts to introduce the dish have been relatively unsuccessful.

Popular Chinese dishes in America include chow mein, egg foo yong, won ton soup, egg rolls, barbecued spare ribs, sweet-and-sour pork, and beef with lobster sauce. Laurence Moore (*Lightning Never Strikes Twice*, 1994) says that of these, chow mein is the only one that came from China. The original, *ch'ao mien* (not *mein*), meaning literally 'fried dough', consisted of diced or shredded meat, vegetables, and fried noodles.

7. Messages from the Cookie Factory

Myth! **American restaurants adopted the fortune cookie from an old Chinese custom.**

Americans consider fortune cookies to be a typically Chinese food and custom. Yet Chinese residents from Canton to Shanghai swear they never heard of them, at least not until some enterprising Chinese tourists saw the cute little doodads in America and decided to bring them to their homeland. In fact, fortune cookies are an American creation. George Jung was a Chinese American noodle maker who invented the curled little cookie in his Los Angeles restaurant in 1918 (some say 1916, the National Geographic News Service says 1920). The cookie was served at first to amuse customers while they waited for their food, and later to cap off their meal and soften the impact of the bill.

Fortune cookie dough is actually similar to a traditional Chinese flat wafer cookie. The recipe calls for butter, flour, egg whites, sugar, a little salt, vanilla extract and tea for seasoning. Topping it off, of course, is that ubiquitous slip of paper on which is written a prophecy or tidbit of wisdom. Early versions simply contained verses from the Bible, but Jung quickly became more creative and included messages, proverbs and predictions.

According to some Chinese experts, the only possible link of the fortune cookie to an early Chinese source is a practice that dates back to the Yuan Dynasty in the 12th century. During the uprisings against the Mongol rulers of China, rebel monks had to devise a way to pass details about the clashes and other important events to the peasants. So they slipped messages into moon-cakes, a sweet holiday dessert, and sold them to the people. The Chinese also used message-bearing cakes on other occasions. In ancient parlor games, for example, players wrote wise and witty sayings on scraps of paper that were then inserted into twisted cakes. It is suspected that Chinese immigrants remembered this bit of history when they settled in the United States, and some may have in fact applied the idea in other ways before Jung hit upon the fortune cookie. One theory is that, in the early period, most immigrants were Buddhists who were accustomed to going to temples to pray and have their fortunes told. Having no such temples or other facilities for prayers and fortune telling in their adopted land, they may have resorted to baking moon-cakes with fortunes tucked inside and selling them in restaurants.

8. Chinese Noodling at Work

Myth! **Marco Polo introduced pasta to Italy.**

We have Chinese noodles and Italian spaghetti, but who started it all by inventing pasta? Some mention the Arabs, whom they believe to have introduced the dish to Sicily. To quote a food historian, "like so much of southern Italian life, the Arab invasions of the 8th century heavily influenced the local cuisine and is the most accepted theory for the introduction of pasta in that region." Others credit the Jews, since the first sure record of noodles cooked by boiling is in the Jerusalem Talmud, written in Aramaic in the 5th century AD. Neither endorsement takes into account the Greeks and the Romans, whose ancient testaments speak of certain types of pasta circa the first century. Even earlier than the Romans were the Etruscans of 400 BC, whose evidence of an Etruscan tomb found 48 kilometers north of Rome shows a group of natives making what appears to be pasta. Although the Etruscan link is historically suspect, this detracts little from the general evidence that, until lately, has placed pasta's beginnings in Italy.

The story of Marco Polo is so intertwined with the explanation for the origin of pasta that, if one has acquired legendary proportions, so has the other. Marco, so the story goes, brought Chinese noodles, called 'spaghett', to Europe in the 14th century after his long sojourn in the kingdom of Kublai Khan. What makes the account pseudo-historical at best is that it also honors Marco for introducing other Chinese 'inventions', such as eyeglasses and ice cream, to the Italians. In the 1938 film *The Adventures of Marco Polo*, Hollywood adds to this anachronistic cornucopia by showing our hero, played by Gary Cooper, trading with his compatriots not only in spaghetti but also in gunpowder. Actually, Marco Polo made no claim of acquainting Italian culinary and fashion tastes to pasta, spaghetti or other Chinese goodies in his book *Il milione*, and neither did any of his contemporaries.

The latest quest for pasta's historical beginnings culminated in an event that has given some credibility to the Polo story, at least the part implying that spaghetti was Chinese. According to an Associated Press report dated October 14, 2005, a 4,000-year-old bowl of noodles has been discovered at an archaeological site in Minhe County in China's western province of Qinghai. The fist-sized clump of noodles was found inside an overturned bowl under three meters (10 feet) of sediment from a flood that researchers suspect wiped out the Qijia Culture of the Late Neolithic era. When researchers lifted up the bowl, they discovered the 50-centimeter-long (20-inch-long) noodles sitting atop an inverted cone of clay that had sealed the bowl.

It has been suggested that the Chinese were overjoyed by the discovery, not necessarily because it corroborates the Marco Polo legend but because it debunks the reverse of that legend, which is that Polo introduced pasta or noodles to China. Nevertheless, many are still reluctant to give the Chinese full credit for inventing the culinary delight, insisting that, since pasta has been discovered independently more than once in the course of history and among specific populations in certain areas, it is probable that more relics even earlier than the one found in China are just waiting to be unearthed elsewhere.

---

9. Mighty Mites

Myth! **The transistor was designed and developed by the Japanese.**

Only a few in the 1950s and 1960s didn't agree with the public perception that the transistor was a Japanese-made gadget. Small but powerful transistor radios coming out of Japanese assembly lines were captivating householders around the world who were used to seeing large and ungainly vacuum tubes in their appliances. Sony, the first to manufacture the tiny radios, would soon mass-produce a host of other transistorized gizmos, including color TV sets and VCRs, in friendly competition with other Japanese conglomerates. Toys, scientific instruments and highly portable and stylized audiovisual equipment powered by transistors, as well as cars equipped with transistorized dashboards, comprised the bulk of Japanese worldwide trade. When the transistor went a level higher to become the microchip, it was to be expected that the latter would also be regarded with awe as something basically Japanese.

The fact is that nothing could have been more American than the first working model of the transistor. Although the Germans had taken out patents on the idea before the 1940s, no prototypes were built and the patents were finally abandoned. Then in 1947 Bell Laboratories organized a three-man team with the sole intention of developing a replacement for the vacuum tube as an amplification device for the telephone industry. A young, brilliant theoretician, Bill Shockley, was selected as the team leader, and experimental physicist Walter Brattain and theoretical physicist John Bardeen were the other two members. With Brattain and Bardeen doing the core work and Shockley the finishing, Bell Labs managed to unveil the invention on June 30, 1948, calling it the 'transistor', a name devised with the help of engineer and science fiction writer John Pierce. Initially, the invention got little attention in the popular press and in industry, but Shockley, seeing its potential, left Bell Labs to found Shockley Semiconductor in Palo Alto, California. Some members of the group would later spin off as Fairchild Semiconductor, Intel Corporation and Texas Instruments, the major US corporations that would turn out the integrated circuit and pioneer the commercial production of computer microchips. Thus was the beginning of Silicon Valley.

Later, American companies would lose their momentum when they chose to apply the new invention primarily to military projects. Japanese entrepreneurs, eager to recover the industrial capacities and trade advantages that had been dissipated in the recent war, stepped in to fill the void in civilian markets. Through engineers-cum-marketers like Masaru Ibuka and Akio Morita, Sony and other *zaibatsus* opened the door to the information age with their breakthrough products and a unique brand of Japanese management. At some point responsibility for the whole transistor enterprise shifted to the Japanese and the transistor became a paradigm of Japanese industry.

10. Familiar Words in an Inscrutable Language

Myth! 'Mandarin', 'pagoda' and 'coolie' are Western words of Chinese origin.

The word *mandarin* is believed to be a Western derivation of Chinese origin, in reference to something typically Chinese. But in fact it is not Chinese nor does it spring from Chinese. The Oxford English Dictionary suggests that its use in reference to oranges of a certain kind may have come from their being identified with the color of the robes Chinese mandarins wore. On the other hand, the latter, meaning a member of the educated, official class of imperial China, looks suspiciously like the Portuguese *mandarino* (language), *mandar* (to command), and *mandarim* (counselor). According to various word experts, the basic source is Sanskrit, one of a family of ancient languages not related to Chinese. The word is "the end product of a series of borrowings from the Spanish *mandarin*, the Portuguese *mandarim*, the Dutch *mandorijn*, the Malay and Hindi *mantri*, and ultimately the Sanskrit *mantrin*, adviser, and *mánas*, mind, all of which makes Mandarin Chinese, mandarin duck, and mandarin oranges cousins to the sacred Sanskrit formula or prayer known as a *mantra.*" Assuming the form of *mandelines*, it entered the English language in 1589 and was originally applied to all Asiatic officials, only to be limited later to the Chinese called *Kuan*.

The Chinese national language is also called Mandarin, based on the dialect spoken in and around Beijing originally and principally by the mandarins. The people themselves speak many languages and many different Chinese dialects, of which the most common is Mandarin, or Putonghua, being known in one variety or another in about four-fifths of the country. The national government has tried several times in the past to impose Mandarin as the official language, but other dialects like Cantonese remain popular with large segments of the population.

Incidentally, the words *coolie* and *pagoda* are not Chinese either. *Coolie* was derived from the Tamil *kuri*, a menial worker, or the western Indian *Koli*, the name of a tribe. The term was brought to the West by Portuguese travelers in the sixteenth century, and was extended in the following century to cover workers in China as well. *Pagoda* is from the Portuguese and Italian *pagode*, a not very precise approximation of an Indian term for a temple—the Tamil word *pagavadi* and the Sanskrit *bhagavati*, meaning a place belonging to a deity.

IV

Key Noting An Event

On the Star Spangled Banner

"Then, in that hour of deliverance, my heart spoke. Does not such a country, and such defenders of their country, deserve a song?"

•

Francis Scott Key

1. Connecting the Stars

Myth! **The stars and colors of the American flag have specific meanings.**

Edward Everett Hale, author of the classic novel *The Man Without A Country*, was among those who popularized the myth that each of the stars appearing on the US flag represents a specific state of the Union. Hale describes a scene in which Philip Nolan, the title character, looks longingly at the flag as he lies dying. Pointing to the stars emblazoned on its blue field, he says, "Tell me their names...The last I know is Ohio...But where are your other fourteen?"

Even today, the general impression is that a star is located on the flag as each state is admitted into the Union, and the star thenceforth becomes a permanent representation of the state in question. Thus, the lower-rightmost star symbolizes Hawaii, which was the last to become a full-pledged state of the US, while the upper-leftmost star refers to Delaware as the first to ratify the Constitution. This does not explain, however, why there were stars in the flag for years before the Constitution was adopted, and what the legal configuration of stars was before 1912.

Needless to say, law or tradition has never sanctioned the belief, although long before Hale wrote his book, the idea of associating a star with a corresponding state had crossed the minds of American legislators. They ruled it out without much discussion during the legislative deliberation on the Flag Act of 1818, effectively maintaining the position that the stars represent the states collectively, and no particular star has any regional or local significance.

The Handbook of the Boy Scouts of America assigns a meaning to each of the three colors of the US flag, namely, bravery for the red, purity for the white, and justice for the blue. These are the virtues the Boy Scouts organization encourages in their young members, but their relevance to the American flag is totally fictitious. There is no historical basis for the contention that the colors of the flag were meant to symbolize anything.

As false as the Scout lore about the flag is the belief that the colors red, white and blue were derived from Washington's family crest. The Father of his Country may have had such a crest, but it is also true that he had his own Grand Union flag which he was flying on the field of battle when the Continental Congress passed the 1777 flag law specifying the three colors for the first time. Obviously, Washington had nothing to do with the new flag, and there is no evidence he suggested the colors earlier when he was supposedly ordered by Congress in 1776 to have a flag designed. The claim that he did so, and that he even took time out from the war to present his idea to Betsy Ross, has long been discredited for being anachronistic and inconsistent.

2. Composed amid the Turmoil

Myth! Francis Scott Key composed 'The Star Spangled Banner' while viewing the British night bombardment of Fort McHenry.

In some paintings of the renowned event that inspired 'The Star Spangled Banner', the figure of Francis Scott Key is seen writing what appear to be the lyrics of the anthem against the background of the British bombardment of Fort McHenry in Baltimore. Many historians scoff at this portrayal, saying our hero may have witnessed the spectacle from some vantage point on that tumultuous night of September 13-14, 1814, but he was in no position to write about it while it was happening.

By describing the bombardment in the past tense and its effects on the American flag in the present, the anthem is itself an attestation that Key composed the poem only after the siege had been lifted. This is as it should be; the war-like conditions of the harbor and its vicinity would have precluded one who was not a professional lyricist from creating a masterful verse on the spot. Contemporaneous accounts of this famous occurrence show that the air had already cleared and Key was on board a British vessel when, transfixed by the sight of the American flag still flying over the fort, he wrote his first stanza on the back of an envelope. Later on, Key added a few more stanzas and adapted the poem to fit the song.

Key, who never attended law school, was district attorney for Washington, DC, when the British invaded that city in 1814 and seized a planter, Dr. William Beanes, as prisoner. President Madison sent Key to negotiate for the release of Beanes from the British vessel where he was being kept. The British agreed to the release provided the negotiating party remained on board during the attack on Baltimore.

3. Enemy Soil in Friendly Waters

Myth! The birthplace of 'The Star Spangled Banner' as an anthem is Baltimore, and as a flag Philadelphia.

Maryland is generally regarded as the birthplace of the US national anthem, but legalists say the circumstances under which the memorable verse was written make this view disputable at the least. Most history books fail to mention that Key at the time of his poetic musings was on board a British ship laying siege on the fort. Except to a layman, the implication of this obviously anomalous setting is that Key was technically on foreign soil and outside US jurisdiction despite his physical presence in Baltimore. Key's situation is defined by a comity of international law, one already in effect during the War of 1812, that deems a naval vessel an extension of its country's territory.

If 'The Star Spangled Banner' as an anthem wasn't born in Baltimore, neither was the Star Spangled Banner as a flag born in Philadelphia. One integral part of the popular Betsy Ross tradition that most Americans continue to have faith in is a nondescript little old house in that Pennsylvania city that travel and art brochures elegantly call the "Birthplace of Our Nation's Flag." It is claimed this was where Betsy Ross resided, and, consequently, where she sewed the first American flag. This was never the official position of Betsy's family, but an enterprising owner of the house who did not want it razed by developers in 1892 nonetheless advanced the idea. Preservationists saved the house at the last moment, and since then have succeeded in enshrining the place as a significant historical spot—at least in the minds of tourists.

Despite the house being dressed up for the benefit of the public, it is doubtful that Betsy Ross ever lived there. According to the Joint State Government Commission of Pennsylvania in 1949, there is no evidence that links Betsy to the place. Reportedly for

39

this reason, both the U.S. Congress and the city of Philadelphia declined when the home was offered as a gift to the government. Today a private non-profit organization continues to manage the site in memory of Betsy Ross and her supposed involvement with the first American flag.

4. They didn't Play it, Sam

Myth! 'The Star Spangled Banner' was one of the anthems played at the signing of the Treaty of Versailles.

It would have been a great day for singing 'The Star Spangled Banner', as the US was one of those that engaged mightily in World War I and had now agreed to end it. Unfortunately, it couldn't have been done even if it was the most desirable thing to do. Firstly, not one of the six countries that participated in the negotiations for ending World War I played an anthem during the signing of the Treaty of Versailles; at least there is no mention of it in the records. Secondly, though the war ended in 1918 through the Armistice, the Treaty of Versailles was not signed until 1919, when the hoopla was all over. Thirdly, as a matter of historical fact, the US did not sign the Treaty, and may not even have had any representative during the proceedings. And lastly, the US would have been mute come anthem-playing time, since it had no national anthem until 1931, the year Congress officially recognized 'The Star-Spangled Banner'.

5. Flagging Interests in Peacetime

Myth! The 18th century is the most revered period for the American flag.

Patriotic Americans are enraptured by the sight of the flag flying in such famous paintings as Bunker Hill, Valley Forge and the Spirit of '76. They are obviously unaware that these depictions are mere products of artistic license, and that not one single land battle of the American Revolution featured the flag in any cognizable form.

It was only in 1814, more than thirty years after the revolutionary war had ended, that the flag began to be considered seriously and widely discussed by Americans as a symbol of the country. This was the year Francis Scott Key made memorable when he wrote about the Star Spangled Banner as it flew over Fort McHenry at Baltimore. In another thirty-two years, American soldiers would fight under Old Glory in the Mexican-American War of 1846-48, but the use of the flag in battle would still be limited.

The flag did not truly become an object of patriotism and a revered institution until the 20th century. During this period attention was finally given to such details as saluting, flag waving and flying, as well as reciting the pledge of allegiance. The symbol attained its greatest glory when, in World War 2, it was not only flown but painted or drawn on aircraft, vehicles and other war materiel disseminated all over the world. These practices were followed similarly in the major post-World War 2 conflicts involving the US. Although hard to believe, the Vietnam War, which had an unusually large number of cases of flag burning and defiling by radicals and rebels, showed more respect for the flag than did the American Revolution.

6. Key Words of an Old Tune

Myth! Key patterned his music after an old American tune.

There is another and much stronger reason for saying that 'The Star Spangled Banner' is not totally American. The tune originally belonged to Great Britain, then an enemy nation, and it probably still does, since it was appropriated without that country's permission and no effort has ever been made to correct the legal infirmity.

Contrary to popular belief, Key made history by writing a poem, not a song. When Congress adopted the US national anthem on March 31, 1931, it chose Key's lyrics but as sung to an old British tune, 'To Anacreon in Heaven'. This was a drinking song

41

composed by John Stafford Smith, an Englishman, in 1780, when the US was waging its war of independence against Britain. The greater irony, of course, is that many Americans today remember the music and hardly the words while wrongly attributing both to a countryman's patriotic fervor.

Incidentally, at least eighty-five other American poems had been fitted to Smith's tune before Key came up with his creation. One of these, 'When the Warrior Returns', was written by Key himself in 1805, nine years before finding the words for 'The Star Spangled Banner'.

7. All Through the Night

Myth! **The Stars and Stripes survived the all-night bombardment of Fort McHenry.**

The words of the US National Anthem would assure Americans that after the unrelenting bombardment of Fort McHenry for a whole night by the British, 'our flag was still there'. Yet, there was at least one eyewitness who refuted Key's claim that what he saw 'by the dawn's early light' was the same one he had hailed 'at the twilight's last gleaming'. Most experts agree such a huge flag could not have survived, with only minimal damage, the rockets from that blistering attack and the rainstorm that followed. It was more likely that, after the shelling had ceased just before dawn, the fort's defenders brought down the torn and tattered flag and replaced it with a fresh one.

As writer Steven Kroll, among others, explains, it was the fort's storm flag, measuring 25 by 17 feet, that flew overhead during the battle, and what Key saw after the bombardment had ended and before he sailed back into Baltimore was the 30 x 42 garrison flag for Ft. McHenry. Mary Young Pickersgill, a Philadelphia tradeswoman, made both flags, and while they are mentioned in the anthem (Key assuming they are one and the same), only the latter has survived. At the time of this writing, the artifact is in the Smithsonian undergoing an $18 million, 3-year rehabilitation and destined to be the centerpiece of the redesigned National Museum of American History.

8. Double Standard

Myth! **The surviving flag from Fort McHenry flies over Francis Scott Key's birthplace in Maryland when it is not in the Smithsonian.**

Contrary to what most people think, the flag that has flown by authority of a Joint Resolution of Congress over the site of Francis Scott Key's birthplace in Maryland continuously since May 30th, 1949, is not the Smithsonian streamer but a modern version of the Star Spangled Banner. The Smithsonian flag has fifteen stars and fifteen stripes, in compliance with the Second Flag Law of 1795 requiring the same number of stripes as stars for the national emblem in representation of the states admitted into the Union. Later, Congress realized that with the increasing number of states to be admitted, there would soon be a problem accommodating all of the stripes in the limited field. In 1818 they passed the Third Flag Law, which returned the number of stripes to the original thirteen but allowed a star to be added for each new state.

Following a bequest made by James Lick in the sum of $860,000, a monument to Key was constructed and placed in San Francisco's Golden Gate Park. Why San Francisco and not Baltimore only Mr. Lick would know, but he has been dead since 1876. The monument, with a height of fifty-one feet, consists of a double arch under which a bronze figure of Key is seated, and is surmounted by a bronze statue of America with an unfolded flag. The material is travertine, a calcareous stone of a reddish yellow hue, extremely porous but of great durability.

9. Rally Round the Flag, Boys

Myth! **Barbara Frietchie defended the flag against the assaults of an enemy army.**

An occurrence during the American Civil War may or may not have been real, but so impressed was John Greenleaf Whittier with its patriotic incandescence and high drama that he chose to memorialize it in one of his narrative poems. The popular verse eulogizes its title character, a real-life widow named Barbara Frietchie, for courageously taking up by her lonesome self a Union flag that had been hauled down in anticipation of the arrival of rebel Stonewall Jackson's army in Frederick, Maryland. On seeing the flag, Whittier writes, Confederate soldiers fired at it, eliciting Frietchie's fiery quotation ("'Shoot, if you must, this old grey head / But spare your country's flag,' she said").

A literal reading of Whittier debunks the two fallacies most often associated with the legend. *First*, it was not the rebels but the men of Frederick town that had hauled down the town's Union flags preparatory to the rebel incursion. *Second*, the flag Frietchie had taken from this bunch was on a staff set in her attic window when it was fired upon, and it was after the shooting that she waved this flag, torn and tattered, at the soldiers while she shouted her famous challenge.

But Whittier himself may have produced the greatest fallacy of all. When his work appeared in the *Atlantic* magazine, some eyewitness residents of Frederick expressed doubts about the poet's version of this piece of Civil War history. The real Frietchie, they said, was 96 years old—not 'fourscore years and ten', as Whittier had written—and bedridden at the time it happened. There could not have been any confrontation because Jackson's troops never got to within three hundred yards of her home. Others reported that Whittier related most everything quite accurately, except that the old woman involved was not Mrs. Frietchie but her neighbor, Mrs. Mary Quantrell. Whittier, who apparently obtained his information from the novelist Mrs. E.D.E.N. Southworth, is said to have admitted his mistake later.

10. It didn't Fly

Myth! **A US flag used in the American Revolution is kept in the Smithsonian Institution.**

There are some who believe that the only US flag to survive the American Revolutionary War was the one that flew on the *Bonhomme Richard*, the vessel commanded by the naval hero John Paul Jones. Jones' biography by Augustus C. Buell relates how a group of young girls sewed the emblem from the materials of their own silk dresses, including the bridal gown that one of them was set to use for her wedding. Not surprisingly, the story proved to be false, like most of Buell's work on Jones, when it was discovered that the owner of the bridal gown, a certain Helen Seavey, never existed.

Congress (if an affidavit purportedly issued by that august body is to be believed) awarded the flag, except for a small piece given to President Lincoln, to James Stafford, the sailor who had saved it when the *Bonhomme Richard* sank. The Smithsonian validated the story by displaying the flag throughout the 1920s, courtesy of the Stafford family. It was only later that the Congressional testimonial was shown to be a fake and the whole story a hoax, compelling the Smithsonian to withdraw the flag permanently from exhibition.

11. A Seamstress's Tale

Myth! **Betsy Ross made the first US flag and called it 'Old Glory'.**

Betsy Ross is the widowed Philadelphia seamstress who, according to her grandson William Canby, was visited one day in June 1776 in her shop by a secret committee of three headed by George Washington. The general asked her to sew a flag for the new nation, and Betsy said yes, but not before convincing the group that the stars should have five points instead of six.

The trouble with Canby's story is that it was presented to the Pennsylvania Historical Society only in 1870, almost 100 years after the supposed occurrence and 34 years after he had heard it as a boy. Moreover, it dated the event a year too early—the first American flag would not be conceptualized until 1777.

Most historians believe the real architect of the US flag was Francis Hopkinson of New Jersey, an artist who helped craft US currency and official seals. Records show that in May 1780 he sent a bill to the Board of Admiralty for designing the "flag of the United States." Congress never paid, citing that "he had not been the only one to work on the project." In effect, this was an admission that Hopkinson was at least one of the designers of the Stars and Stripes.

It is said Betsy was also the one who christened the American flag "Old Glory." This claim is no more credible than the allegation of a daughter of William Driver, a sea captain from Salem, Massachusetts, that it was her father who coined the phrase. But in sympathy with tradition, most critics would rather concede the idea of a simple seamstress designing the American flag than of an unknown mariner inventing what may well be the nation's greatest sobriquet.

12. Mourning Stripes

Myth! **Tradition requires that the flag be flown at half-mast for 30 days on the death of an ex-President.**

Contrary to what most newspapers report, there is no tradition requiring flags to be flown at half-mast for any period of time on the death of an ex-President. It is optional on the incumbent President to proclaim a public mourning period, usually 30 days, as a show of respect on the passing of a revered former high official. He may act alone or on the joint recommendation of the speaker of the House and the vice president acting as the president of the Senate.

There are, of course, traditions that apply to flags at specific locations. Thus, the ones flying on the east and west ends of the Capitol building are automatically lowered to half-staff when a sitting member of Congress dies. It is presumed that a head of department in the Executive Branch can order flags flown at half-staff in his sphere of jurisdiction, since the president has that power on a national level.

Incidentally, when a flag is flying at half-mast, it is not necessarily located halfway at the pole, as one would imagine. The term "half-mast" means that the flag is lowered by the exact length of its side parallel to the pole. Thus, it is lowered until its top corner, the one nearest the flagpole, is at the point where its bottom corner had been. Where both flag and pole are standard, half-mast comes out higher than half the pole. The only time it coincides with halfway on the pole is when the height of the flag is exactly one-third the length of the pole.

13. Image Exposure

Myth! **The most famous photo of the Pacific War is an unrehearsed shot of the American flag being raised by six Marines on Mount Suribachi in Iwo Jima.**

Another major moment for the Star Spangled Banner was the one photographer Joe Rosenthal purportedly captured to become the most famous image of the Pacific War. Called "The Spirit of '45," it showed six GIs raising the US flag on Mt. Suribachi at the end of the battle for Iwo Jima. Rosenthal garnered a Pulitzer Prize for his achievement, and his subject matter inspired an enormous monument in Arlington National Cemetery. The photo symbolized the spirit of the long and bloody struggle against the Japanese, as typified by the charge up Mt. Suribachi, Iwo's highest point, by 252 Americans, of whom only 27 survived the assault. The action caught by Rosenthal's camera was assumed to have been spontaneous, and it was this pictorial quality more than anything else that helped boost the fighting spirit of American soldiers in the fading days of the war.

An anomaly in the ensemble, though somewhat minor, is the fact that not all six flag raisers were Marines, as is commonly believed. One was a Navy man, John Bradley, who would survive the other five until his own death on January 11, 1994 at the age of 70. The more glaring irregularity, however, is the manner in which the photograph was taken. It would be revealed eventually that Rosenthal was not physically present the first time the flag was raised by a group of marines after the hill was captured, and it was not from his memory of that event that the picture was taken. The flag had scarcely been flying when it was hauled down to comply with a visiting politician's request that it be given to him as a souvenir. The scene depicted in the famous photo was a second one staged for Rosenthal on the same site using a different flag and another group of marines from the battalion that had taken the hill earlier in the day.

The Clint Eastwood film *Flags of Our Fathers* (2007) is all about the angst of some of the participants in the photo op who felt

47

afterwards that they were being celebrated as heroes of Iwo Jima for the wrong reason. Others who knew of the staging believed it was a reasonable reenactment of the flag raising, albeit by different actors, and that Rosenthal fully deserved the Pulitzer Prize he had won. However, this has offered little relief from the disappointment of the many who have suddenly realized that a great icon of World War II is not what it appears to be.

14. Burning Questions

Myth! **The American flag must be destroyed by burning when it gets dirty.**

One false notion about the proper disposition of the flag is that it must be destroyed when it gets dirty, and another is that the only legal way of destruction is by burning. Nothing in law or custom forbids cleaning the flag when it is dirty, or mending it when it is torn but reparable, and there is also no specified manner in which the American flag must be destroyed in case it becomes necessary to do so. Public Law 829, generally referred to as the Flag Code, merely states that a flag should be destroyed "in a dignified way, preferably by burning," when it is "in such condition that it is no longer a fitting emblem for display." When an old, tattered or extremely dirty flag cannot be restored anymore, it may be cut up, shredded, burnt or buried. However, burning, though not mandatory, is the preferred means of disposing of flags that are no longer usable.

Incidentally, the Flag Code, which has brought together most of the regulations and customs pertaining to the use of the flag, took nearly 146 years after the Stars and Stripes appeared before becoming public law. Many of these rules prior to their codification, as well as new ones that are still outside the Code, were set forth by flag organizations rather than by statute.

V

Rebel Manifesto

On the Declaration of Independence

"We base all our experiments on the capacity
of mankind for self-government."

•

James Madison

1. Born on the 2ⁿᵈ of July

Myth! **The thirteen original American colonies formally declared their independence from Britain on July 4, 1776.**

If there is anything sacrosanct in American history, it is that, on July 4, 1776, the thirteen original colonies declared themselves independent of Britain. July 4 is the date inscribed on the formal Declaration of Independence, a fact that has led many to believe this was the day the declaration was first adopted by Congress and signed by the members. However, the legal act of severance from the mother country was made two days earlier, on July 2, 1776, when Congress passed the resolution declaring all the colonies free and independent.

The resolution was terse compared to the formal Declaration, which Jefferson wrote for the 5-man committee that Congress had formed for the purpose of preparing the final document. It was the resolution nonetheless that severed all ties with Britain, the operative act that set up July 2 as the real day for celebration. The Jefferson document, which was intended largely to explain the reasons for the July 2 vote for independence, was adopted on July 4 but would not be approved unanimously until later.

John Adams himself, in a letter to his wife dated July 3, 1776, had predicted that July 2 would be "the most memorable Epoch in the History of America" and would be "celebrated by succeeding Generations as the great anniversary Festival." But we are told that a scholar of the 19ᵗʰ century altered the date of the letter to July 5 and Adam's prediction of the holiday to July 4, a fakery that helped settle the matter once and for all.

2. In pursuit of Paul Revere

Myth! **The Declaration of Independence was unanimously supported in the Continental Congress.**

The belief that independence was unanimously supported in the Continental Congress is wrong. In fact, the resolution of July 2, which was in response to the motion introduced by Richard Henry Lee of Virginia on June 7, almost did not make it, as more than half a dozen delegates had opposed the rebellion. In the roll call prior to the last, Pennsylvania and South Carolina voted in the negative, Delaware's delegates were divided, and New York's members, lacking instructions, didn't vote.

Had it not been for a ride—not Paul Revere's, but Caesar Rodney's on July 1-2, 1776—there would have been no declaration of independence and probably no United States of America. Rodney, one of the Delaware delegates, traveled overnight in a thunderstorm from his home to Philadelphia to break a tie in the Delaware delegation and cast Delaware's vote for independence. While most testimonials suggest that Rodney negotiated the entire trip on horseback, dramatically arriving in Philadelphia "in his boots and spurs," he actually rode in a carriage most of the way. This slight historical inaccuracy may be ignored, however, in light of what occurred as a consequence of Rodney's heroic effort. South Carolina and Pennsylvania, not wanting to be left out, also voted for independence. New York, still uninstructed, abstained, but on July 9, it would be among those posting public proclamations of the Declaration of Independence, and on August 2 would sign the Declaration in its present form.

3. Signs of the Times

Myth! **The Founding Fathers signed the Declaration of Independence on July 4, 1776, with John Hancock signing first.**

After passing the resolution declaring independence on July 2, 1776, Congress adopted the formal document prepared by Jefferson's committee on July 4. It is not correct to say that the Declaration was signed on either of these dates, or that all fifty-six signers signed on the same day. The story that each signer proudly and publicly took his turn affixing his signature to Jefferson's handiwork on July 4 was apparently concocted by Franklin and Jefferson himself in letters they wrote after the event.

The signing process was quite gradual and done mostly in secrecy. It started only on July 19, when the body resolved that a parchment copy be made and signed by every member, and indeed this copy was signed on August 2 by every member then present. By August 6 most of those whose names are on the document—fifty of them—had signed, but six signatures were attached years later, the last one being Thomas McKean's in 1781. There are signatories who were not yet members of Congress when the Declaration was adopted, while a few who voted for it in Congress never did get around to signing it. Robert R. Livingston was one of the committee of five who helped to frame the document, and he voted for it but never signed it.

It is not true either that John Hancock's signature was the first on the document, for what he signed on July 4 with the Congressional secretary, Charles Thompson, was the committee original. Nobody knows when Hancock signed or who was the first signatory on the August 2 parchment copy, which eventually became the Declaration of Independence.

4. The Virginia in Sam's Past

Myth! **The term "United States" first appeared in the 1776 Declaration of Independence.**

It is often asked why James I, in granting authority to English companies to colonize the New World, limited the scope of those grants to Virginia. In 1605, for instance, the English king gave one company a grant to 'southern Virginia' and another a franchise for 'northern Virginia'. The answer is that, at that time, the name 'Virginia' did not refer to the colony only but to the entire North American continent from east to west.

'Virginia' eventually became 'United States of America', a term commonly attributed to Thomas Paine, the author of *Common Sense* (1775). Paine had written about it in *The American Crisis II* (1777), but the words actually appeared earlier in the colonies in 'The Unanimous Declaration of the Thirteen United States of America', which was the original title of the Declaration of Independence. According to information relayed by an Oxford English Dictionary researcher to columnist William Safire,

Eldridge Gerry, a Massachusetts representative in the Continental Congress, may have jumped the gun on Jefferson, the drafter of the Declaration, when he wrote a letter dated June 25, 1776, to General Horatio Gates using the name United States of America for the united colonies. Regardless, it was not the intention at that time to use the phrase as a national name, since the federation that has come to be known as the USA would not emerge until 1787. As another historian notes, the word "Thirteen" in the Declaration made it obvious that "United States of America" was just a description for an aggregation of entities and was no more distinctive than, say, "The Thirteen United Colonies of the New World." When the colonists signed the Declaration as "Representatives of the United States of America, in General Congress, Assembled," it was not in behalf of a nation but of individual states 'united' by a common purpose.

The Declaration of Independence notwithstanding, the term 'United States' was not original to the colonists and was actually used to refer to Holland from 1617 to 1769. It didn't firm up for the Americans the way it had with the Dutch until it became "the United States in Congress Assembled" in the Articles of Confederation of 1781. The words finally emerged as a true national name—the United States of America—upon the promulgation of the present Constitution in 1787.

5. The Deed is Gone

Myth! The original of the Declaration of Independence has been preserved and is on display in the National Archives.

What the Library of Congress has is the parchment copy of the Declaration bearing the signatures of those who signed. The original document, reportedly signed only by John Hancock, was the one approved on July 4, 1776. It has since been missing and no one knows if it still exists. Only copies were sent to the printers for the preparation of the final versions, and one of these was made available on August 2, 1776, and signed by members of Congress on that date or later. This August 2 copy is what has been presented to us over the centuries as the original Declaration of Independence, and the one we see on display in the National

Archives. Actually, it is not even a 100 percent true copy of Jefferson's draft, inasmuch as that document had some words changed in the signed copy, giving rise to a substantive difference.

Incidentally, we are used to calling the US's most treasured document "The Declaration of Independence," but that is not its official title. Rather, it is "The Unanimous Declaration of the Thirteen United States of America," which purists say is anomalous because it does not contain the word "Independence." Similarly, "all men are born free and equal," a line beloved to abolitionists in the 19th century and to civil libertarians today, won't be found in any part of the Declaration or, for that matter, the U.S. Constitution.

6. The Young Philadelphians

Myth! **The Founding Fathers who signed the Declaration of Independence were mostly past middle age.**

Quite often, an artist depicts a historical event according to how the public sees it, but because public perception is usually based on sentiment or belief rather than facts, the portrayal ends up wrong. An example often cited is John Trumbull's famous painting, "The Declaration of Independence," which, in an obvious effort to affirm that wisdom goes with old age, shows the Founding Fathers as mostly old men. Historically, however, only seven of the fifty-six signers of the Declaration were past middle age, while seventeen others were of middle age, i.e., between 45 and 60. The rest, or about 60%, were 45 years or younger, and included young adults, such as South Carolina's Edward Rutledge and Thomas Lynch, who were just twenty-six and twenty-seven, respectively, and a large group of thirty-something, notably Thomas Jefferson, who was thirty-three. It seems useless to debate whether or not the shorter lifespan of male Americans during this period had anything to do with the signers being a mere forty-three on the average, since two of them—Stephen Hopkins and Benjamin Franklin—were both seventy. Surprisingly, even such painters as Robert Edge Pine (1730-88) and Edward Savage (1761-1817), who collaborated on the contemporary piece "Congress Voting Independence," saw most of the Founding

Fathers as much older than they really were.

7. The Declarers were Trumped

Myth! North Carolina preempted the July 1776 event by declaring its own independence from Britain more than a year earlier.

While it can be said that all the colonies declared their independence from Britain on July 2, 1776, the act was merely a formality for some colonies that had previously made such declarations on their own in one form or other. Wikipedia notes that more than ninety such 'declarations of independence' were issued throughout the colonies during the three months preceding the July resolution. Some, like North Carolina's Halifax Resolves of April 12, 1776, were formal written instructions for Congressional delegations to vote for independence. Others were legislative acts that officially ended British rule in individual colonies, such as Rhode Island on May 4 of that year.

North Carolina was the first colony to *call* for independence, but Rhode Island, though acting a month later, became the first colony to *declare* independence and preempt the July 2 action of the Continental Congress. For a while, North Carolina would claim Rhode Island's position as well on the ground that, on May 20, 1775, or a full year before any of these events, the citizens of Mecklenburg, N.C., met and made their own formal declaration of independence from the British. The state of North Carolina went so far as to place the Mecklenburg date on the state flag and the state seal and to declare it a holiday. However, reacting to an implied accusation by John Adams that the July 4 Declaration drew heavily from the Mecklenburg document, Thomas Jefferson raised the point that the latter was spurious. He questioned the assertion that, in 1800, after the original document was destroyed by fire, excerpts were recalled and noted down by an old recording clerk named John M. Alexander. It was strange, Jefferson said, that the writing came up only in 1800 and a copy of it printed only in 1820. Historians have since echoed Jefferson's question why so bold and patriotic a statement was ignored for 45 years after it was made.

The better-authenticated fact is that North Carolina nearly broke from Britain on May 31, 1775, when certain resolutions were passed denying the authority of the king. But on this occasion, independence was never mentioned, and the resolutions as a whole were even less impressive than those adopted earlier by Massachusetts on September 9, 1774, at Suffolk.

VI

Let Freedom Ring

On American Democratic Symbols

"Until we are all free, we are none of us free."
•

Emma Lazarus

1. For Whom the Bell Tolled

Myth! The Liberty Bell is a symbol of American Independence.

Most patriotic Americans believe the Liberty Bell got its name from the fact that it was rung in Philadelphia when independence was declared on July 4, 1776. Etched on this relic are words that the Founding Fathers composed: "Proclaim liberty throughout all the land unto all the Inhabitants thereof."

The story is that a gray-headed patriot rang the bell a hundred times, each time proclaiming "Liberty throughout the land!" to a crowd milling below. A blue-eyed boy had signaled that the delegates had just voted for liberty and were poised to sign the declaration of independence.

Experts say the whole incident was a hoax drummed up in 1847 by a young Philadelphian, George Lippard, who wrote it in his book *Legends of the American Revolution*. This notwithstanding, many patriotic citizens and organizations, relying on support given by such impeccable sources as the Britannica (1974 edition), cling to the belief that the bell was rung on the fourth of July 1776, to signal US independence. A group even went so far as to have full-size replicas of the shrine made for every state of the Union, so that the sight might inspire people who couldn't travel to Philadelphia. Obviously, very few realize that no bell ringing could have occurred on July 4, 1776, since the declaration of independence was on the previous July 2. Neither was there evidence that the bell was rung on July 8, when Congress publicly celebrated independence, nor at any time during the entire month of July 1776.

As hard as it is to believe, the term Liberty Bell was coined only in 1839, more than fifty years after the Revolution had ended, and with no intention of commemorating that War or the Declaration of Independence. Its authors were the abolitionists, and what it proposed to honor was the abolition of slavery, using the word 'liberty' in reference to the ideal of freedom for American blacks that the movement was fighting for. The Liberty Bell itself was cast originally as an ordinary bell, to be used for signaling and other normal community purposes. The false idea that it had something to do with certain people's aspirations for freedom, or with an event like the American Revolution, arose because of the Biblical quotation etched innocently on its side: "Proclaim liberty throughout all the land unto all the Inhabitants thereof" (*Lev* 25:10). People thought the inscription was inspired by a political objective, when it was actually the other way around. The inscription inspired the abolitionists to relate the bell for the first time to their freedom movement in 1839, and eventually to promote it as a symbol of black liberty in America. Since then, a great deal of patriotic folklore has sprung up around the bell, much of it untrue.

2. Cracked Symbol

Myth! **The Liberty Bell cracked while it was being rung during an Independence Day celebration.**

It can be categorically stated that the Liberty Bell did not crack while it was being rung for independence on July 4, 1776 or on any other date. The true cause of its present condition is more complicated but less significant than what is popularly believed.

The bell, commissioned in 1751 to hang in what is now Pennsylvania's Independence Hall, was first cast in London and delivered in August 1752. After it was shipped to America, a stroke of the clapper cracked it while it was being tested on the ground, and it had to be recast twice in Philadelphia before being hung in June 1753. Thereafter, the bell was rung for special occasions, one of which was the funeral of Chief Justice John Marshall in 1835, on which date the bell suffered its now famous crack. The fracture worsened and became irreparable while being rung for the last time in 1846 for George Washington's birthday.

Incidentally, it is not widely known that aside from the crack, the Liberty Bell has another defect. Inscribed on its side is the name "Pensylvania," with only one "n" in the first syllable. This was due to a mistake originally made by the English casters of the first Liberty Bell, an error perpetuated for sentimental reasons when the object was recast a couple of times.

3. Vying for the Lady's Favors

Myth! **New Jersey had jurisdiction over the Statue of Liberty when it was first built in the 1880s.**

Frederic Bartholdi and Gustave Eiffel, sculptor and designer, respectively, of the Statue of Liberty, reassembled the great lady on Bedloe Island in the 1880s as it arrived from France. Renamed Liberty Island in 1956, Bedloe, which sits in New York Harbor, is geographically within New Jersey's waters. In 1834 an agreement was forged ceding some control to New York. As a result, sales taxes from the statue's concessions went to Albany, not to Trenton, as did non-federal income taxes paid by the few families who lived there. However, the island's power continued to be provided solely by a Jersey City utility. New Jersey later appealed New York's claim to the island, but after it came under the jurisdiction of the United States as a national monument in 1924, the dispute ended.

It is not clear why there was a dispute in the first place, since the island itself had been federal territory since 1796. In 1937, the National Park Service replaced US Fort Wood, which had been established there in 1841. Equally ironic is that tourists who prefer to travel by ship over the Atlantic are told that the first sight they should expect as they glide into New York Harbor is the Statue of Liberty. All too often, those who make the trip get their first glimpse of American culture in the form of a Coney Island roller coaster and not of the great lady herself.

4. Lighting the Way Home

Myth! **The Statue of Liberty was intended to be a beacon for immigrants aspiring for a better life in America.**

The colossus that stands in New York Harbor is called the Statue of Liberty, but, in effect, this is only a nickname. The lady's proper title to this date is the name given to it by designer and builder Frederic Bartholdi in 1886—"Liberty Enlightening the

World." The formal name is a less than subtle expression of "French republican hopes that it would serve as a galvanizing symbol for the spread of democracy throughout the globe."

The same thought runs through the famous words with which the statue has been identified since 1903—"Give me your tired, your poor, / Your huddled masses yearning to breathe free." They form part of the poem "The New Colossus," written in 1883 by Emma Lazarus, a Sephardic Jew and Zionist, and etched on a plaque inside the monument seventeen years after its inauguration in 1886 and sixteen years after Emma's death in 1887. The poem was not written especially for the lady, as the title would have us believe, but for a literary auction held at New York's Academy of Design.

Actually, "The New Colossus" was meant to refer to America as a refuge for the oppressed, and not to the great statue or the concept of liberty for which it stands. According to historians, this has helped promote a parochial spirit of hospitality and beneficence completely at variance with the original idea of universal militant republicanism. Far from sending Bartholdi's message to freedom fighters around the world, Miss Liberty has become a mere beacon for immigrants, particularly those who seek the material comforts rather than the political benefits of America.

Using Emma's words—a solicitation for the tired, the poor and those yearning to be free—to convey a message for the Statue of Liberty has not been effective in the context of US immigration history. Shenkman cites Senator Patrick Moynihan, who noted that the turn-of-the-century immigrants who came to these shores were energetic and self-sufficient, and hailed from places more blessed and civilized than New York City, then (as now) "a cesspool of intrigue and poverty and corruption." Far from being unkempt, uneducated and uncouth, as they had been painted to be, they were enthusiastic go-getters "who knew exactly what they were doing, and doing it quite on their own."

5. Belle de France

Myth! The Statue of Liberty was designed and constructed by Bartholdi and paid for principally by France.

The Statue of Liberty stands 302 ft. high, but without the pedestal it is merely 151 ft. tall, exactly half the total figure. While it is generally known that the monument was a gift of the French people to the US, only the statue was financed by funds coming from France. The cost of reassembly, including the construction of the pedestal, was put up by Americans—to be precise, by millions of American school children—whose contributions were solicited in a nationwide pitch to make the project feasible. France spent $250,000 for the statue, an amount much less than the $350,000 the US spent for its completion on Bedloe Island.

It is wrong to give sole credit for the design and construction of the lady to Frédéric-Auguste Bartholdi, as much as it is to say France was the sole or main contributor to that monument. The sculptor was responsible for the outer layer consisting of copper sheets hammered into shape by hand, but these sheets could only be laid on a framework of four gigantic steel supports designed by Alexander-Gustave Eiffel. The statue is, in fact, a miniature Eiffel Tower because its inner supporting structure is very similar in construction to the famous Paris tower that Eiffel later built.

It is interesting to learn that France's idea of gifting the US with the statue came only as an afterthought. What Bertholdi had in mind originally was a lighthouse for Alexandria, Egypt, to mark the entry to the Suez Canal, but the Franco-Prussian War interrupted his negotiations with Egyptian authorities. After the war his thoughts shifted to the US, and the great lady was born.

6. His own Sons call him Uncle

Myth! Uncle Sam is a fictional name taken from the initials 'U.S.'

Scholars had thought Uncle Sam was not a real figure but only a name that evolved from the initials "U.S." stamped on government property. Its suspected beginnings was the War of 1812, when people from New York and Vermont who were opposed to the conflict used the term disparagingly. This was the case until, in 1961, someone discovered a copy of the New York

Gazette and General Advertiser of May 12, 1820. In it was quoted a soldier from the War of 1812 claiming to have heard a conversation between a meat inspector and a plant employee. The plant owner was Samuel Wilson, a meat packer from Troy, New York, who supplied the American Army during that war with barrels of pork, each barrel stamped with the letters "EA-US." When the inspector asked what the letters stood for, Wilson's employee jokingly replied that "US" were the initials of Uncle Sam, the butcher. In one variation, the contractor for the meat was Elbert Anderson, nephew of Sam Wilson, so that when asked what the letters "EA-US" stood for, the employee answered, "Elbert Anderson's Uncle Sam."

Sam Wilson was officially acknowledged during President Kennedy's administration by an act of the 87th Congress, which saluted the Trojan resident "as the progenitor of America's National Symbol." But this has not quieted doubts that the Wilson story is just myth, in the light of reports that even Troy didn't know something like it happened until out-of-town papers brought it up.

7. Flagg Waving the Draft

Myth! Uncle Sam was based on the likeness of poster maker James Montgomery Flagg.

James Montgomery Flagg denied the popular belief that when he drew the famous World War I poster of Uncle Sam pointing a finger under the banner heading "I Want You," he made the face look like Abraham Lincoln. The artist claimed he himself had posed for the picture, and the similarity with the great president, enhanced by the patriotic gesture, was purely coincidental. Controverting Flagg in turn are historians who have reason to believe his real model was the popular western star of the silent screen, William S. Hart. One Walter Botts, a professional model who, ironically, was declared ineligible for a veteran's pension, posed for later "I Want You" posters.

But there is no doubt it was Lincoln who was the model for the definitive Uncle Sam caricature drawn by the famous illustrator Thomas Nast. Nast made him tall, thin, hollow-cheeked, and with a beard, all notable Lincoln features. Although it was British cartoonists from the satirical magazine *Punch* that began to present Uncle Sam in caricature in the 1830s, it was Nast's creation in the 1870s that laid the basis for the modern cartoon image of the American symbol.

8. Elephant Man in Donkey Skin

Myth! **Thomas Nast created the symbols of the Republican and Democratic parties.**

Illustrator Thomas Nast popularized the symbols of both the Republican and Democratic parties in his cartoons, but he invented only one—the GOP elephant. This was in 1874, when the political Dumbo appeared in a cartoon the artist drew for *Harper's Weekly* to illustrate two significant stories that year.

The New York *Herald* had accused President Grant of "Caesarism" because of his intention to run for an unprecedented third term in 1876. Several weeks later, the same paper reported what turned out to be one of the most famous hoaxes of that century—animals from the New York City Zoo had escaped and were roaming around Central Park. Nast drew a stampeding elephant and a donkey disguised as a lion to incorporate the two news stories. The donkey marked "Caesarism" was shown scaring all the other animals that were loose in the park, including the elephant labeled "the Republican Vote."

By the time Nast included the donkey in that precedent-setting cartoon, Andrew Jackson, a Democrat, had already invented the symbol. Jackson was the first to use it for his party after his opponents in the 1828 presidential election called him a "stubborn jackass" for his obstinacy. He liked the idea and incorporated the image in his campaign materials.

VII

The Objects of our Affection

On Popular Symbols

"In this sign shalt thou conquer."

•

The Vision of
Constantine the Great

1. Olympian Medical Staff

Myth! **The two most common medical symbols are the Caduceus, the staff of the Greek god of medicine, and the letters 'Rx' found in doctors' prescriptions.**

The symbol of the medical profession is the Caduceus, a staff with two snakes wound around it, an oddity that reputedly belonged to the god of medicine, Asclepius (or Aesculapius), a son of Apollo who was taught the art of healing by the learned Centaur Chiron. Zeus, jealous of Asclepius' skills, killed him when he was a mortal, but he was later deified with the help of Apollo.

Greek mythology revisited tells us that Asclepius' staff featured just a single snake, and seems to have been confused with the Caduceus in the belief that Asclepius and the Caduceus' real owner, Hermes, are one and the same. Hermes himself did not originally own the Caduceus (unlike the broad-brimmed winged hat and winged sandals he wore as the Greek god of messengers), and had only inveigled Apollo into giving it to him. Later, when he found two snakes engaged in a brawl, he tempted them into winding themselves around the staff.

Historically, however, the Caduceus is one of the oldest and most revered holy symbols and long preceded the myth of Hermes. It was an emblem of life to the Sumerians, a healing icon to the pre-Hellenic Greeks, and a serpent-deity in Aztec sacred art. It took on its present form when the Greeks adapted a symbol of arcane wisdom in prehistoric Mesopotamia to the needs of its most enlightened god. The bi-serpented staff eventually became a special emblem of heralds and ambassadors in the ancient world, until, beginning in Europe in the sixteenth century, the medical profession appropriated it to symbolize their Hermetic ability to bring people back to earth from the land of the dead.

Another symbol related to medicine is "Rx", which is most often written in medical prescriptions as though it were two letters. Actually, what is commonly seen as "Rx" is not R and x combined, but R with a diagonal line through its leg, or *R̸*. The belief that it derives from the Latin word *recipere*, which means "take this," is inadequate because it does not explain why the letter R is crossed.

According to the more reliable etymology, Rx has been used for centuries by pharmacies and apothecaries to indicate a Jupiter connection. Jupiter was the ancient Roman deity that had dominion over matters of health and healing, and in those days, medical endeavors were rarely launched without first invoking the god's name or symbol (modern fanciers of astrology follow the same tack when they regard the planet Jupiter's ascendancy to be a good time for gathering herbs and making medicine). It thus became customary to introduce medical prescriptions with the sign of Jupiter as a token of assurance that the medicine would be effective. The sign of Jupiter looked like a merger of the numbers 2 and 4 until this was corrupted to the more familiar R.

2. Wave Lengths and Band Widths

Myth! **The French Tricolor consists of three vertical stripes of equal width sporting the red, white and blue colors.**

The story is that the French insurgents had adopted for their flag only two colors, red and the blue of the city of Paris, but Lafayette persuaded them to add the Bourbon white to show that they bore no hostility to the king. Thus was France's tricolor born on 11 July 1789.

The flag, with just three vertical stripes of apparently equal width sporting the red, white, and blue colors, is a standout for simplicity. What most people don't realize is that the stripes are really of unequal widths, and are so designed precisely to give the optical illusion of equality. If the three stripes were exactly the same width, the differing wavelengths of the colors would have made the stripes appear different, with the red band seemingly narrower. To counteract this, the designers purposely made the bands in a proportion of 100 for the blue, 110 for the white, and 124 for the red.

It is not certain how many other national flags exhibit this unique feature, but it is a fact that the French standard is only one of 45 that are called tricolors, and one of sixteen that are laid out without any emblems or devices on them other than the three colored stripes.

3. Cross of Iron

Myth! **The cross became the symbol of Christianity on the day Christ died on it.**

The cross was not originally Christian, and neither was it introduced through the Roman practice of crucifying criminals. It had religious and mystical, and before that artistic, connotations among pagan peoples, from the Egyptians down to the Incas and Aztecs, all of whom regarded it as a sacred symbol. It was used for ornamental purposes by the Carthaginians, and served as boundary marks to the ancient Scandinavians. Crosses have been found in archaeological sites more than 12,000 years ago, particularly at Herculaneum. According to scientists, they were probably used universally to signify the four main directions of the compass, as well as to represent all of life and everything. It is in this sense that they were regarded as emblems of Quetzalcoatl, lord of the four cardinal points and the four winds that blow from them.

The cross is now associated most directly with Christ, although it did not appear in Christian art until six hundred years after his death. Early Christians were at first indifferent to the symbolization of the Crucifixion because of the fear of persecution and of profaning the image of the Savior. Interest perked up only when it was rumored that the cross on which Jesus died had been discovered and was already in the Church's possession.

Before the cross, the icon most commonly venerated by Christians was the simple drawing of a fish consisting of four or five lines. In the days when persecution drove the movement underground, it became the secret mark of Christians and their faith, appearing clandestinely in the catacombs and in ancient private monuments as the graphic equivalent of the phrase 'Jesus Christ, Son of God, Savior'. The most popular source for the symbol is the miracle of Jesus feeding a multitude of thousands with just a few loaves and fishes, although some significance is also given to the fact that the traditional founder of the Church, Peter, was a fisherman by vocation. In truth, however, the symbol is based on the concept of fish as a word rather than as an object.

The initials of the Greek words in the phrase 'Jesus Christ, Son of God, Savior' form a rebus or acrostic that reads 'fish' in Greek.

The queen mother of Constantine the Great became a Roman Catholic saint principally on the strength of the claim that she discovered Christ's cross in the early fourth century. Converting to Christianity under the auspices of her son, she went to Jerusalem in the 320s to direct excavations at the site of the Crucifixion. According to her account, it was in the debris of centuries-old pagan temples overlaying the site of the Holy Sepulcher that she found not one but three crosses, including the nails that pierced Jesus' hands and feet. The true cross, it is said, revealed itself at the touch of a sick woman who became cured.

Critics note several weaknesses in the story, and Church authorities themselves seem to have second thoughts about its veracity. Most are uneasy that Helena knew exactly where to look despite the general lack even at the time of historical details concerning the holy event. Why the Romans would bury Christ's cross, much less those of the two robbers that died with him, is also troubling, since it was customary to recycle crosses used for this form of capital punishment due to the cost of wooden beams.

Where the relic is today has been the subject of much speculation. Parts of the cross, from splinters to whole segments, have turned up with such frequency that, as one cynic puts it, the pieces can be put together to make more than a hundred crosses. The church festival called the Invention of the Cross ('invention' is Latin for discovery), which used to he held on May 3 to commemorate the finding, was abolished by Pope John XXIII in 1960.

---

4. Veiled Prophet

Myth! **Jesus has the most number of monuments in his name.**

There are few Christian homes, and fewer Christian churches, that do not display an icon of Jesus Christ. But this is no indication that the great founder of the Christian faith holds the record for having the most number of monuments in his name.

Neither does Mohammad have that honor, despite his founding the religion with the widest following in the world. The universe of Islam, though suffused by this prophet's spiritual presence, has not one single statue to his credit. The not so obvious reason for this phenomenon is a covenant of the Islamic faith—one of its strictest—prohibiting the unveiling of Mohammad's face in statuary, art or drama. When the *Jyllands-Posten,* a Danish newspaper, published several editorial cartoons depicting Mohammad in September 2005, the violence that erupted in Europe and the Muslim countries led to Denmark's "worst international crisis since World War II." The prophet cannot be depicted even in cinematic form, as the production of the 1977 film *Mohammad, Messenger of God,* proves. Also called *The Message,* this three-hour megabuck epic about the founding of Islam stars Anthony Quinn, who does not play Mohammad (who is never shown on the screen) but his uncle.

Iconographers theorize that, without the prohibition, Mohammad's likeness would be everywhere in Islam, although it would only come second to that of Buddha. The statues of the oriental philosopher-prince, also called Siddhartha Gautama, proliferate in almost every part of the eastern hemisphere and are popular in the West as well. The advantage of Buddha is that his icons are not restricted to a purely religious use, but are equally applied to antiquarian, artistic and other secular purposes.

5. Healing Mantra

Myth! **Hippocrates devised the famous oath that most medical professionals take before they engage in their practice.**

Little is known about the origins of the eponymic Hippocratic oath. Hippocrates, who is regarded in the West as the father of medicine, is popularly believed to have written it in Ionic Greek in the late 5th century BCE. But some classical scholars say the historical origin of the oath is so obscure that its date of composition can only be placed between the sixth and first centuries B.C. As to the fabled ancient physician himself, nothing certain can be said about his ideas, discoveries, teachings, even the dates of his birth and death. Hippocrates's writings did not survive

70

his lifetime, while those obtainable from secondary sources have been recorded and passed on only by others who lived nearly two hundred years after his death. In short, no one can really tell how and when the oath was formulated or who wrote it, and even those who propose that Pythagoreans wrote the oath are stymied by the lack of evidence for a school of Pythagorean medicine.

Researchers believe it doesn't pay to inquire too much, since the oath itself is as vague and mysterious as its historical antecedents. The oath is obviously not a universal one, but is rewritten from time to time and from generation to generation to suit the values of different cultures. It is not true that doctors take the Hippocratic oath or any version of it as a matter of course before they enter into their duties, or that the very few who do quote essentially from the same version. It is also not true, as laymen generally believe, that most modern medical schools require their graduates to take the oath. If at all, each school follows its own tradition in applying the oath to a purpose, usually as a ceremonial frill during commencement exercises.

The oath, while considered an issue of individual morality for each physician, may serve generally as an ideal for professional attitudes and ethics. But in specific cases and for some individual practitioners, the classic wording is regarded as already way past its prime. For instance, notable provisions in the original that prohibit the dispensing of lethal or abortive drugs are now being subjected to closer scrutiny in light of liberal views about abortion and euthanasia. Be this as it may, there are currently no legal obligations attached to the Hippocratic oath. No professional regulatory board responsible for administering tests for the practice of medicine within a particular state requires a candidate to take the oath or anything similar to it in order to receive their license.

---

6. All that Glitters

Myth! **The beauty, rarity and incorruptibility of gold make it the most valuable commodity in the world.**

Gold is universally regarded as the symbol of wealth, but why it is so when other metals have the same or better qualities is not easy to understand.

The element is a good conductor of heat and electricity, and, as the most malleable and ductile of metals, ideal for jewelry. It is both pleasing and workable, and does not tarnish or corrode. But many other metals have also these features, and more. Gold, which anchors much of its value on its rarity, is only the sixteenth most rare element, while platinum is not only rarer but also far more superior in terms of physical properties and potential use. The most sought-after in the nuclear age is no longer gold but uranium, which is neither very rare nor particularly glamorous. It is, however, the basic ingredient of nuclear power and weapons, and the world's atomic nations have created an urgent demand for it.

Odd as it is, none of the better metals qualifies as 'global money' like gold does. The latter is the only totally acceptable medium of international exchange, a convention made possible by the fact that governments, central banks and investment funds hold most of all the gold mined to date (the top ten largest owners of gold in the world control a total of 24,258.3 tonnes, worth approximately $804.35 billion and representing about 15.4% of all the gold ever mined). Odder still is that the yellow metal enjoys this enviable status because it is universally obtainable—in other words, common. Gold can be found and is dug in almost every part of the globe, although it is probably no longer as common as when it could be panned commercially from the beds of streams or stumbled upon in the unlikeliest places.

7. The Holy Grail of Sailors?

Myth! **The America's Cup is awarded by the US to whoever is the current winner of the international triennial yachting competition.**

Contrary to popular belief, the America's Cup, the symbol of international yachting supremacy, was not named for America and did not originate with that country but with Britain. The Royal Yacht Squadron of Great Britain first offered it as the Hundred Guinea Cup for a 60-mile race around the Isle of Wight during the London Exposition of 1851. The field included 17 British schooners and a lone entrant from the US, a 101-foot schooner sailing under the auspices of the New York Yacht Club. The latter, sporting the patriotic name *America*, came out the surprise winner, leading the runner-up British yacht *Aurora* by more than an hour.

As soon as the *America* returned to the US, the trophy was nicknamed "America's Cup" and deeded by the winning boat's owner to the NYYC with instructions to defend it whenever challenged. It has since been called "America's Cup" even though it is officially the Auld Cup. The next race to offer the trophy as prize, and the one to launch the triennial America's Cup Competition, was on August 8, 1870, when the Australian boat *Cambria*, skippered by Captain J. Ashbury, lost to the American *Magic*, captained by F. Osgood. Contributing to the impression that the concept of the Cup has always been American is the fact that no non-American yacht would win it until 1983, when the eponymic Australia II ended the longest winning streak of any side in sporting history.

8. Flight in the Piazza

Myth! The longest and widest staircase in Europe, called the Spanish Steps, is designed by France, built by Spain and administered by Italy.

The popular name given to this famous landmark in Rome does give the impression to the ordinary tourist that it was financed and built by Spain and then leased to Italy under an international accord between the two countries. Actually, the term 'Spanish Steps' was concocted by the English speaking hoi polloi to refer to what is officially called the Scalinata della Trinita' del Monti; it arose only because the Scalinata was constructed on the Piazza di Spagna, a square that earned its own Spanish connotation when the Spanish embassy moved there in the 17th century while the steps were being conceptualized.

The real connection of the Scalinata is with the French. The

73

monumental stairway of 138 steps was built with French diplomat Étienne Gueffier's bequeathed funds of 20,000 scudi in 1723–1725. As its official name suggests, it ascends to the Piazza Trinità dei Monti, another square dominated by the French-built church and convent of Trinita dei Monti. The church was also financed by a gift from the visiting French king Charles VIII and restored by Louis XVIII, and the square itself features the Bourbon fleur-de-lys, along with Innocent XIII's eagle and crown, as part of the sculptural details. These circumstances have led to the belief in some quarters that France is the rightful owner of the Spanish Steps, although the general consensus is that it is real estate within the legal jurisdiction of Italy and forms part of that country's patrimony.

It is further claimed in behalf of the French advocacy that France suggested the idea of the Steps and the design is "unequivocally French." But in fact, the little-known Italian architect Francesco de Sanctis designed the steps following a competition in 1717, by assimilating the ideas of another Italian, Alessandro Specchi, the alleged winner of the competition. Several Italian popes had initiated the concept and its most powerful patron, French Cardinal Mazarin, who was originally Italian, boosted it into realization.

Artists were the first to move into the area, followed by innkeepers and ultimately tourists and celebrities. Enticed by the avant-garde environment and at times by the political stunts and demonstrations held there, the Steps are today "crowded with loiterers in distinctive dress and students from all over the world, while Rome's smart set can be seen shopping in the surrounding streets at both the top and the bottom of the stairs."

9. Phallic Symbols?

***Myth!* The three golden balls were originally assigned to pawnshops to indicate that there was a 2-to-1 chance of a pawned item being redeemed.**

Two of the most ubiquitous commercial symbols in the American scene during the first half of this century can still be found in some places today although they are no longer as popular.

These are the pawnbroker's three golden balls and the barber's pole.

Contrary to popular belief, the symbol of the three golden balls was not originally designed for the pawnbroker's place, but was taken from the coat of arms of the Medici family and first introduced to London by the Lombard bankers and money-lenders. Thus, the claim that the balls were positioned to indicate that there were two chances to one of the pawned item being redeemed is also a fallacy.

As to the red-and-white-striped pole displayed in front of a barbershop, people generally believe this is just a clever attention-getter for bringing in business. In reality, it's a relic of the days when barbers were also practicing surgeons, dentists, and phlebotomists (or blood-letters). As *Brewer* describes it: "The pole represents the staff gripped by persons in venesection, which was painted red since it was usually stained with blood. The white spiral represents the bandage twisted round the arm previous to bloodletting. The gilt knob at the end of the pole represents the brass basin, which was sometimes actually suspended from it. The basin had a notch in it to fit the throat, and was used for lathering customers before shaving."

10. Names from the X-Files

Myth! **The traditional signature of illiterates or uneducated persons on legal documents is the X or the cross.**

Literature and the cinema have made popular the idea that those unable to sign their names may put their marks on the documents instead. This is not entirely fiction, at least not in the early days, when the law had few formal qualifications for contracts. The most common cachet was the X or the cross, which, surprisingly, was used in the beginning not by the unlettered but their opposites. For many centuries making a cross was the way men of learning in Europe signed papers, even though they could spell out their names if they wanted to. They would kiss the mark so made, after which a witness would be asked to write out his name in full to further authenticate it. It was believed that the cross mark, when kissed by the maker, conveyed the force of a sworn oath.

But in the 17th century, educated people began to feel a distaste for giving the sign of the cross a secular or mercantile purpose, and replaced this with their initials or some other sign recognized as their own. At this point, the symbol was relegated to just being an identifying mark for the uneducated. Contrary to the popular myth, however, the cross or X was not the only mark illiterates utilized for affirming or authenticating documents. Most of them, in fact, created signs or marks for themselves that were almost as distinctive as signatures. Today, the large, crude X's or crosses show up on the dotted line only in fiction and the movies.

11. Tools of a Clandestine Trade?

Myth! **The letter G in the logo of Freemasonry stands for God, to signify a religious motif for the organization.**

As part of the square and compass logo of Freemasonry, the letter G is perhaps the most thought-provoking, if not the most popular, of the many mystical symbols of that organization, the full meaning of which a member is pledged to "ever conceal, never reveal."

To one who is not of the craft, it is an open secret that the G stands for God—not specifically Christian, Muslim, or Jewish, but all of them, to signify the universality of the brotherhood and its impartiality to all religious creeds. In monotheistic countries where the organization is allowed to operate, Freemasonry upholds the concept of the Supreme Being, and has a standing policy against admitting atheists and agnostics into its folds. Even in these places, however, Masons, to emphasize that theirs is an essentially moralist society, assign allegorical rather than religious significations to their symbols. Thus, Masonic prayers and invocations prefer to use the euphemism "Grand Architect of the Universe" in lieu of the word "God."

There is reason to believe that what Masons are told about the letter G depends on clime and place. Where anti-religious sentiments are strong or the leadership is strictly secular, the allusion to a supreme deity is avoided in favor of "Geometry," the major science employed by real masons in the building trade. The square and the compass are even hazier symbols and, having no specific or standard meanings, are meant to be interpreted subjectively by individual lodges.

12. Club Europa

Myth! **The bishops of the Church adopted the mace during medieval times as a symbol of religious authority.**

The mace, one of the first known tools fashioned by prehensile man, became an instrument of power when it developed into a club for use in war. It evolved into a brutish weapon particularly suited to the times "when men went about in armour, and sovereigns needed champions to vindicate their rights." As weaponry became more sophisticated, however, it was slowly transformed from an item of aggression into a benign trapping of authority. Up to modern times, the mace has been a symbol for officialdom, as in Britain, where it continues to be used as a staff of office pertaining to certain dignitaries, such as the Speaker of the House of Commons and the Lord Mayors.

Many historians note that it was the bishops of the Church who popularized the mace in the medieval era, but fail to clarify that in the hands of the princes of the cloth, the item had a functional use, not a symbolic one. They wielded it as a weapon of defense against the assassins and rogues unleashed by power mongers during those dark days of intrigue and conflict between Church and state.

13. Jailhouse Rock

Myth! **Alcatraz prison, a century-old escape-proof penal institution, had cells that could be identified with the convicts that had previously occupied them.**

Popularly called "The Rock," Alcatraz had a 'granite'

reputation for being escape-proof. At least 35 convicts tried to challenge this strictest of all federal prisons, but conditions in the surrounding bay made sure that none succeeded.

Or so it seems. Alcatraz was closed in 1963 based on the official reason that the cost of restoring its crumbling facilities was no longer affordable. But there is evidence of one more reason— the escape on June 12, 1962 of Frank Lee Morris and the brothers Joseph and Clarence Anglin, who were written off as drowned but were later seen in San Francisco.

Contrary to the belief that the prison was a century-old institution when it closed, Alcatraz was originally established in 1868 as a military fortress with penal facilities for deserters. It was only in 1934 that the place was taken over by the Department of Justice and converted into an institution for criminals who could not be contained in regular federal prisons.

Incidentally, the standard spiel dished out by tourist guides when they point to the alleged location of Al Capone's cell is probably not correct. What is more likely is that the gangster did not stay put in one place but was transferred from one cell to another as a security precaution. Even if a permanent cell had been assigned to the mobster, this kind of information was always kept secret while the prison was in operation, and has never been released even after Alcatraz was closed. Another aside: contrary to popular belief, Al Capone's conviction and subsequent imprisonment in Alcatraz was not for failing to pay the income tax. Rather, it was for filing a fraudulent income tax return. A person is criminally liable for filing a false return but not for failing to pay the income tax if the questioned return was properly filed.

14. After the Flood

Myth! **The use of the dove and the olive branch as peace symbols is rooted in the Biblical story of Noah and the Great Flood.**

The modern-day treatment of the dove and the olive leaf as Western peace symbols is obviously derived from the story of Noah and the Great Flood. They were the very first objects Noah saw outside the ark before the large vessel settled on the mountains of Ararat.

A passage in *Genesis* 8:10-11 relates how Noah sent the dove out of the Ark and saw it return to him in the evening. In its mouth was an olive leaf that it plucked somewhere, signaling that the waters of the Great Flood had abated and peace once again ruled on earth. People presume that because of the role each played in the aftermath of the disaster, the dove and the olive leaf have become the favorite symbols of peacemakers around the globe.

Strictly speaking, the dove is a modern symbol of peace but an olive leaf is not; as we all know, one sues for peace by offering an olive branch instead. Nonetheless, it is not true that the dove and the olive branch became peace symbols through the story of Noah. The dove earned its status elsewhere in the Bible, when it appeared as a manifestation of the Holy Ghost, Christendom's bringer of peace, while the olive branch is from Greek mythology, a pagan source. According to the classical account, Pallas Athena presented a gift of an olive branch to Athens to wish it peace after the city honored the Greek goddess by naming itself after her.

---

15. From both Sides Now

Myth! **Janus, from which comes Janus-faced, was the Roman god of hypocrisy and deceit.**

'Janus-faced' means hypocritical in the standard English dictionary, and derives from Janus, the Roman god famous for his two faces. The etymology of the word arose from the belief that Janus showed two different countenances in order to deceive. A moment's thought will tell us the belief is entirely false.

A hypocrite, metaphorically speaking, sports dissimilar, or, what is even more likely, highly contrasting facades. In contrast, Janus' two faces were completely identical. Moreover, this god was not prone to deceit, for he was in fact chosen by the Romans to be their guardian of households because of his trustworthiness. Watching over doorways, with one face looking at those who entered and the other at those who left, he ensured domestic

79

security and the safety of passages. He also protected birth, the first great passage of life, and soon presided over all beginnings.

Janus remained a faithful guardian deity in early English writings, until a wholly negative use of his name was began by Anthony Ashley Cooper, third earl of Shaftesbury. In his *Characteristicks of Men, Manners, Opinions, Times* (1711), Cooper scorned the "Janus-face of writers, who with one countenance force a smile and with another show nothing beside rage and fury."

---

16. A Colossal Mistake

Myth! **Rivaling the size of the Statue of Liberty, the Colossus of Rhodes stood astride the harbor entrance of that ancient city.**

Ancient records attest to the existence of the Colossus of Rhodes, a 100 ft. statue of the Greek god Helios built by Chares of Lindos between 292 and 280 BC. Apparently, the vaunted size of the bronze figure made it the tallest statue during its time and a marvel of construction for its locale, a small Greek island rich in myth but not noted for any other technical or artistic achievement. Thus has the structure merited the modern honor of being counted among the Seven Wonders of the Ancient World.

But 100 feet would not seem colossal in the modern sense of the word. A statue of Nero, executed by Zenodorus, was even higher at 110 feet, but the only recognition it got was to have the name Colosseum attached to the huge amphitheater that the emperor Vespasian subsequently erected in its vicinity. Indeed, 100 feet is not enough to warrant the statement by writer Reena Pathak that the Colossus of Rhodes was "nearly as high as the Statue of Liberty." The Colossus might have had an extra 10 feet for its marble base, yet it would still have been just slightly more than two-thirds the height of Liberty (151 feet) and only one-third the latter's total height with its pedestal (305 feet). After an earthquake felled the Colossus of Rhodes, Pliny the Elder remarked that people congregated around the fallen hand but "few could wrap their arms around the thumb" and "each of its fingers was larger than most statues." However, considering that Liberty's second joint has a circumference of only 3 ft. 6 in., the Colossus' was probably even less, suggesting that the arms Pliny said couldn't be wrapped around its thumb must have belonged to babies or small children.

We have no clue on the origin of the word 'colossus' and whether it antedated or was derived from Helios' statue at Rhodes. But the evidence shows that, at the time, 'colossus' did not necessarily mean huge. According to a historian: "Ancient sculptors were accustomed to make their statutes somewhat more than life size, especially those which were to be mounted upon high pedestals or as architectural ornaments upon lofty buildings. Thus, when viewed from the roadway, the figures appeared in proper proportions and the fine details of the artist's handiwork were not lost through the distance. Any such enlarged statue, however little it exceeded man's ordinary size, was, in Rome, a colossus; in Greece, *kolossos*."

The bigger misconception, of course, has to do with the Colossus' position as depicted in both early and modern paintings, sculptures and commercial illustrations of the now long gone structure. These graphic portrayals, augmented by descriptions in literary works and references, show the statue straddling the harbor entrance as ships pass beneath its huge legs, something that, from the experts' point of view, begs credibility. They say that, assuming such a statue was completed as postured, (1) the entire harbor mouth would have been effectively closed during the 8- to 12-years period of construction; (2) the ancient Rhodians by themselves would not have had the means to dredge and re-open the harbor after the construction; (3) the statue would have totally blocked the harbor when it was felled by an earthquake in 224 BC; (4) since the ancients would not have had the ability to remove the fallen statue from the water, it would not have remained visible on land as it had for the next 800 years; (5) as any engineering analysis would readily prove, the statue being made of bronze could not have been built with its legs apart without collapsing from its own weight; and (6) alternate positions proposed by modern researchers for the statue would have made its construction by the ancients more feasible.

The consensus of those closely associated with the building of the Statue of Liberty is that the Colossus of Rhodes stood with his legs slightly apart on only one side of the entrance to the harbor. Ironically, Emma Lazarus, who wrote the famous poem "The New

Colossus" about the iconic lady in 1883, was one of the traditionalists who didn't agree. The poem, inscribed on a plaque located inside Liberty's pedestal, contains a reference to the ancient Colossus, thus: "...the brazen giant of Greek fame, with conquering limbs astride from land to land..."

17. Sign of the Pagan

Myth! Bertrand Russell designed the 1960 peace symbol, a crude figure of a B-52 bomber contained in a circle.

The belief that it was Bertrand Russell who, prompted by his Communist sympathies, designed the 1960 peace symbol is not true. The famous British philosopher may have had some leftist involvements in his time, but his sole concern with the peace symbol was as president of the Campaign for Nuclear Disarmament. The CND used the symbol for the first time in a peace march in England on the Easter weekend of 1958 to protest the Atomic Weapons Research Establishment at Aldermaston. The symbol was later adopted in the 1960s by a broad range of antiwar and nuclear disarmament groups and eventually came to be associated in the United States with protest against the Vietnam War.

The real creator of the symbol was Gerald Holtom, a British commercial artist and a CND member. Holton was commissioned to produce a design that would promote the antinuclear group and could be easily reproduced on banners for display purposes. Using as his basis letters in the semaphore or flag alphabet that Navy ships use to communicate with each other, he completed the assignment on February 21, 1958. This was readily accepted by the organization to become its official logo.

The symbol was widely visualized in the 1960s as a B-52 bomber in a circle, denoting the idea of bomber containment in the Vietnam War. The symbol was said to be an icon of the left's efforts to stop the bombing in Southeast Asia, which was purportedly being carried out by B-52 bombers in Vietnam and Cambodia. This and other interpretations were all false. In 1970 one CND critic went so far as to suggest that the symbol was a satanic device maliciously designed by Communists, its center

82

portion a "chicken track" used in demonic rituals as an anti-Christian symbol representing the opposite of the cross. In truth, insists Holtom, the symbol is simply an artistic manipulation of the semaphore signals for N and D (arms held at 4 and 8 o'clock, and 12 and 6 o'clock, respectively) inside a circle. N and D are the initials for nuclear disarmament while the circle represents the whole world. Although Holtom and his artists were not averse to giving it other meanings, they were particular about excluding bomber containment because it was never a CND objective.

Incidentally, calling the symbol the "peace sign" is not strictly correct either. The objective of nuclear disarmament is limited to putting an end to the possession and use of nuclear devices as weapons of war. But a peace sign is normally equated with the idea of pacifism, which proposes to eliminate war itself regardless of the kind of weaponry used.

18. Roman Thumbers

Myth! 'Thumbs up' was the ancient Roman's signal for the winning gladiator to spare his opponent's life.

Pollice verso is the Latin phrase for "with a turned thumb", describing a hand gesture the audiences of ancient Rome made to pass judgment on a defeated gladiator in combat. It is also the title of an 1872 painting by French artist Jean-León Gérome, which U.S. department-store magnate Alexander Turner Stewart purchased and exhibited in New York City and is now in the Phoenix Art Museum in Arizona.

Gérome's large canvas portrays a group of Roman priestesses called Vestal Virgins giving the 'thumbs down' sign from a box as a way of urging a victorious gladiator in the arena to strike the fatal blow on his fallen opponent. Historically, the type of gesture suggested by the phrase *pollice verso* is unclear, the records being uncertain whether the thumb was turned up, turned down, held horizontally, or concealed inside the hand to indicate a positive or negative opinion. But Gérome's spectacular work and the suggestive English translation of its title have contributed largely to the belief that 'thumbs down' was the signal that a defeated gladiator should be condemned to death, and 'thumbs up' meant he should be spared. Taking up the cue, Australian artist Norman Lindsay also gave the title "Pollice Verso" to his controversial 1904 drawing of the crucified Christ being shown the 'thumbs down' sign by a crowd of naked pagans. 'Thumbs down' has since become the popular mode in most cultures to show disapproval, and the opposite 'thumbs up' to indicate consent, for a specific course of action.

Nonetheless, there is at least one historical source that goes against the modern interpretation, and this is the Roman text *Satire III* of Juvenal stating that the thumbs down sign was for the winning gladiator to drop his sword and spare his fallen foe. Juvenal is backed by a 1601 translation of Pliny that equates 'thumbs down' with 'assent' or 'favor'. Apparently, the original instruction to most gladiators by their handlers was to kill their defeated opponents, so that 'thumbs up' from the crowds would mean "yes" or "approval" of the default action, while 'thumbs down' would be "no," or "disapproval." Other sources believe that 'thumbs up', particularly if it pointed to the chest, was literally telling the gladiator to stab his opponent, and 'thumbs down' to sheathe his weapon. Finally, there are those who place no particular importance on direction or position provided only that the other fingers of the hand covered the thumb. This, they say, was the meaning of "thumbs pressed" *(pollice primo* or *compresso)*, the signal indicating that the dagger was to be sheathed.

Finally, research has shown that, contrary to popular understanding, only the Roman emperor could allow a gladiator to kill his enemy. The royal gesture for the purpose was not a 'thumbs up' or 'thumbs down' but an open or closed hand, the former meaning "spare his life" and the latter "death." Unless the emperor gave his permission in this manner, a gladiator who killed his opponent would be put on trial for murder and likely executed.

19. Reformed Bastion

Myth! **Seen as a symbol of oppression, the Bastille was besieged by the masses to signal the start of the French Revolution.**

The Bastille as a freedom symbol is clearly overrated. Erected as a royal castle by Charles V between 1370 and 1383, it doubled as a fortress to protect Paris during the so-called Hundred Years' War, then became a state prison in the 17th and 18th centuries. In the 1620s, it was devoted to the detention of important persons charged with miscellaneous offenses under the ministry of Cardinal Richelieu, and during the next hundred years was the most infamous prison in Europe and a symbol of tyranny and Bourbon despotism. Even then, the Bastille was not as notorious a dungeon as Alexander Dumas and other authors pictured it to be. The yearly average number of prisoners was only 40, and most were political troublemakers or individuals held at the request of their own relatives to protect the family name.

Serving for a while as the repository of prohibited books, it was considered for demolition in 1784 because of the high cost of maintenance. Five years later, it fell into the hands of an angry mob to signal the start of the French Revolution, but it was obviously captured for reasons other than to save the seven prisoners who were found inside. After seizing arms from the Invalides building, the besiegers had gone looking for ammunition, and when the prison governor became evasive, they stormed and captured the place. The revolutionaries quickly took advantage of the moment to claim the Bastille as the symbol that ended the *ancien regime*.

Institutions

I

Invasion Of The Body Snatchers

On Slavery in the Americas

"I looks like gwine to heaven,
an't thar where white folks is gwine?
S'pose they'd have me thar?"

•

Uncle Tom

1. Equal but Separate

Myth! **The US was the first Western country to outlaw slavery.**

Americans like to believe that the US was the first country in the Western Hemisphere, and Pennsylvania the first American colony, to outlaw slavery.

They are in for a disappointment. Argentina outlawed slavery in 1811, Colombia in 1821, and Mexico in 1829. The US didn't outlaw slavery until 1866, with the promulgation of the Thirteenth Amendment. Even assuming the Emancipation Proclamation of 1863 was an act of abolition, which it wasn't, this was still many decades after the others had wrote finis to the institution.

Interestingly, while slavery was completely outlawed in the rest of the continent, the Thirteenth Amendment didn't terminate it with the same absolute effect in the US. The constitutional provision to this day reserves the right of the state to impose slavery or involuntary servitude "as a punishment for crime whereof the party shall have been duly convicted."

Slave trading was prohibited in the US in 1808, but not many know that as early as 1776 the Second Continental Congress resolved that "no slaves be imported into any of the Thirteen United Colonies." Our history books also tell us that slavery in the US was abolished, in whole or in part, in the second half of the 19th century, without clarifying that the institution was already anathema in many states in the previous century. The first state of the United States to abolish slavery was Vermont in 1777, and the first to do so of the states that comprised the original thirteen colonies was Pennsylvania in 1780.

In fact, Rhode Island became the first American colony to outlaw slavery as early as 1652. However, because slavery was profitable, it was later permitted in that territory again. Surprisingly, in 1733, Georgia, which would soon be one of the most proslavery states of the United States, became the first colony to be chartered on the premise that no slaves will be imported into its territory. The prohibition, however, was not out of concern for blacks, but to help whites. The founders worried that slavery would be incompatible with the goal of establishing Georgia as a refuge for debtors who wanted a new start in life. It was particularly feared that the institution would render the majority of settlers, who couldn't afford to buy slaves of their own, uncompetitive and underemployed. The ban on slavery lasted fourteen years, at the end of which the trustees, under pressure from big planters, reversed themselves and approved the importation of slaves.

2. Southern Comfort

Myth! **The Union did more than the Confederates to alleviate the conditions of Southern slaves.**

It is not well known that the Confederacy gave the blacks a better break than Lincoln's Emancipation Proclamation ever did. The motive may have been less than sincere—the South knew they couldn't win the war without at least modifying the institution of slavery—but the fact remains: they took more steps to alleviate the conditions of slaves during the Civil War than at any time before or after.

One example was a proposal outlawing the sale of slave children and allowing slave testimony to be heard in court. Another was a law passed in Alabama in 1864 requiring masters to get legal counsel for slaves who were indicted for major criminal offenses. Just one month before the Confederacy finally crumbled, President Jefferson Davis and General Robert E. Lee officially endorsed two measures anathema to the very ideals on which the South stood. The first was for the recruitment of slaves into the Rebel army, and in this regard, the Confederate Congress, at the request of Lee, authorized the arming of up to three hundred thousand slaves. The second was for the abolition of slavery itself. Jefferson Davis instructed one of his diplomats in Europe to inform Britain and France that the Confederacy was willing to emancipate the South's slaves in exchange for official recognition as an independent country. This was, at least in theory, more than what the Emancipation Proclamation proposed to do, which was to free slaves in the South but not in the North, and in any case not to abolish slavery altogether.

3. Captive Resources

Myth! **Because of their genetic make-up, Native Americans proved harder to subjugate than African blacks.**

It is said blacks acquired their freedom and their political rights earlier than Native Americans because they had been easier to enslave. Indians, so the argument goes, preferred to be punished or even be killed before submitting to bondage, a condition inconsistent with their beliefs and culture.

The conflicting experience of the US with blacks and Indians has led many to conclude that it is easy to enslave some races but difficult or impossible to do so with others. Apparently, while the black man was able to reconcile to his fate without much trouble, the Indian could not be forced into slavery even after complete subjugation.

Most scientists see the popular view that this difference has a genetic significance as fallacious. According to sociological evidence, North American Indians proved resistant to attempts at enslavement by the conquistadores, not because of any racial or hereditary traits but because they were largely nomadic. US slave masters no doubt had similar designs on the aboriginals, but in the end so much blood was spilled just to force them onto reservations. Indians in Latin America were different. Coming from strong and relatively permanent agricultural communities, they were often enslaved successfully by the Spanish and the Portuguese. Fortunately, their subjugation was less extensive than that of the blacks because Catholic missionaries insisted that they be evangelized as members of the faithful.

4. Unlocking the Cabin

Myth! **Harriet Beecher Stowe's Uncle Tom is the epitome of a subservient black.**

In modern American usage, an Uncle Tom is a black person who is able to survive in a hostile, racist environment by adopting an abject and servile attitude toward the white man. The term derives from Harriet Beecher Stowe's Uncle Tom, in consonance with the belief that this was how she painted her famous character. Apparently, the belief is entertained only by those who have not read the novel, or who, having read it cursorily, mistakenly see the extraordinary devotion of the Negro slave to the little girl Eva as undue servility to whites. Uncle Tom is actually humble, brave, humane and forbearing to his enemies, maintaining his dignity despite having to suffer constantly from the brutal treatment of the overseer Simon Legree.

According to Stowe's book *A Key to Uncle Tom's Cabin*, the character of Uncle Tom was largely based on the life of Josiah Henson, a slave who escaped to Canada and then published his autobiography in 1848. Henson later became a prosperous and learned preacher who came to London in 1876 and was presented to Queen Victoria. Stowe had been careful to shape Uncle Tom in the image of Henson during his days of servitude, but the result was grossly distorted in the plays that ensued from Stowe's book without her permission. Thousands of poorly written stage scripts and third-rate actors eventually transformed the beloved figure into the bootlicking old man of everyday speech who is willing to endure anything in the hope of saving his own skin.

5. A Dred-ful Decision

Myth! In the Dred Scott case, the US Supreme Court ruled that a black person has no rights which a white man ought to respect.

Sam (Dred) Scott, a Virginia slave, was allowed by his master to live for a period in free, or non-slave, states. But when it was decided for Scott to go to Missouri, where slavery was still constitutional, Dred started legal proceedings, claiming that, having lived in non-slave states, he was no longer a slave. After the Missouri Supreme Court found against Dred, he elevated his case to the US Supreme Court. In an 1857 opinion penned by Chief Justice Roger Taney, the Court decided by a narrow majority that, under the Fifth Amendment, no slaveholder could be deprived of his property without due process, and Scott, as a result, was still a slave.

What makes Justice Taney's majority opinion memorable, and ignominious to many, is a passage that says, "They (blacks) had for more than a century before been regarded as beings of an inferior order, and altogether unfit to associate with the white race, either in social or political relations, and so far unfit that they had no rights which the white man was bound to respect." Legal experts feel the remark, although pure dictum, was uncalled for. Others point out in defense of Taney that his use of the past tense makes it obvious he was not expressing a view but taking judicial notice of a fact—that fact being what the public believed, rightly or wrongly, at the time the Declaration of Independence and the Constitution were framed. In any case, there seems to be no doubt where the jurist's sympathy lay. Taney personally did not practice slavery, thought slavery was "a blot on our national character," and as a southerner sided with the Union during the Civil War. But the words he is best known for are now usually read out of context to tarnish his memory unfairly.

6. Better Nixed than Mixed

Myth! **Almost all slaves in the West were African blacks, and their owners were the most anti-black in the US South.**

The common belief at this time is that almost all slaves in the Western hemisphere were black and most if not all blacks in the Americas were slaves. A corollary observation is that the most anti-black among the Southerners were the slaveholders.

In fact, some slaves were of a different color and did not come from Africa. There were brown ones, like the Indians that the Spanish enslaved in some parts of South America. Unbelievably, there were also white slaves, until legislation banned the practice in 1826. They weren't slaves in the strict sense—the polite term was 'indentured servants', referring to members of poor white families compelled by financial circumstances to be 'sold' as menials for a contract period, usually a number of years.

Even more shocking is that prosperous black families in colonial America could buy the services of whites from England until 1670, when the Virginia Assembly made it illegal for blacks to own white servants. These same families, which were both free and wealthy, also owned black slaves whom they imported from their African homeland. The slaveholders had once been slaves themselves but were later emancipated, some as a reward for faithful service, others as a result of religious convictions newly acquired by their white owners.

There were some 3,953,760 black slaves in the US on the eve of the Civil War in 1860. Only twenty-five percent of white families in the South owned these unfortunates, most of whom worked on large plantations. While it seems strange that the other seventy-five percent who owned no slaves were more resentful of blacks, historians say it is quite logical. Most masters were able to develop strong familial relationships with their slaves during the period of bondage, but no such ties or feelings bound blacks to the non-slaveholding sector of southern society. This latter class consisted mainly of small farmers, artisans, tradesmen and poor whites, most of whom felt only a cut above the blacks and regarded the slaves as an unfair source of competition.

7. Under the Spanish Whip

Myth! **The Spaniards were the earliest to introduce slavery into North America.**

While the Portuguese were the first to engage in slave trafficking worldwide, it is generally believed Christopher Columbus under the patronage of the Spaniards was the earliest to open up the trade in the New World. He did this not by importing slaves to America but by exporting captive Indians to Europe. At first, the Spanish monarchy prohibited the entry of black slaves into the New World. Eventually, it raised the ban on the request of Church authorities in order to stop the exploitation of the native population by the conquistadors.

The Spaniards were among the first to import slaves into the Americas, which was mainly through the Caribbean. But Cortéz reported seeing some Portuguese slavers in the slave markets of Mexico, an indication that the Portuguese were ahead in the slave trade in North America. In the US, a Dutch slaver, not an Iberian, brought the first twenty slaves to the new settlement at Jamestown; this was 240 years before the Civil War, not 100, as is commonly supposed.

Ironically, Africa itself had a slave trade going long before the first white Europeans arrived in that continent and began the mass deportation of black Africans to the West Indies and the Americas. The activity was centered in Timbuktu, capital of the Mali Empire, during the 13th century. There were both black and white slaves, with both being generally treated better than in other countries.

---

8. Cry Freedom

Myth! **The slogan "Abolition!" was first used in America against the institution of slavery.**

Most of those who mouthed the slogan "Abolition!" during the civil rights movement in the US in the 1960s did so believing that it originated with the anti-slavery campaign of the Abolitionists in the 19th century.

Actually, the word was born in the 18th century when the colonies were beginning to struggle against British dominion, and it was not in connection with slavery. To be sure, there were already abolitionists in colonial times—mostly religious and other disturber groups righteously railing against the pernicious practice. The Quakers, who were the first to organize the Abolitionist Movement in 1787, had begun their criticism in 1671, or more than a hundred years earlier. But the word 'abolition"' was not one of their battle cries, and won't be long after slavery in the northern states had been virtually eliminated. The slogan would emerge only in another context—that of the colonists fighting the hated British Stamp Act, which, in their effort to have it removed, became one of the symbols of oppression that planted the very seeds of the American Revolution.

9. African-American History X

Myth! **At least 50% of the slave trade in the Americas was carried on in the US.**

One irony of history is that countries that engaged in the practice of slaveholding stood more condemned than those who brought the institution to them. Yet another irony is that the US bore the brunt of that condemnation despite the widespread hold of slavery in all of the Americas.

Critics didn't seem to realize that the US wasn't even the biggest importer of slaves in the American continent. In fact, contrary to what most people think, it was the smallest. Research would reveal that the US imported only some 425,000 blacks from Africa, or about 4.5 percent of the total imported to the Western Hemisphere via the Atlantic slave trade.

True, the slave stock in the states grew to one of the biggest in the New World—4 million by the start of the Civil War—but this was mainly through internal breeding. Importation was banned in 1808, after which, except for some smuggling, the major source of slaves was the law that a child born of a slave parent was also a slave. Unlike other slave societies in the continent, where deaths greatly exceeded births and new imports had to replenish the black population, the number that survived at the end of slavery in the US came near equaling the number originally imported.

II

Clash Of Colors

On Racism

"Apartheid is part of our national heritage."

•

Louis Botha

1. The Dreams of King

Myth! **Martin Luther King, Jr., introduced the phrases "I have a dream" and "I am free at last" in his Lincoln Memorial speech.**

Dr. Martin Luther King, Jr. was never more awe-inspiring in his crusading life than when he stood near the Lincoln Memorial in Washington, DC, on August 28, 1963, and delivered his emotional "I Have A Dream" speech. His audience was a quarter million people that had just ended a civil rights march that day—the largest rally ever in US history. Singing the movement's unofficial anthem, "We Shall Overcome," they massed before King's podium to listen to his stirring rhetoric about a dream—the dream that his children, along with "all God's children," would one day be judged by the "content of their character" rather then the color of their skin.

King repeatedly used the words "I have a dream" by which the 17-minute oration would later become famous, ranked as the top American speech of the 20th century by a 1999 poll of scholars of public address. Yet not many people realized the phrase was no longer original on that occasion. King had earlier delivered a speech using the same phrase in Detroit on June 23, 1963, and it was perhaps to point out this fact that his August 28 speech started with "I still have a dream." What followed deviated substantially from the text he had prepared, to the discomfiture of some of those on the platform with him. But there was nothing off-hand about the "I have a dream" segment, which he conveyed successfully as though it were drawn from his imagination rather than his recollection.

King's epitaph as it appears on his tombstone is, "Free at last, free at last, thank God almighty, I'm free at last." What he actually said in his "I Have a Dream" speech was, "Free at last, free at last, thank God almighty, *we are* free at last." But even this is far from original. As King himself acknowledged in his speech, the line was a quote from an old Negro spiritual.

2. Black Man's Burden

Myth! Carpetbaggers and scalawags did most of the damage to the cause of blacks during Reconstruction.

The abrupt and unmonitored change in the political status of blacks after the Civil War produced aberrations that eventually caused Reconstruction to fail. The newly freed blacks were largely uneducated and illiterate, and became the targets of exploitation by unscrupulous whites who saw power and profits in the devastated South. Some of these were said to be charlatans from the North who saw an opportunity to manipulate black politics or use black votes to gain office. They were called 'carpetbaggers' because they traveled with all their possessions carried in a carpetbag, a type of soft luggage made of carpet material.

But historians who have made incisive studies of the post-war South tell us the carpetbagger is largely myth. They were not the lowlifes that political cartoons, both in the North and South, made them out to be, but middle-class professionals who believed the new South provided means for personal advancement and opportunity. Of the so-called carpetbaggers, quite a few were idealists who had moved south before blacks got the vote.

Even more maligned than the carpetbaggers were the Southern-born white Republicans called 'scalawags' by Southern Democrats. Seen as traitors to the Confederate cause because of their anti-slavery stance during the war, conservative Southern politicians depicted them as corrupt profiteers exploiting illiterate blacks. But historians believe scalawags were no more contemptible than carpetbaggers, and view the accusation against them as a backlash from the bitterness caused by the South's defeat in the war. One of the most prominent scalawags was General James Longstreet (Robert E. Lee's top general after Stonewall Jackson), who, despite an impressive record during the Civil War, was accused of disloyalty to the South for joining the Republicans and batting for Negro suffrage.

3. Days of the Locust?

Myth! Blacks took advantage of their dominant political power during Reconstruction to commit unprecedented graft and corruption.

An issue that still haunts the political campaigns of minority candidates in the South is whether blacks should carry the blame for the failure of Reconstruction because they were the dominant political power at the time. It is charged that blacks took advantage of this period of readjustment and committed unspeakable graft by, among other things, robbing state and local treasuries, imposing taxes designed to work unfairly against the whites, disfranchising whites so as to be able to take complete charge, and electing illiterate and ignorant politicians to high office.

Experts explode the myth by pointing out that in only two states, South Carolina and Georgia, did blacks form a majority of the legislatures during Reconstruction, and in those places blacks happened to outnumber whites in the general population. No black governor was elected in any state, and only in South Carolina was there even a single black Supreme Court Justice. State constitutions were rewritten after the war by a majority of whites, for in only two constitutional conventions did blacks have the major voice in drafting provisions that could have allowed them to participate in power. To be sure, taxes increased after the war, but they were necessary for the rebuilding of the devastated cities and countryside. The claim that the Reconstruction governments were corrupt is neither more nor less cogent than the observation that governments everywhere in the United States were corrupt during this era.

4. Scared Crow

Myth! The term Jim Crow was formed by combining the name of a black bird with that of a black man.

"Jim Crow," a term for the systematic practice of discriminating against and suppressing black people, has various origins, none of them dating later than the 1830s. According to the Negro Year Book for 1925-26, Jim Crow was the name of a Negro born in Richmond about 1800, who was later emancipated and acquired "quite a fortune" in England. Where the Year Book got its information is a mystery, and whether or not it suffices as a record of a black person whose name had something to do with the etymology of the term is uncertain. Some word historians bring Jim Crow back to an earlier period—1730, when black people were beginning to be described as crows because of their color. The combination of Crow with Jim seemed natural, since Jim was one of the most common names for male slaves.

Not being hard evidence, however, both sources must yield to a documented one—a popular song copyrighted in 1828 by Thomas D. Rice and forming part of a skit, "The Rifle", written by Solon Robinson. The song and its accompanying dance were reportedly based on the chance observance of an old Negro in Louisville, Kentucky, who shuffled as he sang, "Weel about, turn about, do jist so." In the skit produced in Washington in 1835 and taken to London in 1836, where it became equally popular, a black-faced Rice sang, "And ebery time I wheel about I jump Jim Crow," with no indication that Jim Crow was a name and referred to any specific person. From there, the phrase was used in American English to refer to a black person or anything associated with him, and eventually to racial segregation imposed by whites on blacks.

---

5. Sub Rosa in Alabama

Myth! **Founded by American blacks, the NAACP is best known for instigating the Montgomery incident that sparked the civil rights movement.**

Two fallacies that persist about the NAACP are, one, it was organized by Afro-Americans, and, two, it instigated the Montgomery, Alabama, incident that sparked the civil rights movement in 1955. The black writer and educator W. E. B. Du Bois is generally reputed to be the founder of the NAACP, but actually, he was only a co-founder and, moreover, he was a Ghanaian. The chief founder was the liberal New York journalist W. E. Walling, who, after a race riot in Springfield, Massachusetts, in 1908, met in his apartment with other concerned citizens, including social worker Mary W. Ovington, to discuss the launching of the organization in 1909. The new set of officers was all white except for Du Bois, who served as the first editor of the magazine *The Crisis*.

Many believe the December 1, 1955, incident in Montgomery, Alabama, involving the 43-year old black seamstress Rosa Parks, was a planned operation under the auspices of the NAACP. Parks was arrested for refusing to yield her seat in a bus to a white man, and, for refusing to pay the fine, was jailed. Her case led to the widespread boycott of buses in Montgomery under the orchestration of Martin Luther King, Jr. Because Parks was active in the local chapter of the NAACP and King was the pastor of her church, word got out that she was an NAACP operative under King whose protest had been arranged by the civil rights organization to challenge Alabama's segregation laws. But Rosa herself made clear that she was not a rebel, and that what she did was not because she had a righteous cause to promote but because she was tired and her feet hurt.

6. Crossing the Bar

Myth! **South Africa introduced apartheid officially in the early 1900s and gave blacks the right to vote only in 1994, when they had their first colored prime minister.**

White supremacists were aghast at South Africa's decision to dismantle apartheid and fully liberate the black vote. They warned that their country's blacks had never been trusted with the franchise before, and could not share power too long with the whites without corrupting their newfound freedom.

This premise was and has always been false. South African blacks have proved their merit to hold and exercise the franchise as far back as 1853. On July 1 of that year, a constitution was introduced in the Cape Colony giving each British citizen there—

101

both white and black—the right to vote depending on job and salary.

Not many realize that the official policy of apartheid, which separated whites from nonwhites as well as one nonwhite group or indigenous African tribe from another, was introduced only in 1947, and the society had had a high degree of racial mix up to that time. The best proof of this was General Louis Botha, who in 1910 became the first prime minister of the Union of South Africa. Botha was actually descended from a black slave, Lijsbeth van die Kaap, who in the late seventeenth century had five daughters, three by an Indian and former slave, Louis van Bengale, and two by Johann Herfst, a German settler. Four of these daughters married white men. According to research released by Professor Leon Hattingh of the Institute for Historical Research of the University of West Cape, Lijsbeth is the ancestor of more than 200,000 living Afrikaners who think they are 'pure white'. The same study revealed that the average 'white' Afrikaner is really 7 percent black.

7. Reversal of Fortunes

Myth! **Virginia was the first US state to have a black governor.**

Virginia, birthplace of several US presidents, is often made host to the claim that it was the first state of the US to have a black governor. It came about in 1990, when L. Douglas Wilder, grandson of slaves, a Korean War hero and a millionaire trial lawyer, was sworn in as the Democratic chief executive of Virginia.

Wilder deserves every bit of respect for his achievement, which broke a 118-year-long dry spell, but according to historians, he wasn't the first black governor and Virginia wasn't the first state to have one. A black Reconstruction-era politician and lawyer with a name straight from a W. C. Fields movie—Pinckney Benton Stewart Pinchback—was duly elected lieutenant governor of Louisiana when that state was about 50 percent black. The son of a white father and a free black mother, Pinchback subsequently became governor of Louisiana for four weeks in 1872 and 1873.

He had been appointed to that position to replace Governor Henry Clay Warmoth, who was suspended while his impeachment case was being heard by the Louisiana legislature. When Warmoth's term expired during the impeachment proceedings, Governor Pinchback stepped down from his caretaker role and yielded his office to a white man, William Pitt Kellogg, who was sworn in as the new governor.

The fact that Pinchback was elected senator in 1873 but was not seated has not detracted one bit from the honor earlier garnered by Louisiana when it chose him governor. This was the second civil rights breakthrough for the state, once a bastion of the deeply conservative south, the first one being the draft of black soldiers to fight for the Confederacy in the Civil War.

III
Strangers In Their Own Land

On Native Americans

"Every human longs for peace and love."

•

Hiawatha

1. Don't ask How, just say How

Myth! 'How' is the universal American Indian word for 'hello'.

However we've been led to believe about this purported custom, there is no such thing as a universal Indian greeting. American Indians speak some 500 different languages, with not many words common to more than a few. Most native vocabularies have their own forms of salutation, and any similarity one may have with another is generally limited to their meanings.

'How', long regarded as the Indian ice-breaker in American pop culture corresponding to the English word 'hello', is an obtrusive Hollywood creation either wholly invented by a scriptwriter or derived from a remote and corrupted Indian source. 'How' did have some variants in the native speech of the Plains Indians, who spoke versions of a major language called Siouan, but these were mostly interjections indicating surprise or anger rather than goodwill. The Tetons said *howo* and *ho*, the Dakota *hao* and *ho*, and the Omaha *hau*. All served as a sort of introductory adverbial ejaculation along the lines of 'well', 'hey', 'so', or 'now', with the precise meaning of each depending on the ethnographer who recorded it.

Modern Native Americans, whether or not they still speak in their dialects, are as proficient in English as their white brothers, and most if not all prefer to say 'hello' when greeting others.

2. Most Chiefs have Hatchet Men

Myth! The tomahawk was invented and named by American Indians.

The tomahawk may well have been the favorite war weapon of the American Indians, but it did not originate with them. It was the white settler who invented the metal hatchet and, like the rifle and the steel knife, sold it to the natives, not caring or realizing that it would be used eventually against him. The item was accepted enthusiastically and spread rapidly to tribes even in remote areas not yet known to the whites. The Indians were not a metalworking people, hence every single piece was traded rather than manufactured.

But what came to be known as the tomahawk was not the same weapon that the Indians invented the word for. 'Tomahawk' derives from the language of the Powhatan (Algonquians of Virginia) and originally meant the stone or wooden war club, which was the only indigenous weapon extensively used by the American Indians. When John Smith introduced the word to the English vocabulary, spelling it *tomahak*, he defined it simply as 'ax', although he later remarked that the term was also applied to the native war club. Only with the passing of the years did 'tomahawk' come to be used exclusively for the metal war hatchet that has become so familiar to devotees of western novels and movies.

It was an Old West belief, fostered in the last century by the popular TV series featuring Fess Parker as Daniel Boone and Ed Ames as his Indian sidekick, that the tomahawk was aerodynamically balanced for throwing, particularly since it was supposed to have been originally based on a Royal Navy ballistic. The fact is, the tomahawk was rarely thrown in combat, and for an obvious reason: a weapon thrown is likely to be a weapon lost. Worse, it could be picked up in case of a miss and used against the thrower. Similarly, serious fighters did not throw their knives the way it has been commonly shown in war and cowboy movies. In modern times, however, the use of better materials and expert craftsmanship in the manufacture of the weapon has promoted tomahawk throwing as a popular sport among American historical groups and a category in competitive knife throwing.

3. Return of the Natives

Myth! Native Americans are fast disappearing from the North American continent.

The misleading names that have been given to the American Indians reflect a lack of understanding of these people. First is the word 'Indian', which is a perpetuation of Columbus' mistake when he landed in the New World thinking it was India. Second is the phrase 'The Vanishing Americans', a popular epithet with writers who believe the race is disappearing from the North American continent. The nickname might have been coined in reference to those periods when the original numbers of the native population were declining at an alarming rate because of disease, massacres and wars. But recent polls reveal that in modern times, Native Americans have actually been increasing at an impressive pace. Against only 248,000 American Indians in 1890, the number surpassed one million by the late 1990s, resulting in a growth rate of one percent per annum. This is considered one of the highest, if not the highest, of any minority group in the US, excluding immigrants.

Some sociologist-historians think the euphemistic 'Native Americans' is the only appropriate term for the Indians, but even this is not politically correct. Indians who, as the sole aborigines of the continent, should have been the first of the national groups to enjoy American citizenship, were in fact the last. Blacks earned full political standing upon their emancipation in 1866, yet it was only after 1924, when Congress passed a law making American Indians citizens, that the latter were allowed to discard their status as "subjects of domestic independent nations." This puts the US in the unenviable position of being the only country in which some of its naturalized citizens have roots thousands of years older than those of natural-born ones!

4. Wampum Talk

Myth! **American Indian currency in the New World was called 'wampum'.**

Most everybody thinks *wampum* was the money the American Indians were using when the New World was opened up for colonization. Actually, *wampum* was the sole creation of the whites. The Indians had absolutely no concept of money before contact with the Europeans.

The term *wampum*, although rooted in the Algonquian dialect, was coined by the British, not the Indians. It referred to the tubular shell beads assembled into strings, woven into belts or formed into embroidered ornaments, and used primarily as records of important agreements or treaties and as objects of tribute given by subject tribes. According to 16th-century documents, eastern Indians at that time used *wampum* for decoration and ceremonial gift exchange. Because of the inadequate supply of European currency, strings of *wampum* were used as money in what is now the eastern US, beginning in the first decade of the 17th century and continuing up to the first half of the 18th century. The value of the *wampum* came from its desirability to inland tribes and from the skill and expense involved in making it, not from its sanctioning as an official currency.

That *wampum* was used as a trading medium only among the North American Indians is a common misunderstanding. Actually, it was legal tender for both Indians and palefaces in the East, until mass production of the beads by machines produced inflation and limited their use to belts for ceremonial gift-giving. In the West, Indians continued to use *wampum* as money until about the middle of the 19ᵗʰ century.

5. Smoke Gets in your I's and U's

Myth! Smoke signaling is the most common form of long-distance communication among Indians.

Smoke signaling was not universally practiced by American Indians, as is generally believed. Only tribes isolated geographically (i.e., those at the northern and southern extremes of the Americas) or economically (by virtue of being nonagricultural or nomadic) used the method, and oftentimes it was for a special purpose. Anthropologists have noted, for example, that the Yahgen people who lived at the southern tip of South America used smoke signals to summon neighbors whenever a whale was caught or found beached. In what is now the southwestern US, smoke signals carried news about the location of a buffalo herd or the approach of enemies. Some of these signals resembled Morse code, with different numbers of long and short puffs carrying different messages.

On the whole, there were more Indians who used drums instead of smoke signals for telegraphing information, although the great majority relied simply on mounted runners and other forms of courier service. Hollywood westerns showing Indians using smoke signals to communicate with each other must undoubtedly be blamed for the false stereotype. An anecdote concerning the making of *The Fabulous Texan* (1947), a B effort from Republic Pictures, illustrates the point with some humor. A scene required that the local Indian tribe send smoke signals, so producer Edmund Grainger hired Indians from a nearby reservation to make sure it was performed correctly. Afterward, he congratulated them for a job well done. "No problem," replied one of the Native American consultants. "We learned it from the movies."

6. Um's the Word

Myth! Old West Indians spoke economically worded English phrases ending with 'um'.

The Old West Indians weren't supposed to be any different from the non-English white settlers in the way they spoke English, but it is often shown that they were. Movies, in particular, have been so unrelenting with their lampooning of Indian speech that they have unintentionally created a whole new jargon for the Native Americans. This consists of economically worded phrases, pronouns in the wrong case, and one-tense verbs ending with the inexplicable 'um', on the whole a vocabulary generally no better than Tarzan's.

The Oscar-winning *Dances With Wolves* (1991), in an attempt to get Native Americans out of the mold, has them conversing among themselves in their own dialects. But the effort has not been sufficient to erase the stereotyped image of the Indian in his tepee grunting out words such as 'paleface', 'warpath' and 'forked tongue' as he tries feebly to communicate with white negotiators. These three terms, picturesque enough to be admitted into the English language as colloquialisms, lead all others in demonstrating that the Indians have a knack for verbal allegory. But experts swear no Indian has ever uttered 'paleface', 'warpath' or 'forked tongue' outside the silver screen or the pages of Western fiction. It was James Fenimore Cooper who, in his various stories of Indians and pioneers, coined the words, and

Hollywood, thinking they were authentic, made them part of its stock-in-trade for the Western genre.

7. Cardboard Indians

Myth! **Hiawatha's Longfellow is fictional, but James Fenimore Cooper's Chingachgook is real.**

Melodic names like Minnehaha, Chibiabos and Gitche Gumee gave Henry Wadsworth Longfellow's epic poem, *The Song of Hiawatha,* the flavor of pure fantasy. The story may well be fantasy, but save for a few changes, the hero is not. In the poem, Hiawatha belongs to the Chippewa from Gitche Gumee on the shores of Lake Superior; in real life, he was a Mohawk who lived in upstate New York at the end of the sixteenth century. Why Longfellow moved Hiawatha several hundred miles from New York to the Great Lakes is a mystery, but his choice of the Indian leader as the central character of his myth is obvious. Among the notable achievements of the historical Hiawatha was the founding of the Iroquois League around 1570. Through his influence, the Five Tribes or Nations—the Cayuga, Onondaga, Seneca, Mohawk and Oneida—were able to put aside their factional differences and forge what they called the Great Peace. For two centuries, the confederacy held sway over much of the northeast in a cohesive but liberal spirit that identified it as the first democratic government on the continent.

Longfellow's inspiration for Hiawatha's legend came from reading the anthropologist Henry Schoolcraft, whom he thanked in his notes to the poem, and from mixing the latter's ideas with the folklore of the Dakotas and other colorful tribes. Longfellow took Hiawatha's name and fictionalized all else, including his tribe. Historians believe no Chippewa lived near the Great Lakes or anywhere else. Native Americans from north of Lakes Huron and Superior were called Chippewa by undocumented alien immigrants from Europe, but they were really the Ojibwa group of the Algonquin people.

Chingachgook, on the other hand, is Hiawatha in reverse. This Native American and his son Uncas, the title heroes of James Fenimore Cooper's novel *The Last of the Mohicans,* are fictitious

110

participants in a real-life milieu—that of the Mohicans that inhabited the colonial American frontier in the 18th century. The Mohicans, an Algonquian-speaking confederacy of tribes that allied with the British during the French and Indian Wars, used to hold regional sway over New York and eastern Connecticut, but war with the Mohawks and white settlements pushed them out of these areas and they almost entirely lost their identity. Cooper's famous story made their extinction complete, although it now appears that, at the least, mixed-blood remnants of the confederacy have survived near Norwich, Connecticut, and in Stockbridge, Massachusetts, where they are part of the so-called Stockbridge Indians. At last count, some 800 are still around today.

8. Scalping causes Permanent Hair Loss

Myth! **American Indians introduced the barbarous practice of scalping.**

There is evidence that Indians were already scalping people thousands of years ago. European explorers reported finding tribes that resorted to the practice as early as the 1500s, and archaeologists have recently discovered proof of scalping in ancient Indian corpses. Scholars say Indians created rituals only around ancient behaviors, and would never have ritualized scalping if it had been borrowed from the Europeans.

However, prior to the arrival of Europeans, the idea of scalping was more related to the Indian custom of cutting off various body parts as trophies following warfare. Because they lacked the steel knife, scalping consisted merely of slicing off a small patch of skin only an inch or two in size, usually behind one ear, and it never proved fatal to a live victim. It was the white settler who introduced and popularized scalping in its more brutal form, and the Indians were originally the victims. Scalping was an old European tradition dating back hundreds of years, having developed independently of the Indian native ritual. The Dutch and English colonists decided to apply it to the New World in response to money offered by the government for the killing of an Indian. The idea caught on and before long, scalps had become a stock in trade for Indian fighters and bounty hunters. Eventually, even the white settlers were offering bounties for each other's scalps and those of their respective Indian allies.

9. The two Sides of Genocide

Myth! **The red man massacred a large number of white settlers, and would have killed many more had the US Army not stepped in.**

The script of the typical Hollywood 'cowboy-and-Injun' action picture is predicated on the scenario that the red man was beginning to wipe out whole communities of white settlers in the American West when the US Army intervened. There is not a grain of truth in this despite the veneer of authenticity of three films produced in 1970—*Little Big Man, A Man Called Horse* and *Soldier Blue*. At least a thousand massacres of Indians by whites are recorded, but in *The Gospel of the Red Man* (1939), Ernest Thompson Seton cannot identify a single massacre of whites by Indians. The Native Americans were actually the victims and the whites the aggressors in a genocidal campaign that began with the Pilgrim Fathers and other colonists. The 17th century saw the extermination of whole tribes, such as the Wappingers by the Dutch and the Pequot by the Puritans. Scenes of mass killings perpetrated by white colonists on native non-combatants punctuated King Philip's War, the French and Indian War, and even the War of 1812.

The US Army entered the picture at the height of the campaign, not to prevent mayhem or to mediate between peoples, but as the whites' surrogate exterminators. The great Indian wars they fought during the late 1800s were only a mopping-up effort, because by that time "the Indians were nearly finished, their subjugation complete, their numbers decimated." The fallacy is sometimes garnished with the Hollywood line that the white settlers became a target of Indian animosity because they were hunting the bison indiscriminately. Actually, it was the US Army that was killing off the animals as a way of starving the Indians pursuant to the genocidal policies of Jackson and Van Buren.

112

10. Give and Take in the Old West

Myth! **The practice of 'Indian giving' started with Native Americans.**

The expression 'Indian giver' is applied generally to one who, for some reason (usually the break-up of a relationship), demands the return of a gift he has given. The name implies that this was how it was when the practice originated with the Indians.

But the assumption is wrong. According to the genuine Native American custom, a gift was never returned and the giver never asked for its return under any circumstance. The giver expected reciprocity not in the sense that he wanted his own gift back, but that a reciprocal gift of at least equal value should be given him. Since the failure to reciprocate a gift was an affront against the Indian's values, gift giving was actually a way of causing the impoverishment of a disliked person or of humiliating a rival more than of establishing status. Large gifts would be given in the hope that the receiver had little or no means of matching them. In some cultures this practice of reciprocity often became quite intense and competitive.

White people, at least those not familiar with Indian culture, misinterpreted the Indian's concept of reciprocity to mean that the Indian wanted his own gift back. Hence, the term 'Indian giver' came into popular use as an erroneous description of both the American Indian and a person who gives something and then wants it returned.

11. Como sabe 'Kemo sabe'?

Myth! **'Kemo sabe' is American Indian for 'faithful friend'.**

Those who had a brush with the pop culture of the 30s, 40s and 50s are not liable to forget the Lone Ranger, the masked cowboy hero of American radio, film and TV, who was called *kemo sabe* by his faithful Indian aide-de-camp Tonto. Despite its use at the time in the sense of 'faithful or trusty friend', the phrase *kemo sabe* continues to fascinate wordsmiths, who tend to draw elaborate histories for it from absurd sources. Some believe it is indeed American Indian in origin, less because Tonto was a brave than because the words happen to be Apache for 'white shirt' and Navajo for 'soggy shrub'. A widely accepted theory is that the words were lifted from the name of a boys' summer camp at Mullet Lake, Michigan, which had adopted it in 1911 without any idea what it meant.

More likely, the phrase was just cooked up by The Lone Ranger's scriptwriters, in particular Fran Stryker, who developed the characters of the masked man and his sidekick for the radio serial. The words suspiciously look like the Spanish *como sabe*, meaning 'how do you say', and might have been intended as a conversation filler for the inarticulate Tonto the way *como sabe* was used as a meaningless expression by cowboys and vaqueros of the Old West. Probably later, when it was realized that the corrupted form *kemo sabe* had the sound of certain Indian words, it was decided to give it a definite meaning as part of Tonto's idiom.

12. Tippling in the Tepees

Myth! **Frontier Indians couldn't handle their drinks and were not really adept with the bow and arrow.**

The ability of the Old West Indian to handle his drinks is belittled by some writers, who say liquor was one of the weaknesses that his enemies exploited to bring about his downfall. Army agents sometimes pretended to be white traders and sold whiskey to the Indian, in the belief that his very low tolerance for alcohol would distort his senses and add to his vulnerability. The braves drank before going on the warpath, and, like Sitting Bull and Geronimo, ended up going to the Happy Hunting Ground loaded to the gills.

The principle this is supposed to uphold is that people of some races metabolize liquor at a lower rate than do others. It's myth, of course—and all meant to be a racial aspersion, for what is said of the Native Americans is sometimes also said of minority groups in other races. Sociologists have established that, although the rate of alcoholism among Indians is twice the national average, the reason is not physiological at all.

A less serious slander on the frontier American Indian—this one involving his skill with the bow and arrow—is that he stood very little chance against a modern archer. In rebuttal, one writer says, "The only way to find out is to send a modern archer out to kill a buffalo. From horseback. With no saddle. Without a modern, fiberglass bow. It is fairly obvious that the Plains Indians were highly expert with bows, arrows, and spears; their lives depended on them."

13. How to Program a Pogrom

Myth! White Europeans caused the near extinction of American Indians through constant warfare and massacres.

There is almost complete agreement that white Europeans had much to do with the decimation of Indians in the New World. But, contrary to common belief, it wasn't through constant warfare and its attendant massacres. A less conventional agency used, albeit unwittingly, was killer diseases, such as cholera, smallpox, tuberculosis, measles, influenza and syphilis, which were introduced into the continent by white men and slaves from Africa.

Lacking any racial immunity to the new viruses and germs, Native Americans declined in number within decades. In America, the prehistoric Indian population was estimated at about 2,500,000; by 1890, this number had fallen to a mere 250,000. As early as 1640, the Iroquois confederation in the US had lost nearly half of their people to the European scourges. Smallpox cut the Blackfeet population in half in 1787 and by another 2/3 in 1837, while cholera took away twelve hundred of the Pawnees in 1849. The Indian massacres, such as those perpetrated by John Chivington at Sand Creek and George Custer on the Washita, contributed to the decimation of the native population, but not as near to the point of extinction as disease did. The same goes for

115

the Indians of South America, ninety percent of whom died from disease within the first fifty years of contact with whites.

14. All Wet and Hot Air

Myth! **Forced to sell tribal lands, Chief Seattle asked, "How can you buy the sky? How can you own the rain and the wind?"**

Reputedly the best message ever spoken by a Native American was a complaint against man's exploitation of his natural environment for commercial gain. The message appeared in one of the biggest bestsellers of 1991-92, a children's book entitled *Brother Eagle, Sister Sky: A Message from Chief Seattle.* "My mother told me, every part of this earth is sacred to my people," the message read. "Every pine needle. Every sandy shore. Every mist in the dark woods. Every meadow and humming insect. All are holy in the memory of our people." This was one of the four known versions of Seattle's words, but by the time the book was published, politicians, scientists and environmentalists, including the famous mythologist Joseph Campbell, were quoting them.

The eloquence of the message was not diminished one bit even after it was discovered that a screenwriter by the name of Ted Perry had composed them for a documentary on the environment in 1972. Unable to find any authentic speech by a prominent Native American to argue for the earth's sanctity, Perry made one up by mixing his thoughts with some of Seattle own words. The name 'Chief Seattle' was made to appear in the writing credits in lieu of Perry's, because, as the show's producers explained over Perry's objections, this added authenticity to Seattle's words.

Actually, the most eloquent English speech by a Native American-—at least in the opinion of Thomas Jefferson, who likened its author to Demosthenes and Cicero—was not a speech at all but a written memorandum. In the spring of 1774, two Shawnees ambushed some settlers on the frontiers of Virginia, provoking the whites to retaliate by waylaying several Indians who were in a canoe near the mouth of Yellow Creek. Claiming that some of those murdered were his relatives, the Indian leader Logan (native name: Tah-gah-jute), who had long been known as the white man's friend, came out of his peaceful hibernation at Old Chillicothe on the Scioto River in Ohio and perpetrated fearful barbarities upon the isolated settlers. After the Indian allies were defeated in the same year in what is known as Lord Dunmore's War, the governor of Virginia invited their chiefs, including Logan, to attend a peace meeting at Chillicothe. It was here that Logan supposedly delivered his celebrated speech in which he justified his retaliatory action against the whites.

Jefferson was the first to call public attention to this piece in his *Notes on Virginia*, but he apparently didn't know that Logan was not at the meeting and did not deliver his speech in person before Lord Dunmore, the Governor of Ohio. Logan had refused to go, and only sent a message to the royal official in the form of a memorandum written down from the chief's verbal statement and read before the meeting at Chillicothe. According to historians, the transcription produced inaccuracies that to this day have been attributed to Logan.

---

15. Shout before you Chute

Myth! **Government troops killed Geronimo while the fierce Apache chief was on a drinking spree.**

There are several misconceptions about this colorful American Indian. *First*, although he had an enormous reputation as a warrior leader, Geronimo was never a chief of the Apache or of any tribe. He was only a renegade leader who succeeded in harassing the US Army time and again with his small pack of Chiricahua Apache braves. *Second*, Geronimo's real name was 'Goyahkla', or 'Goyathlay', meaning 'one who yawns', implying that he wasn't always as fierce as people thought he was. He started becoming hostile after the Mexicans killed his family, and it was then that they gave him the name Geronimo, after St. Jerome, to whom they pleaded for help after a particularly bloody battle with the wily Native American.

Third, contrary to his popular portrayal, Geronimo was not a ruthless brave who loved to kill and scalp. Despite a reputation for always scalping their slain enemies, the Apaches rarely did so, and Geronimo was no exception. Apache raids were conducted mostly for plunder and for such items as weapons, horses, and money, and there was no particular status attached to the number of enemies that a brave killed and scalped.

Finally, Geronimo was not killed in any encounter with government troops, as is generally believed. He was captured, ironically, by Apache Indian scouts serving in the US Army, and placed under house arrest for fifteen years. During that time he became a farmer and an active member of the Dutch Reformed Church on an Oklahoma reservation. He sold souvenirs of himself until, at the age of eighty, he died in the army post at Fort Sill from pneumonia that he had caught through overexposure while in a drunken stupor.

---

16. Forrest's Little Tree

Myth! The 1991 national bestseller *The Education of Little Tree* is the autobiography of a persevering Cherokee orphan who became a well-known writer and politician.

At the age of five in backwoods Tennessee, Little Tree was taken in by his grandparents and taught survival skills, along with courage, self-reliance, and profound tolerance for other people. Growing up without schooling, he was at first a cowboy ranch hand, but taught himself well enough to be appointed later as official Storyteller in Council to the Cherokee Nation. In 1991, the American Booksellers Association gave the book their ABBY Award because of its humanitarian values.

Becoming Forrest Carter in his adult life, the 'Cherokee' author was praised in the New York Times and interviewed by Barbara Walters on the 'Today Show'. But dying in 1979, he did not live long enough to face the embarrassment caused when an Emory University professor disclosed that Little Tree was non-existent and his life story pure fiction. The publisher of the book was both shocked and chagrined to learn that Forrest Carter was not the Native American whose childhood is documented in *Little Tree*. He was really Asa Carter from Alabama, not Tennessee, he was not an orphan, and he and his relatives were not Cherokee but white. Worse, Asa was a white supremacist who promoted his principles through violence, from his student days to the time he

118

established a branch of the Ku Klux Klan and ran against Governor George Wallace on a racist platform. According to his brother Doug, Asa invented lovable Little Tree as a way to finance a political comeback. After Forrest's widow India admitted all, the book was moved to the fiction category in November 1991, after 19 weeks in the New York *Times* bestseller list.

17. The One with the Funny Haircut

Myth! **The punk hairstyle called the Mohawk was patterned after the way members of the Mohawk Indian tribe wore their hair.**

The head that sported a Mohawk haircut was shaved bare except for a two-inch-wide strip of hair standing erect from forehead to neck. Purportedly, this was the hairstyle common among the Mohawk Indians, members of the Iroquois League who lived (and still live) in what is now Quebec and upstate New York. A statue of the Mohawk leader Thoyanoguen ("King Hendrick") in Lake George, New York, shows him with something resembling a Mohawk, but the whole front half of the statue's head is bald, so the haircut is at most a half-Mohawk. Many paintings of Mohawks show a third style: the head mostly bald, except for a single tuft of hair on top or in the back, adorned with feathers.

Students of Indian culture insist the style was originally set not by the Mohawks but by the Mohicans, or Mohegan (meaning either wolf or river people), who settled in Connecticut and along the Atlantic coast with fifteen other tribes speaking the Algonquian language. English authorities, on the other hand, claim that even Mohican is a misnomer for the punk hairstyle, as it should appropriately be called the 'Huron'. It was the Huron (French for 'bristle-head') tribe that sported the "Trojan plume" hairdo, which punk devotees later popularized under the name 'Mohawk'. The mistake arises obviously from the film versions of Cooper's *The Last of the Mohicans*, in which there are only two Mohicans (Chingachgook and Hawkeye) and the rest are Hurons fighting the French while wearing the haircut. The Mohican style, in fact, is the long combed hair parted in the middle and knotted in

119

the back, just like another anti-establishment group, the Hippies, in the sixties.

18. Imitations of History

Myth! **Daring frontier encounters with Native Americans made heroes of Daniel Boone and William Penn.**

Enrico Causici's marble sculpture above a door in the rotunda of the Capitol shows Boone fighting two braves at the same time. This fantasized encounter boosts the Kentuckian's popular image as an Indian fighter, but contradicts the little-known fact that he killed only one Indian in his whole life. Some believe Boone is a false icon, an unheroic frontiersman whose doings have been dressed up in tall tales or confused with the exploits of more intrepid adventurers like James McBride and John Findlay.

In Penn's case, a painting shows the famous English Quaker entering into a treaty under an elm tree at Shackamaxon for the purchase of Pennsylvania from the Indians. But it's all a figment of the artist's imagination. In the first place, the only credible portrait of Pennsylvania's founder was painted by a druggist, who did it from memory years after his subject had died. More significantly, there was never any treaty between Penn and the Indians over Pennsylvania, and certainly none that was drawn in Shackamaxon that day. Penn journeyed to America in 1682 to acquire the territory under a deal called the 'Walking Purchase', which allowed him to buy as much land as he could walk in three days. Penn already owned the land through a proprietary grant from the Duke of York, but the Quaker believed the Indians had certain prior rights that deserved to be respected. This gesture was lost to the critics, however, who claimed that Penn's son put one over the Indians by hiring three runners to cover more ground than usual.

Incidentally, although William Penn founded the state of Pennsylvania, he did not lend his name to it nor did he have much to do with its naming. The Penn in Pennsylvania came from Admiral Sir William Penn, his father, who died in 1670. Admiral Penn had lent Charles II $16,000 and his son inherited this claim against the crown. As repayment William Penn asked for "a tract of land in America north of Maryland," and in March, 1681, the grant received the king's signature. The younger Penn wanted to call it New Wales originally, but after the King's secretary, a Welshman, refused, he proposed Sylvania, Latin for "wooded place." The King accepted the new appellation provided that Penn tacked on his name in honor of his father the Admiral, and overruled him when he complained.

Plagued by bad business decisions and on the verge of bankruptcy, Penn suffered a massive stroke in 1712. His wife Hanna discovered that, unlike the father, who had been a lender, the son was an inveterate borrower, mostly from the Crown. To stave off repossession of the colony by the British, Hanna went into action. As a woman, she could not legally take over the affairs of her husband's colony, but as a factual surrogate, she practically ran it. She masterfully utilized her contacts in the British government, signed her husband's name to colonial documents, and appointed a governor for the colony. Biographers agree that she had more savvy than Penn, particularly in the way she managed pressures from both the Crown and local leaders to disband the colony.

19. Squaw Guide for Explorers

Myth! **The Shoshone Indian woman Sacajawea was the official guide, interpreter and envoy of the Lewis and Clark expedition and one of the few survivors of that arduous journey.**

In many illustrations and paintings of the Lewis and Clark expedition, the tableau is dominated by the figure of Sacajawea leading the way through the Rockies or pointing to the Pacific Ocean in the distance. Though she was nursing an infant son at the time, she was undoubtedly helpful to the success of the mission, but the real guide of the expedition was her husband, a French-Canadian trapper by the name of Toussaint Charbonneau. Sacajawea, who was born in what would later become either western Montana or eastern Idaho sometime around 1784, was kidnapped in late 1800 by a band of Minnetaree that eventually traded her to Charbonneau. She is officially recorded as having died at the age of 24, contrary to the oral Indian tradition that she lived to the ripe old age of 96 (it was Charbonneau who died an octogenarian).

However, like most of the others in the group, she survived the arduous 28-month-long journey, begun when she was only 17. Americans may find hard to believe the fact that the expedition encountered hostile Indians, accidents, sickness, grizzly bears, rattlesnakes, exposure and near starvation, yet it had only one casualty, a man who died of bilious colic.

20. Losing the Tent and Getting the Sack

Myth! Several American Indian tribes were forcibly relocated in the 1830s because of their open hostility and incompatible lifestyles.

One of the saddest events in Native American history occurred when the Choctaw, Chickasaw, Creek, Cherokee and Seminole were forcibly moved from their home grounds in the southeastern states to unsettled lands across the Mississippi in the 1830s. Those who ascribed humane motives to Andrew Jackson's call for the wholesale migration insisted it was necessary because the Indians were hostile and their lifestyles were incompatible with white culture. The President, it was claimed, wanted them transferred to avoid friction with the white settlers or else they would be slaughtered, which was already happening.

According to most modern historians, nothing could be further from the truth. The Indians involved belonged to the 'Five Civilized Tribes' of the Southeast, so-called because they had developed societies that were compatible with white culture and even emulated European styles in some respects. These tribes had more than conceded to the presence of the whites, and were only too willing to live in peaceful co-existence. The last to be removed in 1838 were the 15,000-17,000 Cherokees of Georgia, who were not nomadic savages but had assimilated Western customs, including the wearing of gowns by their women. They had built roads, schools, and churches, had a system of representational government, and were becoming farmers and cattle ranchers. A warrior named Sequoya had also perfected a written Cherokee language. But because their tribal lands happened to be valuable cotton-growing territory, the government forced the whole tribe to follow a 'Trail of Tears' through Tennessee and Kentucky, leaving 4,000 of their people dead along the route.

21. The Crazies get the Monuments

Myth! General Philip Sheridan devised the saying, "The only good Indian is a dead Indian."

General Sheridan, so goes the story, was once approached by Chief Toch-a-way of the Comanche, part of an Indian delegation paying a visit at Fort Cobb in Oklahoma Territory in January 1869. The chief beat his chest and proclaimed, "Me Toch-a-way; me good Indian." It was then that Sheridan tossed off his famous but impolitic remark, "The only good Indian is a dead Indian."

According to a cavalry captain who claimed to have been present, his actual words were only slightly subtler: "The only good Indians I ever saw were dead." In any case, Sheridan denied making either statement, alleging that the incident didn't even happen, and blamed his friends for making the attribution and his critics for repeating it until it was widely believed. The truth may never come out, but some biographers thought the quote had "the ring of typical Sheridan rhetoric," and was likely to have been said in view of the prevailing popular sentiment against Indians at the time. Sheridan was known far and wide to have acquired an intense distaste for Native Americans, which was why, after defeating the Confederates in the last major battle of the Civil War in 1865, he took up a peace time job commanding an Army force dedicated to wiping them out in the West. One writer says the quip summed up his feelings and those of almost "every ranch house, military post, overland stage station and mining gulch in the Western states and territories."

Whether or not Sheridan was heard right, it is almost certain the essence of the infamous quote originated elsewhere. Only a year before, on May 28, 1868, Montana Congressman J. M. Cavanaugh said on the floor of the House, "I have never in my life seen a good Indian—and I have seen thousands—except when I have seen a dead Indian."

IV

Way Out West

On Cowboys and the Old West

"But the West of the old times, with its strong characters,
its stern battles and its tremendous stretches of loneliness,
can never be blotted from my mind."

•

Buffalo Bill

1. West Point

Myth! Horace Greeley gave the famous advice, "Go west, young man."

Horace Greeley came to be known by the statement "Go west, young man, go west," which appeared in one of his editorials in the New York *Tribune*. Still, traditionalists who insist he said it can't agree when he said it. Biographer Henry Luther Stoddard says he first said it as early as 1837. According to the author of a recent book of quotations, Greeley wrote it in *Hints Toward Reform* in 1850. Another biographer, William Harlan Hale, cites an 1854 letter in which Greeley used the expression.

What Greeley did write was, "...turn your face to the great West, and there build up a home and fortune." Greeley himself acknowledged in the editorial that the quote, "Go west, young man, go west," was originated by John Babson Lane Soule, a little-known Indiana journalist, in an article in the Terre Haute *Express* in 1851. Soule's line was, "Go west, young man, and grow up with the country." Greeley reprinted Soule's article in his newspaper, the New York *Tribune*, but to no avail; the phrase stuck to Greeley. Despite attempts by the politician-editor to disclaim credit for the remark, most people continue to believe he originated it.

2. City Slickers or Country Slackers?

Myth! American cowboys were native to the West.

The cowboys of American folklore are a far cry from the first men who went by that name. 'Cowboy' was originally spelled as two words, and represented a figure that did not come from the American West at all.

When the British seized New York City in 1776 after the beginning of the American Revolution, both sides formed mounted guerrilla outfits that were sanctioned to commit acts of robbery and murder. Those on the British side gained the nickname 'Cow-boys' from the way they used cowbells simulating the sound of lost cattle to lure their unsuspecting victims into the woods before doing away with them. They were also accomplished cattle rustlers, and as a result of their activities, the term 'Cow-boys' became synonymous with terror throughout the neutral areas of Westchester County, Connecticut, New Jersey and Long Island.

These last-named places eventually became the common hunting ground for both sides, with the Cow-boys swooping from the British position and patriot brigades, or 'Skinners', coming down from the American lines. Although the Skinners professed allegiance to the American cause and the Cow-boys to the British, the distinction was lost on the unfortunate inhabitants caught in the crossfire. The two sides often banded together, and they had a working agreement for the disposal of their loot, which was mainly in New York, and for the sharing of the profits more or less equally.

---

3. Years of the Horse

Myth! **The era of the American cowboy lasted a mere twenty years.**

Much of the folklore dramatizing the role of the American cowboy is drawn from a period spanning only 20 years, from 1867 to 1887. The cowboy saga is actually much longer, and covers the American Revolution, California under Spain, and Texas from the 1820s. During this earlier stretch, however, the cowboy was just a ranch hand tending the cattle as one of his duties. He didn't take on his more familiar and legendary role as a cattle-driving trail hand until 1867, when the image of the self-reliant, silent hero of the west began to form.

It was in 1867 that a livestock trader named Joe McCoy—some say he was the original 'real McCoy'—hired ranch hands to bring longhorn cattle from Texas along the Chisholm Trail to the railhead in Abilene, Kansas. Other cattle businessmen soon took up the practice. The new jobs were not only higher-paying, they also provided greater independence and allowed for skills to be honed during the grueling and often rowdy journeys. The many

126

risks to which the trail hand was exposed—cattle stampedes, Indian attacks, rattlesnakes, disease and gunfights—added glamour and enriched the literary and screen adventures of many a fictional Western.

By 1887, bad weather, the spread of homesteaders' barbed wire, and the extension of the rail line ended the reign of the cowboy as the cattle-driving vagabond of the West. The majority returned to their more sedentary duties as ranch hands, but the few made famous by the publicity retired and moved elsewhere to become lawmen, journalists, entertainers and Hollywood consultants.

4. Ride, Vaquero!

Myth! **The style, techniques, equipment and language of the American cowboy evolved in Texas.**

The prevailing notion is that the culture of the cowboys, which consisted of their techniques, fashion, art and patois, developed in Texas contemporaneously with the development of the beef industry there. However, this is true only to the extent that cowboys became movers of large herds of cattle in that vast territory.

On a broader scale, cowboy culture started more than fifty years earlier with the *vaqueros* (Spanish for 'cowboys' and the basis for 'buckaroos') of Spanish California. The *vaqueros* spread their knowledge and way of life throughout the west, including Texas, and it was in this state where a technology transfer, so to speak, occurred between them and white settlers in the 1820s. Pushing westward into Texas, these settlers had discovered the local Spanish and Mexican ranches that lodged the vaqueros, who had mastered both the handling of cattle on horseback and the tools of the trade—horse, rope, saddle, spurs, and branding iron. The newcomers readily absorbed these methods, then applied their newly found skills to the herds of ownerless horses and cattle that dotted the plains.

When the Texans won their independence in 1836, they not only took over the land but everything they learned from the Mexicans. Texas joined the Union nine years later, by which time the Texas cowboy was teaching *vaquero* lore to his neighbors.

5. Not Suitable for a Pinhead

Myth! **A ten-gallon hat can hold several gallons of water.**

The ten-gallon Western cowboy hat, whose commanding presence earned it the nickname 'The Boss of the Plains', was invented in the 1860s. Also known as the Stetson after its creator, a Philadelphia haberdasher named John B. Stetson, this classic symbol of the Old West had been designed especially for cattle kings and Midwesterners with inflated egos. But it soon became both fashionable and practical for cowboys and outlaws alike, and even women like Annie Oakley and Calamity Jane took a liking to it.

Contrary to its general appearance, the Stetson is not an oversized hat. It comes in the same head sizes as any other hat and looks huge only because of the tall crown and very wide brim. The hat holds nothing like ten gallons, nor even a gallon, but only about three quarts of liquid. What gave rise to the term 'ten-gallon hat' would seem to be the practice of cowboys off and on the movie screen to use the hat's crown as a bucket for taking water to their horses and to small fires that needed dousing. But in fact, the name comes from the Spanish term *sombrero galon*, which referred to a fancy braided hat worn by Mexican vaqueros in the 1800s. The *sombrero galon* had the base of its crown decorated with a leather strip containing ten braids, or 'galloons', and was thus jokingly called a 'ten-*galon*' hat, later Americanized to 'ten-gallon' hat.

6. Bronco Bluster

Myth! **Rodeo broncos, broken or not, buck from instinct.**

One who sees a rodeo for the first time won't wonder why a bucking bronco bucks and rears; he will simply take it for granted. He will think the animal was once wild but has not lost its bucking reflex, or is uncomfortable with an unfamiliar rider on it, or was trained to display this reaction when ridden.

The view popular among debunkers is that a bucking bronco bucks because a rigging device, called a flank girth or strap, has been secured tightly around the animal's midsection and across the sensitive side flanks while it is in the chute. This technique is apparently used in bareback and saddle-bronco riding to make the horse react like a wild, untamed animal to the discomfort of the strap.

But those who debunk the debunkers insist flank straps are used in rodeos only to assure that bucking horses continue to buck for an eight-second count. They claim that, with or without them, a rodeo horse will follow its instinct, which is to buck and kick in every direction when first mounted by a rider. All the literature on Western lore and the illustrations by such renowned artists as Frederic Remington, Charles Russell and others attest to the natural instincts of these horses to buck.

There seems to be no disagreement between the two views. The pro-strap argument says "broncos and bulls have no natural tendency to be ornery when a rider is on their back unless they are unbroken mustangs or have something bothering them." The antis assume that rodeo horses are unbroken, which is why most of the time they buck even with an empty saddle.

---

7. Range of Colors

Myth! **There were very few black cowboys in the Old West.**

A famous black cowboy, Nat Love, once wrote of the West: "There a man's work was to be done, and a man's life to be lived, and when death was to be met, he met it like a man." It was a West in the process of formation by Mexicans, blacks, Indians, and Englishmen, many of whom were cowboys long before the white settlers knew the meaning of the term. In short, it was a West quite unlike the virtually lily-white world that popular media has portrayed.

The concept of the Western cowboy started with the Mexican vaquero and the English buckaroo, first in California and later in many parts of the west. This concept would eventually assimilate the many blacks working as cowboys on Texas ranches before the Civil War, mostly as slaves. After attaining freedom, and having acquired the skills of the cowboy on these ranches, they moved to other more socially receptive places. In the first thirty years after the Civil War, about 5,000 of them rode out of Texas and up the Chisholm Trail with the cattle drives to escape the faltering economy and the backlash of Reconstruction politics.

At the turn of the century, about one in every three cowboys in the American West was black, with the ratio higher in some states. A popular reference book points out that "Oklahoma, for example, saw thirty all-black towns spring up between 1890 and 1910, and 26 of the first 44 settlers of Los Angeles were black." Ironically, the myth that these minorities had helped to build eventually cleansed itself of their presence, refashioning the image of the American cowboy as white and native-born.

8. The Hip Shooter was a Deadwood

Myth! **The prototypical Western cowboy was a white American named Deadwood Dick.**

Those who expect their prototypical cowboy to be a white American named Deadwood Dick may be in for a surprise. Of the several Deadwood Dicks in the history of the American West, two stand out for their contribution to the popular lore of the region. One was white but not American, and the other was American but not white. Both were also a little short of the standards set by the fictional Deadwood Dick, the fearless Indian scout and outlaw fighter created by the 19th-century dime novelist Edward L. Wheeler and whose exploits were published between 1877 and 1897.

The first ever real-life Deadwood Dick was an Englishman named Richard Clarke (1845-1930), who was the model for Wheeler's hero. He won fame as both an Indian fighter and a Pony Express rider, who lived to see his adopted country make peace with the Sioux tribe even while he often had to defend against them on his postal missions. It was once thought it was Clarke who had written the dime novels, based on his experiences, but this and many of the Deadwood Dick myths about him have since been debunked.

The other standout historical figure called Deadwood Dick was the black cowboy Nat Love (1854-1921), who was born in a Tennessee slave cabin. He went to Dodge City at age fifteen, worked as a cowboy, and ended up in the rodeo. A colorful character, he ordered drinks for his horse in a Mexican bar and boasted of having fourteen bullet wounds on his body. In his autobiography, he wrote of the West as only a real cowboy who lived it could.

There were others—mostly actors and stagecoach drivers living in Deadwood, South Dakota—who took advantage of the name because of the reputation attached to it. But the only other notable among them was Cornishman Richard Bullock, who is often confused with his compatriot and contemporary Richard Clarke. Bullock was a quick-shooting gunfighter on the Deadwood stage and an express guard for gold shipped from the mines in and around the Black Hills of South Dakota. Contrary to the myth that gunmen of the Old West met violent and early deaths, all three famous Deadwood Dicks lived healthy lives well into the twentieth century.

9. The Front in Frontier

Myth! **The six-shooter was the single most important mobilizer of frontier progress, while the false front made no contribution at all.**

The panoramic star-studded film *How the West Was Won* (1962) encompasses three generations of pioneers who helped open up the American West. Unfortunately, the film places too much emphasis on the gun as a frontier mobilizer, and gives relatively little attention to what historians say were the real heroes that won the West, namely, the steel plow, the barbed wire and the portable windmill. These were technologically insignificant objects that made larger-than-life imprints on frontier progress— the plow for the farms, the wire for the ranches, and the windmill for both.

Careful to avoid turning itself into a parody, the film omits the slightest reference to the frontiersman's single contribution to architecture: the false front. This was the phony facade a property owner added to his downtown building to make it look like it had a second story. Although the origin of the practice is unknown, almost every nineteenth-century Western town had this feature. The idea was to put up an appearance of prosperity for the purpose of attracting business, but whether or not it worked seemed to be beside the point. Its mere presence was "a reassuring sign of confidence in the future at a time when frontier towns had to worry whether they had a future at all."

A combination of 19th century history and folklore confirms there was indeed a 'gun that won the West', but this was the repeating rifle, not the six-shooter. It all began with the long rifle, which replaced the smooth bore musket on the American frontier through the efforts of German (others say Swiss) gunsmiths who had settled in Pennsylvania and Virginia as early as the 1740s. Though it had nothing to do with Kentucky, the long rifle gained its more famous nickname, the Kentucky rifle, after a popular song, 'The Hunters of Kentucky', about Andrew Jackson and his victory at the Battle of New Orleans in the War of 1812. From the mid to the late 19th century, the Kentucky rifle developed into a weapon of choice for both civilians and the military especially after the addition of a mechanism that made it a repeating or multi-shot affair.

The Kentucky rifle eventually came to be called the Winchester repeating rifle, seeming to suggest (erroneously) that the repeating feature originated with the Winchester line. Inadvertently or not, Oliver Winchester created this impression when he produced his first model after he had changed his company's name from the New Haven Arms Company to the Winchester Repeating Arms Company. In fact, the Winchester was only the culmination of a long series of previously designed repeating rifles, the last of which was the Henry rifle of 1860, the brainchild of Benjamin Tyler Henry. Earlier were other design pioneers whose works Henry redefined for use by the Union Army in the Civil War. After that war, the Winchester Repeating Arms Company had the basic design of the Henry rifle completely modified to become the first Winchester rifle, the Model '66, which fired center fire cartridges and had not only an improved magazine but also, for the first time, a wooden forearm. In 1873 Winchester introduced the steel-framed Model '73, which became the focal point of the eponymic James Stewart movie.

10. Phony Express

Myth! **The Pony Express was a unique but casualty-prone system of mail delivery.**

We like to think the Pony Express was a unique American experience, but it was not. The system was, by 1860, ancient history, having been used in Cyrus the Great's Persia around 540 BC, in Alexander's empire two centuries later, and in Genghis Khan's Mongolia in the early second millennium. The pony express reached its full development among the nomads of the Asiatic steppes, thriving until the 1920s in Outer Mongolia, where it had made its first *anno domini* appearance.

That the Pony Express was the first of its kind anywhere in the world is not the only fallacy about this phenomenon. Since ponies didn't have what it took to carry heavy mail loads over long distances, fleet horses were used, ridden for stages of 10 to 15 miles. Most of the riders were not the toughened cowboys they are depicted to be, and many were not even adults but orphaned teenagers whose services as skillful riders were secured through newspaper ads. There is the persistent myth that both horse and rider were exposed to all sorts of dangers—Indian attacks, outlaws, sickness, and sunstroke—because of the ruggedness of the Old West, and as a result there were many casualties. In truth, riders didn't normally go beyond 30 to 45 miles before they handed over the wallet, so the risks were considerably lessened. Also, the relatively small area serviced between St. Joseph, Missouri, and Sacramento, California, helped keep the casualty rate practically nil. Only one rider in the history of the Express was killed in the line of duty, and his horse on its own managed to reach the next station and deliver the mail intact.

11. Defense Circle

Myth! **Wagon trains, used in the Old West primarily to transport pioneer families, pulled into a circle when defending against Indians.**

A wagon train consisted typically of a group of pioneer families moving west on wagons pulled by horses. The train was often used to defend against Indian attacks by pulling into a large circle.

Although the popular image of a wagon train is that of a group of pioneer families moving west, this was not really the case. Wagon trains were first seen in the 1820s, when the first big push into the West began, but most of them were used to transport freight, not to carry settlers. According to one estimate, over three-quarters of all wagon trains carried merchandise, with only enough people and animals to get the goods safely to market. The movement of people did not really begin until after 1841.

It is also not true that mostly horses were used to pull the wagons. Oxen and mules were the usual draft animals, and a 20-mule team—which, oddly enough, consisted of only eighteen mules—was quite common. Mules were found better than horses, since they could thrive on a diet of all grass and no grain. Grass could be found along the way, but grain for horses had to be carried and added to the weight of the wagons. Oxen were even better because they shared the mules' food requirements and were less attractive to thieves. Horses were undoubtedly faster, but speed was not of the essence in these journeys, movie scenes showing wagons running faster than attacking Indians notwithstanding. While all animals could be eaten if food ran critically low, most settlers and wagon masters had little preference for eating mules and horses.

Hardly a Hollywood western omits a scene showing a wagon train pulling into a large circle when it stops to rest from its journey. In real life, this was done once in midday and once at night, and was appropriately called "corralling," not "circling," as we are often told. The purpose was not to put up a defensive circle against attacks by Indians and outlaws, but to keep the horses, mules, oxen and other livestock within the circle and prevent them from straying.

134

Although death on the westward trail was a way of life, the danger from Indians has been much exaggerated in folk history. Except for a brief period in the 1860s, there were hardly any Indian attacks on wagon trains. Wagon masters had the good sense to direct travel on territory in which Indians had no interest. Of about three hundred thousand deaths believed to have taken place on wagon trains heading west, only three hundred sixty-two deaths have been confirmed as resulting from Indian attack. The greatest killer on the trail by far was disease.

12. The Horseman called Death

Myth! The common cause of death of cowboys was gunshot wounds.

The cowboy who can't be separated from his trusty six-shooter and the town citizen who becomes easy prey to the outlaw because he can't use a gun—these are two of the legends that Hollywood has built around the Old West, and neither one was true.

Typical real-life cowboys didn't like to carry guns because they got in the way when they were riding and scared their horses or cattle. Consequently, only a few died by the gun, contrary to what is popularly believed. The most common cause of death was pneumonia or riding accidents, from being dragged along by a galloping horse when the cowboy's foot was caught in a stirrup during a fall or when mounting or dismounting. There were other risks, such as stampedes and rattlesnakes, but a gunshot wound was not likely.

To provide the rationale for its gun-slinging heroes, Hollywood often portrays settlers as gun-shy victims who must be protected against ruthless outlaws. Observers say this was hardly the case in real life. The settlers knew how to use firearms, as many had seen combat during the Civil War or in Indian fighting. Outlaws were successful only because they used the element of surprise or were able to hide in the rugged terrain. When prepared, the citizenry weren't as easily abused.

13. New Kid from the Block

Myth! **The practice of branding cattle originated in the West and was unknown to Eastern tenderfoots.**

A tenderfoot—'greenhorn' is an associated term—is popularly believed to be any person new at the game. Surprisingly, the original meaning of the word had no reference to people but to cattle. A tenderfoot was a cow raised in a corral and then released to fend for itself on the range in the West. It did not necessarily have a tender foot or a green horn, but it usually had a brand to identify the ranch to which it belonged.

Apropos of branding, another popular belief is that it originated in the West during the nineteenth century. This happens to be the wrong place and two hundred years too late. In 1644 legislation was enacted by Connecticut providing that all cattle and swine be earmarked or branded and that the marks be registered. The West later adopted the custom without giving the slightest nod to its primary source, which was *not* the American East but the Middle East. Cattle branding was observed 4,000 years ago in Egypt, as evidenced by old tomb paintings showing Egyptians branding their fat, spotted cattle.

V

Invitation To A Beheading

On Capital Punishment

"The criminal shall be decapitated;
this will be done solely by means of a simple mechanism."
•

Joseph Guillotin

1. Killed by his own Device

Myth! **Joseph Guillotin was executed using the device he invented.**

There are four fallacies attached to the origin and history of the infamous execution device that decimated the ranks of royalists and revolutionaries alike during the French Revolution. The *first* is that the concept came from the French. Actually, beheading devices had been in use in Europe since the 14th century. One was used in 1307 in Ireland, and others may have been in use even earlier in Germany, Italy, and England. A beheading machine known as 'the maiden' was already widely used in Europe when the French began considering the idea in their own country. However, due credit should be given to the French model for being the first perfected 'head-remover' of its kind.

The *second* fallacy is that Dr. Joseph Ignace Guillotin, a physician-member of the French National Assembly, designed the machine. The real designer was Dr. Antoine Louis, and the builder was a German piano maker, Tobias Schmidt, who completed a working model from Louis' designs. Dr. Guillotin did no more than introduce the idea of the guillotine and campaign intensively for its adoption by the French government. Being a confirmed opponent for humanitarian reasons of the cruel 18th-century devices of torture and execution, he believed that hanging as a form of capital punishment for the poor, and the sword for nobles and those of high rank, should be abolished and decapitation should instead be applied to all. On his suggestion, the Assembly commissioned Louis to meet the requirements of a 'simple machine' that would carry out future decapitations efficiently and humanely, and the contraption was adopted on March 25, 1792.

The *third* fallacy is that the French device was named after Dr. Joseph Guillotin. Obviously, this became true at some point, but not in the beginning. The guillotine was called the *louisette*, after Dr. Louis, when it was first introduced in France. A writer notes that over the next several years, "as the blade's human toll climbed higher and higher, the public began to reassociate the machine with Dr. Guillotin. Songs were written about the doctor and his speech before the National Assembly (endorsing the device), and before long the 'louisette' began to be called the 'guillotine'."

Finally, there is the fallacy about Dr. Guillotin being the first victim of the deadly machine he himself had recommended. The doctor is no doubt being confused a second time with the machine's designer, Dr. Louis, who died a political martyr under the blade during the Reign of Terror. But even Dr. Louis was not the first victim of the guillotine, as is supposed. That dubious distinction belongs to Nicolas Jacques Pelletier, a highwayman, who was executed on April 22, 1792. Though Guillotin was also condemned to die for supporting enemies of Robespierre, he was spared by a change of government that sent Robespierre to the guillotine in his place.

By way of postscript, Dr. Guillotin survived the Revolution, though he lived out his life stigmatized by his connection with the dreaded contraption. After he died in 1814 of a carbuncle on his shoulder, his children petitioned the authorities to have the name of the device changed. When this proved unsuccessful, they were allowed to change their name instead.

---

2. Cutting a Ridiculous Figure

Myth! **Beheading is the most humane of the traditional modes of capital punishment.**

In some countries, beheading is still occasionally employed as punishment because of the belief that it's the most merciful. Such work used to be done with a high degree of efficiency by the guillotine, which is probably why people have the impression that this instrument is the fastest and most humane mode of carrying out the supreme penalty.

There are stories, too, to suggest that death by beheading may not be as quick or as painless as imagined. Often told, for instance, is the experience with Marie Antoinette, the queen consort of Louis XVI, who was sent to her execution by the French revolutionary tribunal in 1793. It is claimed that as soon as Marie's separated head landed at the foot of the guillotine, one of her eyes 'winked' at the gaping crowd. Essentially the same thing has been said of many beheaded royalties, including Charles I of

139

England, whose mouth 'twitched' after his head had been lopped off with an ax.

Medical opinion has been cited in support of the view that the body may show signs of life, but not consciousness, immediately after a beheading. Cecile Adams, in *The Straight Dope*, says, "The fatal blow in a beheading induces immediate unconsciousness, even though the brain may not actually expire for several minutes." There is thus no pain, only shock, which may cause involuntary muscle spasms, such as the eye appearing to wink or the mouth to smile.

---

3. Just a Pain in the Neck

Myth! Hanging produces a slow kind of death.

The more deliberate view is that 'the kindest cut does not come from the blade but from the rough strands of a hangman's rope'. According to studies, hanging has been so refined that death is now almost always instantaneous, much quicker than in the case of the guillotine, lethal gas or electrocution. These other methods were devised after the eighteenth century in reaction to the notion that hanging produces a slow kind of death. In those days, the person to be hanged was simply pushed off a short height with a rope casually placed around the neck, and slow strangulation was the result. But by the latter half of the 1800s, and contemporaneous with the newer forms of execution, various types of drops and knot placements were developed to cause a quick death.

The present system ensures that during the fall the head is jerked with sufficient force to break the neck. Death occurs less by strangulation than by injury to the upper part of the spinal cord from the fracture or dislocation of cervical vertebrae.

In the US unfortunately, media has not helped bring back hanging in its improved form as a preferred mode of capital punishment. Graphic but erroneous depictions in Hollywood films (e.g., the villain's fate in *Schindler's List* and Clint Eastwood's ordeal in *Hang 'Em High*) have even promoted horror stories about botched jobs that never happened. Thus, many states that have been persuaded to abandon the electric chair because of the

140

high cost of energy and evidence of massive burning (Louisiana in 1991 and Florida in 1997) have also eschewed hanging and have converted to lethal injection.

4. Death in Small Pieces

Myth! **'Drawn, hanged and quartered' describes the sequence of an execution process once followed in medieval England.**

'Drawn, hanged and quartered' was the term for one of the most terrible of punishments, a cruel and undignified form of execution meted to political prisoners, particularly those adjudged guilty of high treason by the English. The words 'drawn,' 'hanged,' and 'quartered' referred to the three phases of the execution process, but not in that order. The victim was first hanged (*suspendatur*), and then while still alive he was drawn (*devaletur*), meaning that his bowels were torn out and burnt before his face. After which, he was beheaded and his body quartered (*decapitetur et decolletur*), or divided into four pieces. The quarters may be buried separately or together, or further dishonored by being hanged from the gibbet for public viewing.

The last few frames of the 1995 Oscar-awarded movie *Braveheart* misinterpret the sequence in this execution process by showing Mel Gibson's character being prepared initially for the 'drawing' phase. In earlier judicial pronouncements of the sentence, drawing was indeed first in the process, and the sequence 'drawn, hanged and quartered' was quite correct. As then used, however, 'drawn' had a different meaning and referred to the act of taking the prisoner to the place of execution on a hurdle or at a horse's tail. It was an indignity that formed part of the punishment, but it was done prior to the execution, which consisted merely of hanging and quartering. It was only later that disemboweling, which by coincidence was also called drawing, was added as the middle step in the whole operation. The exact phrase should have been 'drawn, hanged, drawn, and quartered,' but the second 'drawn' was eliminated apparently to avoid confusion.

5. Little but Lethal

Myth! Lethal injection has proved to be the most painless
and stable mode of execution in modern times.

Lethal injection as a mode of execution is gaining ground with
many governments and fast becoming universal, but the verdict on
whether or not it is 'quick and humane' remains pending. Much of
what has come out of the US as the sole provider of information
and the main practitioner of the 'art' has not been conclusive or
has led to controversy.

Opponents believe that lethal injection is not humane because
the anesthetizing agent used, thiopental, is an ultra-short acting
barbiturate that may wear off too soon and lead to consciousness.
After the thiopental, pancuronium bromide is given, and this not
only dilutes the thiopental but paralyzes the convict as well. What
ensues is an 'excruciatingly painful death' for the condemned
person who regains his senses prematurely but is unable to express
the intense burning sensation caused by one of the constituent
chemicals, potassium chloride, because he or she has been
immobilized.

The procedure is further exacerbated by a flawed method of
administration characterized by (a) administering personnel that
usually lack expertise in anesthesia; (b) dosages that are restricted
to a set protocol and not customized to each individual; and (c)
remote applications that result in an increased risk that insufficient
amounts of the drugs have entered the bloodstream. Opponents
conclude that the system of lethal injection is "entirely
unnecessary and is aimed more towards creating the appearance of
serenity and a humane death than an actually humane death."

Jurists and humanists agree that, considering its limitations,
lethal injection could go the way crucifixion in ancient times or
the electric chair in recent years did. But given proper attention,
lethal injection offers the best chance of closing the gap between
compassion and justice in the execution process and ending the
constant bickering about the morality of capital punishment.

6. Not a Capital Idea

Myth! Capital punishment is the only sure deterrent to crime.

Statistical studies respond differently to the question whether or not forfeiting the life of the criminal has a deterrent effect on the homicide rate. Some make the point that society can't have an impact on killer types if it's not prepared to deal them the supreme penalty. According to this view, the greatest of all forms of punishment works two ways: it discourages those who would commit murder, and it ensures that those who did do not plague innocent people again.

Other studies just as easily prove that capital punishment will not prevent murder. Murder is an irrational act, and insofar as those who kill weigh their desires against the possible penalties they will incur, the prospect of spending a long time behind bars has shown to be just as effective a deterrent. In the United States, according to figures released by the FBI in 1994, states with a death penalty had about twice the murder rate of states without one.

The preponderance, however, favors the proposition that capital punishment should be imposed at least for murder and heinous crimes. The US Supreme Court, in the 1976 case of *Gregg v. Georgia*, reasoned that for some crimes, such as murder for hire and murder by a life prisoner, the penalty of death is the only adequate sanction. Americans have consistently supported capital punishment for murderers, except in the 1960's, when public opinion went below 50 per cent. Since the 1970s, it has gradually gone up again and, lately, has attained higher than 65 per cent.

While it may seem the word 'capital' in 'capital punishment' means 'principal', or that the phrase derives from death being the most major of all penalties, it does not. Neither does 'capital' mean 'final', based on the German word *kaput*, for 'finished', in allusion to the finality of capital punishment. Word mavens confirm that the root word of 'capital' is the Latin *caput*, meaning 'head', a reminder that capital punishment originally referred to the penalty of beheading as the supreme punishment for malefactors.

143

7. Fry and Fry Again

Myth! A convict who survives a botched execution is entitled to be pardoned under the principle of double jeopardy.

Two principles in the US Bill of Rights are often cited in support of the view that a convict is automatically entitled to a pardon if he survives a hanging or other execution. The first is double jeopardy and the second is the Constitutional prohibition against cruel and unusual punishment.

Double jeopardy is invoked in the belief that the concept covers not only the prosecution aspect of criminal procedure but the execution phase as well. It is argued that a convict who has gone through a failed execution, like one who has been acquitted, should not be placed in jeopardy of the same process again. The argument is misleading, of course, since there can be no legal or moral equation between an acquittal and a botched execution. It also runs smack against the requirement that a death sentence must be carried out until the convict is dead, a mandate in most verdicts that is no more unconstitutional or illegal than the idea of capital punishment itself.

The Constitutional restraint on cruel and unusual punishment is said to apply to a failed execution on the ground that the hanging or electrocution of a convict is cruel enough, but to do this repeatedly to one who must be almost dead from previous attempts is to make him suffer the same cruelty many times over. The false logic misses the fact that an unsuccessful execution is repeated precisely to end the needless suffering that the technical failure may have caused. There have been notable cases of reprieves where equipment failed or the victim recovered, but in every such case, the basis of the amnesty is humanitarian, not legal.

Beliefs
&
Traditions

I

Brother, Can You Spare A Rib?

On Adam and Eve

"The serpent beguiled me, and I did eat."

•

Eve

1. Madam, I'm Adam

Myth! **God gave Adam his name.**

Whether Adam was named ahead of or at the same time as Eve is of little concern in light of the revelation that it wasn't God who gave them their names. *Genesis* 3:20 tells us Adam himself called his partner Eve to signify that she was "the mother of all the living." How Adam acquired his own name is another story. In the original text, the name Adam is nowhere mentioned; rather, every time God speaks to or about Eve's husband, he refers to him as *adham*. Not surprisingly, *adham*, a Hebrew common noun meaning 'the man', transposed into the proper noun Adam in later versions. Biblicists say God's term of address for the original *Homo sapiens* was always meant to be generic, to stress the fact that in history as in allegory, Adam is the symbol of all humankind.

2. Therein lies a Tail

Myth! **Men have one rib less than women.**

The notion that man gave up a rib for woman is an age-old belief originating from the Biblical account of Adam and Eve. But the belief is not confined to adherents of Scripture alone. Ancient peoples like the Sumerians incorporated the tradition about woman's origin in their popular culture. An extension of the belief is the claim that every male human is born with only eleven ribs, one less than what Adam had in the beginning. When Adam ceded a rib, so the theory goes, the loss was imprinted in his genes and transmitted as a male peculiarity to every succeeding generation.

However it may have begun, the claim that man has one rib less than woman is unabashed medical quackery. Any anatomist can prove that the male and the female of the human species have the same number of ribs, which is twelve. A 29-year-old Belgian doctor named Andreas Vesalius discovered this anatomical truth as early as 1543, when he published his seven-volume work *On the Structure of the Human Body.* As expected, Vesalius' colleagues and, for a time, the Church and society at large, initially rejected the finding.

A numerical difference may sometimes occur in the coccygeal or tail vertebrae of the sexes. But aside from the fact that this has nothing to do with the ribs, it is more often the woman who has fewer bones in that part of the anatomy. This is probably why, in some cultures, the belief is reversed, with woman having eleven ribs and man twelve.

3. Look, Ma, there's a Hole in my Tummy

Myth! **Adam and Eve were perfect human specimens.**

Most works of art depicting Adam and Eve reflect the popular belief that, anatomically, the first couple looked exactly like their descendants today. If at all, Renaissance art made them healthier, more handsome (oftentimes devoid of unsightly body hair), and better proportioned than the average modern human being.

What these portrayals have apparently overlooked is that the original couple was missing one body feature common to *Homo sapiens*—a bellybutton. The two lacked navels because they were not born in the conventional mammalian way, a condition not biologically possible for all other humans.

Michelangelo, Van Eyck and Titian have been criticized for their 'unrealistic' paintings of the Creation showing the first man and woman sporting this human vestige. But Renaissance apologists maintain there is no reason the two should be shown as less than perfect humans in a Creation scenario that is perfect in all other respects. Their sentiment hews to the fundamentalist thinking that man was crafted, navel and all, in the eternal and immutable image of God. Evolutionists think it's useless to argue the point, saying Adam could have been anything, even a blob.

4. Apple Polisher

Myth! **The devil tempted Eve in the guise of a talking snake.**

In the grand morality play that unfolded in the Garden of Eden at the beginning of time, God was Good personified and Evil was a charmer dressed in snake's clothing. Or so we are told. Etched in the minds of most Christians is the gratuitous belief that the cunning tempter in the Garden of Eden was Satan in the guise of a talking snake. But the Bible nowhere suggests that the serpent was a snake, or that it was the devil in disguise.

In the early days, 'serpent' was a generic word that referred to any kind of venomous creeping animal with or without legs. In the 15th and 16th centuries, the term was applied to mostly reptilian creatures, including salamanders and crocodiles. What the Garden variety looked like is anybody's guess, but if it had been a snake, God would not have bothered to condemn it to a life crawling on its belly in the dust.

The Bible itself provides the clue that the serpent was not the devil but an ordinary beast. In *Genesis* 3:14, God cursed the tempter "above all the livestock and all the wild animals" for having deceived the woman. At this point, one may well ask how a beast capable of beguiling humans with its speech could be ordinary. As any Bible enthusiast knows, the concept of a talking and thinking animal in Scripture is not new. Balaam's ass in *Numbers* (22: 28-30) was concededly no devil, yet it also possessed the ability to speak.

5. Hey, Doc, there's a Lump in my Throat

Myth! **Only men have Adam's apples.**

Most cultures see the Adam's apple as a symbol of masculine strength and a smooth neck without it a symbol of feminine beauty. The rugged male can't have the youthful (and effeminate) attractiveness of Adonis or Narcissus because of the Adam's apple sticking out just above the tie knot on his collar. And it's Adam who gets the blame for this apparent imbalance between the sexes.

Those who believe the hokum that man has fewer ribs than woman are apt to fall for the story that only men have Adam's apples. The anatomical condition purportedly arose when Adam, who couldn't get enough of the apple Eve offered him, bit off more than he could chew, almost gagging on a piece of the forbidden fruit that lodged in his gullet. He paid for this indiscretion (called original sin) by having an enlarged larynx, a condition that, like his missing rib, attached genetically to every male descendant thereafter.

The myth persists due to a wrong perception of the male and female anatomies. Although unnoticed, women also have Adam's apples, medically called thyroid cartilages. The male protuberance, however, is larger because his larynx has to accommodate longer vocal cords and he has less fat around the neck to hide it.

Biblical experts say the real change brought on Adam and Eve by their eating of the forbidden fruit was intellectual and emotional rather than physical. In the words of the Good Book, the woman saw that the fruit was "desirable for gaining wisdom," and after she and her husband ate it, "the eyes of both of them were opened, and they realized they were naked." In less metaphoric terms, the couple, unperturbed in their innocence until then, learned the difference between good and evil and, more importantly, the feeling of elation or guilt that goes with choosing one over the other.

6. A Tree grows in Eden

Myth! **Evil originated with the tree of knowledge in Eden.**

God banished man and woman from the Garden to prevent them from eating of the fruit of the tree of life. This empyreal scene is often referred to as the Fall of Man, but that should not detract from the fact that the real defining moment for man's downfall was their eating of the fruit of the tree of knowledge against God's wishes. The English poet John Milton posited a sensible view when he wrote that it was "Man's first disobedience" that "(b)rought death into the world." With everyone in Eden

150

living in ignorance of good and evil, the only form of wickedness possible was disobedience.

Some Biblicists believe evil can be traced to a time earlier than Adam and Eve—for example, when God planted the tree of knowledge in the Garden. Like the tree of life, the tree of knowledge had a special quality, which the serpent described to Eve, thus: "When you eat of it your eyes will be opened, and you will be like God, knowing good and evil." According to the theory, it was this power of the tree, bestowed through its fruit, that corrupted Adam and Eve and caused original sin.

There is also a niche in Christian tradition, though a very small one, for the thinking that evil preceded Creation itself, when the archangel Lucifer aspired to be as God and rebelled against the Supreme Being. The story of Lucifer, while essentially apocryphal, is compatible with Scripture, particularly the Book of *Job* and parts of the New Testament.

The consensus nevertheless is that sin or evil originated with man's act of disobeying God in his first exercise of free will. There was nothing magical about the tree of knowledge, as it was a mere prop in the heavenly plan to test human nature. Had the fruit been intrinsically tainted, the original sinner would have been Eve, since it was she who took the first bite. Adam was only enticed to take the second bite, but because he was the one God commanded not to eat of the forbidden fruit, he was the first to fall.

---

7. Curses!

Myth! God cursed Adam for eating of the forbidden fruit.

For listening to his wife and eating of the forbidden fruit, Adam was chastised by God in these words: "By the sweat of your brow you will eat your food until you return to the ground, since from it you were taken; for dust you are and to dust you will return" (*Genesis 3*:19).

These words have come to be known as 'Adam's curse', but only because they appear in the Bible in a heap of other Godly retributions that use the word 'curse'. Scripture is explicit in naming the serpent and the ground, not Adam and Eve, as the objects of God's damnation. In Adam's case, God made the point

151

that man must thenceforth endure the human suffering that was to come from the curse placed on the ground. Far from being a condemnation or admonition, it was to remind Adam of the mortal state of things awaiting him outside Paradise.

The only 'Adam's curse' alluded to in Christian precepts is original sin, which, unlike 'Eve's curse' (in reference to childbearing), is spiritual and not temporal. Both, however, are designed to add to life's burden, though not in the manner of a real curse.

8. Garden Variety

Myth! The forbidden fruit of the Bible is an apple.

Even as the apple is praised as a health food, it gets blamed for making Adam and Eve irreversibly unhealthy. Bible thumpers tell us our first generation ancestors fell for a dirty trick played by a sinister apple polisher. If those German folk spinners, the Grimms Brothers, are to be believed, a similar fate befell one of the more famous residents of their fantasy wonderland, Snow White. Sadly, unlike the fairy tale princess, our former 'Edenites' were never relieved of their ensuing worldly distress.

Lacking details, many of us simply take for granted that the forbidden fruit was an apple. Actually, no one has really said it was an apple, and no amount of catechizing should tell us otherwise. The only reference in Scripture ("the fruit of the tree of the knowledge of good and evil") gives the thing metaphorical identity and nothing more. The orthodox view that it was an apple is eons younger than the Old Testament, and apparently originated from parallels drawn between the Garden of Eden and the Garden of the Hesperides when Greek mythology was in vogue. The latter was a dragon-guarded place in which there was a tree laden with golden apples belonging to Hera.

Another theory is that St. Jerome, in translating the Old Testament from Greek to Latin, adopted the erroneous interpretation of Aquila Ponticus that an apple tree mentioned in the Song of Solomon was the same tree that grew in the Garden of Eden. Alternatively, it is claimed the saint wrote *malum* in his translation, having in mind the word 'evil', not realizing that

152

malum is also the Latin equivalent for 'apple'.

In Genesis, according to Biblicists, while no mention is made of the apple or of the apple tree, a passage stating that Adam and Eve "sewed fig leaves together and made coverings for themselves" somehow acknowledges the presence of at least one fig tree in the vicinity. Michelangelo himself painted the non-conforming image of a fig on the Sistine Chapel ceiling, seemingly convinced that Eden was located in the Middle East, where figs are abundant. Some would even surmise that, on the assumption it was the fig tree that brought the curse on Adam and Eve, this should be reason enough for Jesus Christ to curse it back and make it barren. As we all know, Jesus did that precisely in one of the Gospel incidents in the New Testament.

Carbonized apples, rock-hard and soot-black and resembling chunks of coal, have been unearthed and dated to 6500 BC. However, this, or the fact that apples thrive in some parts of Iran, proves nothing more than that the apple requires long periods of cold weather to nurture and would not have adapted well to the temperate climate of Eden. This is probably why the Hebrews, among the many religious cultures that have their own concepts of the forbidden fruit, choose the pomegranate as their standard. The Koran has its own candidate in the banana despite the inability of this fruit to thrive indigenously in the Middle East.

9. The Banishing Truth

Myth! **For their disobedience, God evicted the first couple from the Garden of Eden.**

A common tableau in religious art is of the first couple, wrapped in animal skin and cowering in shame, being driven out of Eden by seraphim brandishing flaming swords. Unlike many other depictions of the *Genesis* stories, this representation of Man's expulsion from the Garden is reasonably faithful to the description of the Bible.

But while most everyone is familiar with what happened on man's last day in Eden, many seem to have been transfixed by the drama of the moment and forgotten why it happened. Surprisingly, the usual explanation given for the eviction is that it

153

was to punish our first parents for disobeying the Almighty, who had commanded Adam not to eat of the fruit. According to the Good Book, the true reason was God's apprehension that man, having become wise like God after eating from the tree of knowledge, would aspire to also become immortal by eating from the fruit of the tree of life. In the exact words of *Genesis* 3:22, God drove man out 'lest he put forth his hand, and take also of the tree of life, and eat, and live forever'. This passage, incidentally, also debunks the popular belief that there was only one forbidden tree in Eden.

10. Noah Connection

Myth! The Bible does not say who among Adam's children is a common ancestor of humanity.

Of the hundreds of sons and daughters Adam begot during the eight centuries he spent on earth, the Bible names only three: Cain, Abel and Seth. Abel, a celibate when Cain slew him, is obviously not an ancestor of humanity, and this goes for all the Biblical characters that died childless or whose descending lines ended too soon. To get a fix on the others, one has to track a genealogical route through countless ages that have not been— and most likely will never be—bridged by conventional history.

It may seem an impossible task, but there's a simple method of knowing who among Adam's children are, like him, a common ancestor of mankind. All that's needed is a bit of deductive thinking and a closer reading of some of the quiet passages of *Genesis*.

For instance, one passage tells us that Noah, his wife, his children and their spouses were the few who survived the great flood that wiped out all life on earth. Undoubtedly then, Noah is a common ancestor of man. Although Noah is not a son of Adam, Seth is, and Seth is designated in *Genesis* 5 as a direct ascendant of Noah. This means that the whole of humanity, from Noah to the last baby born in the world, descended from Seth.

Quite possibly, Noah's maternal line and the ancestry of Noah's wife began with a Seth sibling and not with Seth

154

himself. Still, Seth is the only one in Adam's brood whose lineage to Noah is clearly defined. This same lineage reveals several other common ancestors of man in the antediluvian period after Seth. The names Enosh, Kenan, Mahalalel, Jared, Enoch, Methuselah and Lamech may sound arcane to most, but each (representing a generation down to the ninth, Noah being the tenth) rings a bell in the context of man's efforts to determine his Biblical heritage.

11. His son Seth

Myth! **Cain was the eldest child of Adam and Eve.**

If Cain had not turned out the way he did, many a first-born male child would probably be carrying his name today. In cultures with strong family traditions, it is ordained that the first male child, as Cain has been thought to be, should grow up to be a 'keeper' of siblings especially in the absence of either or both parents.

However, while Cain is sometimes regarded as 'the first religious man' or 'the first killer,' there is no indication in the holy writings that Cain was 'the first born of human'. That he was the number one son and Abel the number two in the world's first family is merely an impression that the faithful, through eons of belief, has endowed with the near quality of Biblical truth. In *Genesis* 4:25, Eve gave birth to a third son and named him Seth. An Old Testament source, the P-document, reveals that Seth was actually the firstborn and not the third, a statement that may have been unwittingly omitted in the Bible. The Good Book does say, though, that our first parents begat a large number of children, estimated in the hundreds, raising the odds that at least one of them was older than Cain.

155

12. The Mark of Sorrow

Myth! The mark of Cain is a visible red spot placed above his eyebrow.

One of the many arguments about the 'mark of Cain' has to do with its appearance. The simplistically minded believe it was a red spot above Cain's brow, while the more imaginative—among them the poet Shelley in 'Adonais'—see it as a crimson or scarlet band around the forehead. Others don't notice it on any part of Cain's face but on some other part of his body.

All these descriptions are speculative, as there is nothing in *Genesis* to indicate that the mark was visible or physical. The mark may well have tagged Cain as the world's prime criminal, reminding him constantly of the heinousness of his crime and shaming him into becoming an outcast. But *Genesis* 4:15 tells us the real purpose of the mark was not to punish Cain but to protect him. God was worried the slayer would himself be slain by those who wanted to avenge Abel, so he put out a warning, "Whosoever slayeth Cain, vengeance shall be taken on him sevenfold." It is this malediction or curse that has come to be known as the 'mark of Cain'—clearly a misnomer, since it wasn't a mark nor was it directed against Cain.

In the modern context, the 'mark of Cain' is the tag of a fratricide, or one who kills a sibling. This is a departure from its original Biblical sense as a symbol proclaiming that only God can punish a murderer.

13. Population Postulation

Myth! There were no more than four people on earth at the time of Abel's death.

A casual reading of the Bible would suggest that Adam and Eve had only one other child at the time of Abel's death, and this was his murderer Cain. The chances are there were others. Calculating that Seth was born when Adam was 130 years old,

156

and this was a year after Abel's death, St. Augustine placed the crime in the 129th year of Creation. Before this date, Adam and Eve must have had ample time to procreate in accordance with God's advice to be 'fruitful and multiply'.

Various passages of *Genesis* strongly imply that the couple had numerous children during this period. Verse 4:14 speaks of Cain being fearful that 'others' might kill him in retaliation for the murder. And verse 4:17 relates how Cain, soon after being expelled to the land of Nod, lay with his wife, who could only be a sister.

One expert estimates the world's population at an astounding half a million on the date of Abel's murder. This, he says, is based on the reasonable assumption that Adam and Eve and their adult descendants had a child from each marriage every year for 129 years, and the sexes were evenly divided between them.

14. Abel is able but Cain can't

Myth! Abel was a carnivore.

In *Genesis* 4:2, "Abel kept flocks, and Cain worked the soil." From this many infer that Cain, the planter, was a vegetarian whereas Abel, the shepherd, was a carnivore. A further reading of the chapter proves this deduction false. Both brothers could not have eaten anything other than fruits and vegetables because God had prohibited the eating of meat during this early period. God lifted the interdiction only after the Great Flood, when he told Moses, "Everything that lives and moves will be food for you. Just as I gave you the green plants, I now give you everything" (*Ge* 9:3). Abel tended sheep most probably for their wool, to be used for making garments and tents.

II

According To The Book

On the Age of Patriarchs

"And all my days were nine hundred sixty
and nine years; and I died."

•

Methuselah

1. Solar Standoff

Myth! **NASA scientists discovered the 'lost day' that resulted when Joshua commanded the sun to stand still.**

On the day the Israelites were fighting the Amorites, Joshua commanded the sun and the moon to stand still until his army had conquered the enemy. Accordingly, the sun stood still in the middle of the sky and did not go down for a whole day (*Jos* 10:12-13).

This Biblical account was supposedly confirmed by NASA's discovery of a 'lost day' in its computer models of the earth's orbital history. According to the report, the research was conducted at the Goddard Space Flight Center in Maryland. Unfortunately, NASA denies having made any such discovery, nor having conducted a study that produced the momentous serendipity. When the rumor started in the early 1960s, NASA was doing computer studies of the earth's orbit and the movement of other planets to determine optimum rocket launching times and trajectories. But there was no effort to delve into the history of the orbit, as this would have involved a calendar study reaching back thousands of years, a feat way beyond NASA's scope and capability.

The NASA disavowal is seconded by many Biblical scholars, who doubt Joshua's miracle literally happened. They have reason to suspect that the passage describing the event was only lifted from a poem or prayer in the now missing *Book of Jasher.*

2. Blast from the Past

Myth! **The walls of Jericho collapsed from the sound of seven trumpets.**

The belief that the walls of Jericho were brought down by the "sound of seven trumpets" is a gross misreading of the Bible. As described in *Jos* 6, the Israelite warlord Josue ordered his soldiers to march once around the city, with seven priests blowing on

159

ram's horns ahead of the Ark, each day for six days. On the seventh day, the soldiers marched seven times around the city, again with the priests ahead of the Ark. On their last round, they gave a long blast on the horns—at which point popular misconception cuts in to assert that the sound collapsed the walls of the city.

This folk interpretation of the Jericho event misses one important line of text, to wit: "As soon as the men heard it (the trumpets), they gave a great shout, and the walls collapsed" (*Jos* 6:20). In other words, the trumpets were only meant to signal the thousands massed around the walls to shout in unison. It was this great shout, not the trumpet blast, that literally shook the earth and brought down the already weakened walls of Jericho.

Scientists speculate that the shout was timed precisely with what they believe to be the real cause of the collapse—an earthquake. Geological records of the Holy Land indicate that the town lies on the Jordan Fault separating the Arabian plate from the Sinai plate, and that over the last 10,000 years, quakes, the latest of which occurred in 1927, have repeatedly destroyed it. This theory is buttressed by the archeological observation that Jericho's walls often collapsed in a single direction, a tendency that's normal in a quake but not in any other scenario.

3. Soup Sale

Myth! **Esau sold his birthright to Jacob for a mess of potage.**

Bible preachers are not telling it right when they say Esau sold his birthright to Jacob for a mess of potage. The popular retelling of the story of the brothers does not mesh with Scripture in two respects. Most people are made to understand that Esau asked Jacob for a "mess of potage," but this phrase is nowhere in the Bible, and only the word "mess" can be found in a few versions. The food Jacob gave Esau was actually bread and red stew, which is why Esau is sometimes called Edom, meaning "red".

There is also the notion that Esau was so foolhardy—and hungry—as to cede his valuable birthright to Jacob in exchange for food. *Hebrew* 12:16 of the New Testament confirms that Esau

160

"for a single meal sold his birthright," but the original story in the Old Testament conveys a somewhat different sense. In *Genesis* 25:29, Esau is not allowed to eat of the red stew until he promises ("swears") to sell his birthright to Jacob. Obviously then, the food is being given not in exchange for the birthright but for Esau's commitment (or "earnest," as it is called in the trade) to sell the birthright to Jacob in the future. Lawyers will insist that, in this case, the meal is in consideration of the promise of a sale and not of the sale itself, the real price not being due until the transfer becomes legally or morally binding.

---

4. Onan the Barbarian

Myth! **Onanism is a euphemism for masturbation.**

Onanism is popularly believed to be a euphemism for masturbation. But while masturbation is deemed sinful in religious circles, onanism was punished in the Bible only because it violated Hebrew tradition.

Judah told his younger son Onan to marry his brother's widow and continue their line in conformity with the time-honored Hebrew tradition of *levirate*, or widow-brother marriage. Onan obeyed, but knowing the children from the union would be considered his brother's and not his own under the unwritten law, he was reluctant to consummate the marriage. Therefore, each time he performed the sexual act with his new wife, he withdrew and spilled his seed on the ground (*Gen.* 38:8-9).

Technically speaking, what Onan did was not masturbation, as is commonly assumed, but *coitus interruptus*, or premature withdrawal. Centuries of secular misinterpretation have confused the two and brought undeserved opprobrium on masturbation not only from religious but, until recently, from medical quarters as well. Ironically, while the Roman Catholic view now agrees that masturbation is different from onanism (albeit still as reprehensible), most English dictionaries maintain their synonymity.

It is generally assumed that Onan was punished for spilling his seed on the ground, an assumption that has formed the basis for the moral condemnation of this form of sexual activity. Actually,

161

Onan's real sin, for which Yahweh slew him, was refusing to obey the law of *levirate*.

5. Man for all Seasons

Myth! **Methuselah, the oldest person ever, outlived his father Enoch by more than 600 years.**

Methuselah set the world's record as the oldest person who ever lived, by dying at the age of 969 years (*Ge* 5: 27). His father Enoch, who was himself 365 years old when "God took him away" (*Ge* 5:23-24), was 65 at the time of Methuselah's birth (*Ge* 5:21). Gerontologists may easily deduce from this that Methuselah, who was 300 years old when Enoch passed away, outlived his father by 669 years.

But Biblicists don't think it's that simple. In *Heb* 11:5, "Enoch was taken from this life, so that he did not experience death." He was the first of two characters in the Old Testament (the second was Elijah) who ascended body and soul into heaven without going through death and resurrection. Enoch did not die in a human way, and in a technical sense is still alive and living a life that has already surpassed Methuselah's by several millennia.

Because of the infinite duration of Enoch's physical being, his age is limitless and cannot be fixed for record purposes. Methuselah's primacy over Enoch has been maintained in the record books only by measuring longevity on the basis of time spent on earth rather than of physical existence.

6. What is Truth?

Myth! **The God of the Old Testament never lied.**

Only pagan gods lie, apparently. The ancient gods of Olympus had no qualms about lying to each other or to their human constituents. But with the Hebrew God of the Old Testament, the idea is believed untenable, even anathema. The whole moral

162

foundation of Christian theology rests on the proposition that the Giver is incapable of violating his own commandments and his omnipotence precludes any need to deceive or lie.

Yet the Old Testament recounts that on one occasion, God lied. When Sarah learned she was going to have a child, she said, "After I am waxed old shall I have pleasure, my lord being old also?" God reported Sarah's reaction to Abraham, but changed what she had said to, "Shall I of a surety bear a child, who am old?" God deliberately omitted parts of Sarah's statement to conceal her doubts about Abraham's own procreative powers. It was a white lie, but a lie nevertheless.

There are people who echo Sarah's sentiment and assume that the one-hundred-year old Abraham was, if not sexually impotent, incapable of producing offspring. In truth, the "Father of Nations" was just hitting his stride when he fathered Isaac. In *Genesis* 25, we are told that, after Sarah's death, "Abraham took a wife and her name was Keturah. And she bare him Zimran, Jokshan, and Medan, and Midian, and Ishbak, and Shuah." Abraham was a prolific patriarch up to the ripe old age of 175, when he died, proving that, as God had intimated to him in a lie, it was Sarah who had the problem.

7. Technicolor Dream Coat

Myth! Jacob gifted his son Joseph with a coat of many colors.

As most everybody knows, Joseph's coat is the garment that catalyzed his fabulous adventures in *Genesis*. But moving from Biblical lore to popular fantasy, what was originally a simple robe has flowered into a coat of many colors, becoming the centerpiece of various literary and artistic productions, including a popular Broadway musical entitled *Joseph and the Technicolor Dream Machine*.

According to *Genesis* 37:3, Jacob loved Joseph "more than all his other sons, because he had been born to him when he was old." To prove this, he made him "a long robe with full sleeves." Nothing more is said about how the robe looked, although some versions call it a "decorated robe" without mentioning its color.

Actually, the only time the apparel became colored was when Joseph's brothers, after abandoning him in the well, slaughtered a goat and dipped the robe in its blood, to make it appear to Jacob that wild animals killed the boy.

8. Game of Patience

Myth! Job was a very patient man.

According to *Jas* 5:11, "Ye have heard of the patience of Job." And who hasn't? To test Job's faith, God allowed Satan to throw every conceivable misfortune at him and his family. The popular impression is that he took it all with quiet fortitude and was vindicated in the end.

As the Bible itself attests, this proverbial patience happens to be overrated. The paragon of perseverance that is supposed to be Job is able to keep his cool for only the first two chapters of the book that carries his name. In more than thirty of the later chapters, he is an angry and rebellious man, complaining loudly about his unexpected turn of luck and bitter to a point where he accuses God of being unjust, questions his wisdom, and even challenges his authority. It is only after being severely rebuked by God that he relents and submits completely to his mercy.

Incidentally, Job's lament in 19:20 ("I am nothing but skins and bones; I have escaped with only the skin of my teeth") has produced a metaphor that deviates entirely from its original meaning. By the phrase "with the skin of my teeth," Job obviously meant that he had escaped with practically nothing left but the skin of his teeth. The preposition "with" has been supplanted popularly by the word "by", and the resulting phrase "by the skin of my teeth" now refers to the margin of a very narrow escape, a margin so thin it can only be measured by the skin or lining of a tooth. This Americanism is fairly modern, having appeared only at the beginning of the nineteenth century, and may have been influenced by the belief that Job used the word 'with' to actually mean 'by'.

9. He ain't Heavy, he's our Brother

Myth! His brothers sold Joseph into slavery.

Joseph was the youngest of the twelve sons of Jacob and his father's favorite. Hating him for this, his brothers plotted his assassination. At the instance of one of them, they decided not to do it directly but to strip him and throw him into a dry cistern.

In *Acts* 7:9 and *Genesis* 37:23-28 and 45:4, the brothers later pull Joseph out of the well and sell him to some Ishmaelite merchants going to Egypt. But in other versions of *Genesis* 37:23-28, the brothers are no longer around when a band of Midianite traders pass through, draw Joseph up out of the cistern, and sell him to the Ishmaelite for twenty pieces of silver. These divergent accounts of how Joseph was initiated into Egyptian life cast a cloud on the popular belief that it was his brothers who sold him into slavery.

10. A Lot of Salt

Myth! For looking back at the destruction of Sodom, Lot's wife was transformed into a pillar of salt.

Lot was warned to escape the iniquitous city of Sodom before God destroyed it with fire and brimstone. He was instructed to take his wife and two daughters and not to look back at the burning city. His wife, however, disobeyed. Clinging to the past, she was unwilling to turn completely away, and for this indiscretion she was turned into a pillar of salt.

Tourists even now are directed to the bizarre salt formations in the Dead Sea area and told that one of them is Lot's wife. But Biblicists have long agreed that the transformation of Lot's wife into salt is not to be taken literally. "Being transformed into salt" is only a figure of speech that means to become barren, or to be incapable of conceiving, the rationale being that salty regions are barren because nothing can grow there. Lot's wife was rendered barren, and it was not for looking back at Sodom in the literal sense. The term "looking back at Sodom" is often used as an allegory for "looking back longingly at sin while moving forward with God"—in other words, insincere penitence. What this tells us is that the destruction of Sodom may have been an actual event, but the incident involving Lot's wife is pure metaphor—to symbolize the belief in ancient times that God makes barren those who ask for absolution of sin when they have no resolute desire to avoid its repetition.

11. Stairway to Heaven

Myth! **The ancient shrine at Bethel was erected to commemorate Jacob's dream.**

The story of Jacob's ladder offers an explanation for the origin of Bethel, a place about ten miles north of Jerusalem, as an important center of worship. The relevant passage is *Genesis* 28:10-22: "And Jacob...dreamed, and behold a ladder set up on the earth, and the top of it reached to heaven: and behold the angels of God ascending and descending upon it. And behold the Lord stood above it...And Jacob awakened out of his sleep and said, Surely the Lord is in this place and I knew it not...and he called the name of that place Bethel, though the city used to be called Luz." Following his vow, Jacob established a house of worship in Bethel to commemorate the event. The city later degenerated into a place of idolatry, was condemned by the prophet Hosea, and was finally put to the sword by the house of Joseph (*Jdg* 1:22-25).

Despite the strong images the story of Jacob's ladder projects in both Jewish and Christian traditions, modern Biblical research has shown that Bethel, far from being a Jewish center in ancient times, served as a pagan shrine from its inception to the date it was destroyed. Visitors used to sleep in its premises not to worship but to consult pagan oracles in dreams. Scholars conclude that the concept of Bethel as a house of God was just an attempt by the early fathers to fuse the local cult with the worship of Jacob's god Yahweh. There is a tendency today to set aside the literal import of Jacob's ladder and show the story in its true light as a metaphorical allusion to the communion between man and God.

166

12. Old Boy

Myth! Isaac was only a boy when Abraham set him up to be sacrificed.

The story of Abraham and Isaac in *Genesis* 22 explores the theme of faith, specifically faith in God. The patriarch is put to the test when, for no obvious reason, God commands him: "Take your son, your only son, Isaac, whom you love, and go to the region of Moriah. Sacrifice him there as a burnt offering on one of the mountains I will tell you about." We are told that Abraham obeyed blindly, proceeding to the place with Isaac and two servants. But at the last minute, God reveals his true purpose and the sacrifice is aborted.

Most versions of *Genesis* 22 consistently call Isaac a "boy," but critics are not sure what the term really means. They think it likely that "boy" is used only figuratively, to emphasize the vast difference in age between Isaac and the old man Abraham. Some have worked out by cross-reference with other sources that at the time of the incident, Isaac was already thirty-seven years old. Using his own method, the ancient Jewish historian Flavius Josephus estimated Isaac's age at twenty-five.

Two circumstances in the story support the notion that Isaac was a young to middle-aged adult when it happened. First, Abraham didn't bother to ask leave of Sarah for his projected trip with Isaac, and second, Sarah showed no concern upon discovering that they had left. No parent would have acted so nonchalantly knowing that the only child in the family, a mere youngster, was going on a long week's journey to the mountains with an extremely old companion.

13. Gay City

Myth! God destroyed Sodom because of its homosexual practices.

The traditional view is that Sodom was destroyed because of its

167

homosexual practices, not the least of which was sodomy, the sexual aberration for which the city became an eponym. In some versions of the Bible, the "homosexuality" of Sodom is dramatized by a scene in which a large number of men surrounds Lot's house one night to demand that he bring out his two male guests so they can "have sex" with them. Lot offers his own two daughters instead, but the crowd is not appeased.

Historically, Sodom never had a reputation for being a homosexual haven before the Christian era. It is believed that what damned Sodom were vices that had to do with materialism, e.g., pride, greed and wealth, not lust or sex. Older forms of Scripture, in describing the incident involving Lot's guests, used the vague word "know" in lieu of "have sex," implying that a sexual connotation may not have been intended.

Still others claim the real cause of God's anger at Sodom was the inhospitality of its people to strangers. Hospitality in Abraham's time was a holy and serious custom, and one was careful to treat every stranger as a highly honored guest because of the possibility that he was entertaining angels or even God himself. The custom was in keeping with stringent laws that protected travelers against the common crimes of rape, robbery and murder.

14. Mountain Suspense

Myth! Noah's Ark settled on Mount Ararat after the great flood.

The King James version of the Bible speaks of "the mountains of Ararat"—not "Mount Ararat"—as the final resting place of Noah's Ark after the Great Flood receded (*Ge* 8:4). Explorers and archaeologists periodically go in search of the actual site, hoping to find some artifacts that would serve to bridge the gap between history and Biblical tradition. So far, there has been no trace of the spot, much less of any part of the fabled vessel.

Neither is Mount Ararat mentioned in the Vulgate and Douay versions. Catholics, in fact, prefer the mountains of Armenia to those of Ararat, a view supported by the Syrians and Nestorians, who single out Mt. Judi in southern Armenia as Noah's point of

168

disembarkation. The Kurds also favor Armenia, ignoring the claim of some ancient writers, including Josephus, that the mysterious site is somewhere in the Kurds' own home country of Kurdistan. Surprisingly, the spot chosen by the Armenians themselves, in agreement with the Jews, is a mountain range in present-day Turkey near the USSR border, where once the Urartu (the Assyrian equivalent of "Ararat") kingdom flourished. The highest peak in the Turkish range is called Great Ararat and its nearest rival is Little Ararat, but exploration there has failed to yield anything of interest.

15. We're no Angels

Myth! **Angels are winged humanoids whose young ones are known as cherubims.**

Renaissance art has made popular the image of angels as long-robed humanoids with beatific faces and oversized bird wings. These representations are incompatible with broadly held religious and philosophical views on the matter. From Plato to Aquinas, the consensus is that angels are spiritual in substance and nature—faceless, bodiless and wingless, just as God is. In many places of the Bible, angels take on a human form, but mainly to relate to their milieu when on an earthly mission as messengers of God.

What may have started the idea that an angel has a body and wings is a combination of Scripture and pagan lore. Ancient peoples, such as the Assyrians, painted or sculpted winged men with the heads of hawks to adorn or guard their buildings. The Hebrews borrowed these figures to form their own concept of the heavenly host, which they substantiated in *Ezekiel, Isaiah* and *Revelation.* The winged creatures that appear in these prophetic books have monstrous visages that deviate almost entirely from the conventional image of angels, and their descriptions are so thoroughly cloaked in allegory that it is impossible to say whether they represent actual beings. These impressionistic images were later humanized in other parts of Scripture to make them look like men with wings, and it is this configuration that artists have portrayed through the years.

A cherub is traditionally portrayed as a baby angel with its head

169

resting on a pair of small wings, oftentimes without a body. In the Bible, the description of a cherub is utterly different. *Ezekiel* 1 states that in appearance "their form was that of a man, but each of them had four faces and four wings...their feet were like those of a calf." One of the four faces was human, and the rest were those of a lion, an ox and an eagle. These surrealistic creatures—part of the apocalyptic vision—are clearly not ordinary angels but belong to a separate order of heavenly beings. Some Biblicists believe their hideous appearances prove they are pure metaphorical illusion.

Incidentally, the words "cherubims" and "seraphims" have their place in the Holy Book—they are used routinely in *Ezekiel* 10 and *Isaiah* 6—but elsewhere, they are considered to be grammatically improper. The conventional plural forms of "cherub" and "seraph" are "cherubim" and "seraphim," respectively.

III

Might And Mane

On Biblical Longhairs

"I am the voice of one crying in the wilderness,
Make straight the way of the Lord."
•

John the Baptist

1. Long and Short of ancient Hairdos

Myth! The ancient Israelites generally wore their hair long.

The Old Testament is believed to be the only written record about the cultural life of the ancient Israelites, from the time of Seth to the hiatus preceding Jesus. Even so, Scriptural text gives no indication of which hairstyles were popular with either sex among the Jews and the Gentiles of that period. Colorful Biblical incidents that draw attention to the opulent hair of Samson and Absalom have inspired Renaissance artists to portray most OT male personages, specifically the patriarchs Noah, Abraham and Moses, in the image of these hirsute gallants. Consistently with the Renaissance model, modern Biblical art has helped form the widely held opinion that medium- to shoulder-length hair was the standard observed by the Israelites in ancient times.

Taking a different view are some who rely on archaeological and other deductions to prove that longhaired Israelites were the exception and not the rule. They see God's 'chosen people' as originally nomadic tribes that would not acquire any degree of cohesiveness until, scripturally speaking, Moses came along to lead them to the Promised Land. Before then, these wanderers had to settle in alien places and undergo assimilation into the culture and lifestyle of their hosts. The latter included the Egyptians, whose relics of that period show they were a nation that maintained a strong tradition for short hair. Thus, with the exception of cult members, priests, elders, teachers, religious eremites, holy men and others who were required to keep their hair long in order to uphold a vow or a theme, the ancient Israelites had no choice but to adopt Egyptian hair fashion, particularly during the time they were enslaved by the likes of Ramses II. If this were not so, it is asked, why would Moses tell his sons not to let their hair grow long? (*Lev* 10:6, 20:1,5-15, 1 *Cor* 11:14).

The hairstyle prevailing in the Christian era is apparently a throwback to what was in vogue during the days of the ancient Israelites. *Corinthians* of the New Testament is frequently cited in support of the claim that most Hebrew men in Jesus' time wore their hair short and women long. Saint Paul states, "Both not even nature itself teach you, that, if a man have long hair, it is a shame

172

unto him?" (1 *Cor* 11:14). Lacking evidence to the contrary, this passage is strong affirmation that Jesus wore his hair short rather than long. Late Renaissance art remained orthodox for its own reason, however. Because the fashion then current favored long hair for men of distinction and short for the masses, artists of this period stuck to the idea that the Great Teacher had long, richly textured hair. Thus, in Jacopo Bassano's 1542 oil on canvas of the Last Supper, Jesus with his hair flowing to his shoulders stands out in the company of his 12 shorthaired apostles.

2. The Hair is human, the Strength divine

Myth! Samson derived his extraordinary strength from his long hair.

Various literary and artistic interpretations of Scripture have induced the widespread notion that the source of Samson's extraordinary strength was his hair. However, the Bible itself does not say this. What it does say is that each time Samson performed one of his deeds, "the Spirit of the Lord came upon him in power" (*Numbers* 6). There is nothing to suggest that Samson drew his strength from a special part of his body or from some other earthly item.

Many experts believe that Samson's physical prowess, though remarkable, was not superhuman. He sometimes performed feats of strength and daring with the aid of divine inspiration. On most other occasions, he was able to magnify his natural strength with an inner vigor developed from years of discipline with the Nazarite sect. Samson had been a member since birth of this elite corps of ascetics dedicated to the service of God and to a vow never to have a haircut. A Nazarite's uncut hair symbolized his independence, will and courage, and cutting it was, in effect, breaking him totally in spirit.

Hollywood and art would have us believe that Samson had a good hair on his head but none on his chest. There is a tendency in their portrayals to show that the source of Samson's strength was magical (his long locks) rather than physical (manliness, as shown by hair on the chest). However, hair on the chest as a sign of virility and strength, the two main components of mature

173

masculinity, is a popular myth that stems from people associating the hairy quality of a gorilla to its brute strength without realizing that a gorilla is hairy all over except on the chest. Hair on the head, unless it's magical, is no guarantee of physical strength either. Experiments have shown that baldness may in fact be a more reliable sign of mature masculinity than long hair.

3. That Philistine woman

Myth! Delilah was the Philistine woman who betrayed Samson to her countrymen.

The common belief that Delilah was the Philistine woman who betrayed Samson to her countrymen is unwarranted. *Judges* 16:4 describes Delilah in curt terms as "a woman in the Valley of Sorek" who later conspires with "the rulers of the Philistines" to subdue Samson. But nowhere does it say she was a Philistine herself. More likely, she was an Israelite under Philistine jurisdiction.

In focusing undue attention on Delilah, there is a tendency to omit a whole passage of Scripture describing Samson's own wife as the Philistine woman who betrayed him to her countrymen. This she did by beguiling him into giving her the answer to a riddle that he had posed to his Philistine guests at their wedding, and passing on the information to her tribal kinsmen to make them win their bet with Samson. Unlike Delilah's betrayal, his wife's perfidy caused Samson no harm and instead prompted him to kill thirty Philistines.

Samson did not learn a lesson from the incident, and had one more experience with a scheming female before his fateful meeting with Delilah. The strong man, who was fond of making recreational visits to the coastal cities of the Philistines, once went to Gaza to spend the night with a harlot. It is not known if this woman was also a Philistine, but she certainly had the attitude of one. She told Samson's enemies of his whereabouts while he was asleep. Fortunately, before they could make a move, Samson got up and tore loose the doors of the city gate, carrying them off to the top of the hill that faced Hebron.

174

4. Shearing her Love

Myth! **Delilah cut Samson's hair to rob him of his physical strength.**

People need not be Bible smart to wager that Samson's hair was cut to rob him of his physical prowess. But people need to be Bible literate to accept a wager that it was Delilah who did the barbering after putting drugs in his drink.

To say that Delilah clipped Samson's hair after tricking him into taking a sleeping potion is to usurp the Bible on several counts. The precise words of *Judges* 16:19 are, "She had him sleep on her lap, and called for a man who shaved off his seven locks of hair." Nothing can be plainer than that Samson's hair was shaved, not clipped, and it was not Delilah but a man, probably a servant, who did the job. Samson must have voluntarily dozed off on the woman's lap, probably after a hectic bout of lovemaking—a far cry from that famous scene in the 1949 Hollywood blockbuster *Samson and Delilah* showing Hedy Lamarr surreptitiously putting knockout drops in Victor Mature's wine.

5. The Nagging Truth

Myth! **Samson revealed the secret of his strength to Delilah out of love for her.**

Delilah kept asking Samson for the secret of his strength, and each time Samson lied to her. It was on her last try that Delilah, almost losing hope, said, "How can you say 'I love you' when you won't confide in me?" Samson finally revealed all, and this she duly passed on to the Philistines, who succeeded in capturing him.

Delilah's seductive lament is probably what accounts for the popular belief that Samson disclosed his secret to Delilah out of love. It may come as a disappointment to unmitigated romanticists, but a closer reading of *Judges* tells us that love had nothing to do with it. Later on in the same passage, we learn that she 'importuned him continually and vexed him with her complaints till he was deathly weary of them'. In simpler terms, it was Delilah's constant nagging, not her feminine charms, that prevailed on Samson.

6. Neither Hide nor Hair

Myth! **The ancient Israelites were light haired and white-skinned.**

There are those who would press the point further and argue that the ancient Israelites were not only short-haired but were actually black-skinned like most Africans. Their premise is the well-debated contention by, among others, the English writer Gerald Massey, the 19th century explorer Sir Richard Francis Burton, the anthropologist Count Constantin de Volney and the ancient Greek historian Herodotus, that ancient Egyptian communities like those with which the Israelites intermingled were black.

Joseph, the son of Jacob, had to be black-skinned—so the argument continues—because, "(i)f he were white skinned, as over half the world's Jews are today, his brothers would have recognized him easily among the black- skinned Egyptians....Moses had to have the same physical characteristics because again, he was raised in the house of Pharaoh, as the grandson of Pharaoh, when Pharaoh ordered all other Hebrew males to be killed at birth. If the Israelites were a white-skinned people, how could Moses the Hebrew survive (secretly) in the house of Pharaoh among black-skinned Egyptians for 40 years, and not be noticed?"

7. Heir Head

Myth! **Absalom was slain when his hair got caught in the branch of a tree.**

Most everyone who has read his catechism knows about Absalom, the rebel son whose defiance of his father King David led him to an unprecedented fate. According to the popular account of Absalom's death in the battle of Ephraim, this prince-warrior was riding his horse when the animal went under an oak tree and his hair got caught in the thick branches. While hanging thus, he was slain by David's men.

The Bible in 2 *Sa* 18:9 says he was riding a mule, not a horse, and "his head caught hold of the oak," without mentioning his hair. A moment's thought should tell us that had his hair been entangled, he could have easily cut it off with his sword. The impression that it was his 'hair' rather than his 'head' that entrapped him may have come from a previous Biblical passage that describes Absalom as a handsome man with long hair weighing as much as five pounds.

On the other hand, Esau's hair may have indirectly caused his fall from grace as the dominant successor to his father's estate. In *Gen* 27, his younger brother Jacob pretends to be Esau so their father Isaac can bless him from his invalid's bed. Isaac, who is almost blind, is fooled by the kidskin that Jacob wraps around his hands and neck to simulate Esau's hairiness.

8. The Seventh Veil

Myth! **Herod had John the Baptist bcheaded at the request of his stepdaughter Salome, whose sexual advances John had spurned.**

The tetrarch Herod Antipas had John the Baptist, a longhaired ascetic like his cousin Jesus, imprisoned for purportedly accusing him of entering into an unlawful marriage with Herodias, his brother's wife. Mark and Matthew, two of the New Testament Gospellers, tell us that the martyr eventually lost more than his hair when Herod ordered him executed at the instance of Herodias' daughter, who had asked for his head as her reward for dancing to his satisfaction at his birthday.

In neither Gospel—indeed, nowhere in the Bible—is the young woman named, although in some ancient Greek versions of Mark "Herodias' daughter" becomes "Herod's daughter Herodias", prompting scholars using these texts to believe that both mother and daughter had the same name. The Latin Vulgate Bible translates the same phrase as "daughter of the said Herodias", following which western Church Fathers chose to refer to the younger female as "Herodias's daughter" or just "the girl". Needless to say, the idea that both mother and daughter were named Herodias gained currency for quite a time in early modern Europe.

It was only later that popular tradition started calling Herodias' daughter Salome, evidently in acceptance of the ancient historian Flavius Josephus, who provided the name in his book *Jewish Antiquities* (Book XVIII, Chapter 5, 4). However, as the only source for the name prior to the 19th century, Josephus presents no real evidence that his character and the person referred to by Mark and Matthew are one and the same. In fact, he makes no mention of her involvement in the death of John the Baptist, and in other parts of the *Antiquities* states that Herod had John beheaded not because of Herodias or Salome, but for political reasons, i.e., his sermons were prodding the populace to rioting and sedition. Moreover, Josephus does not describe Salome as a dancer or entertainer, merely as Herodias' daughter and the widow of Herod's son Philip who later married Philip's sibling and raised three children with him. The name Salome is common enough in the Bible (there is, e.g., Salome the disciple who was present at the Crucifixion), but Josephus makes no suggestion that he might be referring to any of them. It is perhaps for this reason that the name Salome did not catch on until the 19th century, when French writer Gustave Flaubert used the Josephus reference in describing the biblical dancing lady in his short story "Herodias."

Why Herodias' daughter would ask her stepfather Herod to gift her with the head of the Baptist is also something of a mystery. Mark and Matthew concur that, contrary to the popular impression, the real instigator was her mother, who bore a deep grudge against John for accusing her and Herod of committing adultery. But in a play launched in Paris in 1869, Oscar Wilde's fertile imagination took exception to the Biblical account and painted Salome as a femme fatale who acquires a perverse taste for the Baptist and causes him to be executed when he spurns her affections. The idea, made even more memorable by the opera that Richard Strauss based on Wilde (and by various film portrayals of Salome dancing the "dance of the seven veils"), has become the surviving myth even though totally inconsistent with both the Bible and Josephus's account.

Interestingly, the earliest known Hollywood treatment of the Biblical episode is the 1918 *Salomé* starring Theda Bara, with Flavius Josephus given tongue-in-cheek credit for the story.

---

9. Harlot Times

Myth! The oldest profession in the world is prostitution.

Quite a number of characters in the Old Testament—Rahab in *Joshua* 6:17 is one of the very first named—are prostitutes, which is probably what accounts for the popular belief that prostitution is the oldest profession in the world.

But the mention of two other trades in *Genesis* effectively denies prostitution's claim to its venerable status. The first is tailoring, as suggested by the passage that describes Adam and Eve's reaction when they found themselves naked ("...they sewed fig leaves together and made coverings for themselves"—*Ge* 3:7). The second is an even earlier passage, and refers to what must be the world's oldest occupation—farming or gardening. After God had formed man, he planted a garden in Eden and put Adam in charge as the first—albeit inconstant—gardener ("The Lord God took the man and put him in the Garden of Eden to work it and take care of it"—*Ge* 2:15).

---

10. The Bigger they Come

Myth! David slew Goliath with a stone from his slingshot.

The dictionary defines Goliath as the giant Philistine warrior in the Old Testament who was slain by David with a stone and sling. This is shortchanging another Goliath in the same book of the Bible, the one David did not slay but only caused to be slain. In *1 Sa* 17:48, David is just a shepherd boy in the Israelite camp when he fells Goliath the Philistine with a stone hurled from a sling. In

179

2 Sa 21.19, David has become king of the Israelites and there is war again with the Philistines. At the battle of Gob, one of his warriors, Elhanan, son of Jaare-Oregim the Bethlehemite, fights Goliath the Gittite and kills him in hand-to-hand combat.

Both Goliaths are giants and are described as having "a spear with a shaft like a weaver's rod." Because of these oddly similar circumstances, some critics suspect the two characters are one and the same and the incidents in which they figure are versions of the same story.

There are also two contradictory stories about young David's rise to King Saul's attention. In *1 Samuel* 16, David is in Saul's service as his official harpist when Goliath challenges Israel. But in the very next chapter, David is still a shepherd boy who has just arrived in the middle of the challenge—the youngest son fresh from his father's flocks—to bring food to his brothers in Saul's camp.

IV

Moses With The Mostes'

On Moses

"What if they do not believe me or listen to me
and say, 'The Lord did not appear to you'?"

•

Moses

1. The Burning Truth

Myth! God appeared to Moses as a burning bush.

While tending a flock of sheep, Moses strayed towards Mount Horeb and there had his first encounter with God. Even Bible thumpers make the mistake of saying God appeared on this occasion in the shape of a burning bush, a belief that is not completely faithful to the phrasing of the Bible.

Exodus 3:2 ("an angel of the Lord appeared to him in fire flaming out of a bush") makes clear that God took the form of an angel and not of a burning bush. This is one of many instances in the Old Testament where an angel comes down to earth to convey a heavenly message as an embodiment of the Deity Himself. Biblicists say the bush and the flame are added symbols of God's presence; the bush alludes to his immanence in nature and the fire that burns without consuming itself represents his eternal power.

Unfortunately, most film portrayals of the burning bush completely ignore the angelic image. There has also been a tendency to sacrifice accuracy for visual tone by showing the entire bush burning and becoming almost indistinct because of the flames. *Exodus* is quite specific that only the middle of the bush burnt, indicating the holy presence within, and the outline of the bush, if not of the angel, remained cognizable.

2. Tribal Travel

Myth! One to two million Israelites joined the Exodus led by Moses.

An estimated one to two million Israelites joined the Exodus, but not all were followers of Moses. Of the several Hebrew tribes that left Egypt for the Promised Land, only the House of Joseph were in the flight led by the patriarch.

Exodus 12:37 says: "The Israelites journeyed from Rameses to Succoth. There were about six hundred thousand men on foot, besides women and children." Based on the most reasonable estimates of family size in those days, the "women and children" were at least a million in a column marching ten abreast with the men and nearly 100 miles long.

Some historians judge the Biblical estimate as too high, saying the large number quoted was more likely the entire population of Israelites. Paul Kuttner notes that during the actual Exodus only those related to the House of Joseph—i.e., descendants of Manasseh and Ephraim—participated in the flight led by Moses. Other Hebrew tribes, then despised as "Asiatics", left Egypt also but by different routes, crossing the Sinai Peninsula into Canaan. Although the whole experience is collectively called the Exodus, the Biblical book of that name limits itself to the part involving Moses.

3. Manna Matters

Myth! **Moses and the Israelites were sustained in the desert by manna that fell from heaven.**

The entire Israelite community had only been in the desert three days when they started complaining to the brothers Moses and Aaron about the lack of food. The Lord heard their grumbling and caused bread to rain down from heaven.

The people called the bread *manna*, meaning "What is it?," because nothing about it was known except that it was "white like coriander seed and tasted like wafers made with honey." Manna, according to *Exodus*, fed the Jews as they walked relentlessly in the desert for forty years. Tradition traces the source to heaven, but experts say the phrase 'manna from heaven' is only a Biblical metaphor for a life-giving nourishment that was in all probability of the earth. The likely reference is the tamarisk (*Tamarix Gallica*), familiar then as now as an evergreen shrub in the various oases and plateaus of the Sinai Peninsula. The secretion of this plant from perforations that certain insects make in it around June and July is collected as it solidifies in the cool morning air. The substance is both nutritious and palatable and has proved beneficial to desert travelers even in modern times.

The Bible says that after eating the manna, the people started complaining again because they were thirsty and had no water to drink. Thereupon, Moses, on God's instruction, struck a rock with his staff, and water gushed forth. Once again, we are warned not to take things literally. 'Striking a rock' is an Aramaic figure of speech for finding something significant, which for Moses simply meant finding a method to quench his people's thirst. Moses could have "struck a rock" by actually striking a rock, but he could also have accessed a more practical source of water, such as a hidden spring, rainwater, desert plants or an unexpected oasis in the desert.

4. Grandpa Moses

Myth! **Moses had a full set of strong teeth when he died at age 120.**

The Vulgate version proclaims that when Moses died at age 120, "his eye was not clouded, nor were his teeth loosened" *(Deut.* 34:7). This biblical bit has become fodder for trivia books, which claim Moses is the only Old Testament patriarch who died with a 20/20 vision and a full set of teeth. Proponents of the Latin Bible believe the Vulgate version is in error with respect to Moses' teeth, and that the phrase, which correctly translates as "his eye was not dim, nor his natural force abated," actually refers to the sexual potency that Moses maintained to the very end. Most other experts suspect that the use of the word "teeth" by the Vulgate writers was not a slip-up—only a cover-up to make their characterization of Moses fully consistent with the high moral tone of the *Book of Deuteronomy.*

5. Lambkill

Myth! **Thousands of one-year-old healthy lambs were slaughtered for the first Passover.**

Jewish tradition has always favored the lamb as the centerpiece in the celebration of Passover, following the Lord's prescription in *Exodus* 12:3. The unswerving belief shared by Jews and Christians alike is that lamb's blood, and nothing else, stained the Israelites' doorframes during the night the angel of the Lord came on his mission of death.

But most hard-lining critics tend to shun a literal interpretation of *Exodus* 12:3, which describes the celebration of the first Passover. The passage tells us God had specified that the animals to be offered should be year-old males without defects and chosen not later than the tenth of the current month. In practice, it would be difficult enough to assemble ordinary lambs for a community as large as a million souls, but to bring to slaughter 250,000 perfectly healthy year-old male lambs (assuming four Israelites to a lamb) in such a short time would be nigh impossible. Experts say the Israelites could not have performed the ritual without God relaxing his requirements beforehand (say, by allowing a mix with less than perfect animals) or helping with a miracle.

6. Trinity is my Name

Myth! God told Moses to call him Jehovah or Lord.

In *Exodus* 3:7 God, speaking from within the burning bush, tells Moses that he has been designated to lead the Israelites out of Egypt. Moses asks God by what name he should call him when he breaks the news to the Israelites. God replies: "I am who I am. This is what you are to say to the Israelites: 'The Lord has sent me to you.'" He adds: "This is my name forever; this is my title for all generations."

It seems settled in both popular and Biblical lore that God chose to be called Lord, or *Jehovah* in Hebrew. Semantically speaking, however, *Jehovah* is not a name or even a title, but an artificial construct devised by ancient hagiographers from the Hebrew phrase "I am." It results from pronouncing the letters *Y, H, V, H* (called the tetragrammaton), although even this is only a presumed pronunciation in the absence of the actual one, which was lost. The Hebrew text is limited to using the anonym *Jehovah* when referring to God because the Hebrew faith strictly prohibits the mention of his real name under any circumstance. Experts believe ancient texts had a name for God, but this was erased from the Hebrew due to the proscription. In actual speech, the Jews avoid uttering the name *Jehovah* altogether, pronouncing it "Adonai" or "Elohim" when reading scripture ("Adonai" is the source of the vowel sounds *a, o,* and *a* that were inserted into the letters YHVH to produce the word YaHoVah and *Jehovah*).

7. Plague with Doubts

Myth! **The Plague on Livestock destroyed all of Egypt's farm and work animals.**

Using Moses as a medium, God brought ten plagues upon Egypt to pressure Pharaoh into releasing the Israelites from captivity. One of these, the Plague on Livestock, was designed to destroy that nation's entire farm and work animals save those that belonged to the Israelites. *Exodus* 9:6 would have us believe that the plague did the job with utmost thoroughness, but this may not be quite an accurate interpretation. Subsequent passages reveal that many of the animals—apparently remnants from the Plague on Livestock—were ravaged by the later Plague of Hail (*Ex* 9:19) and Plague of the Firstborn (*Ex* 12:29). Even after all ten plagues had passed, the Egyptians were still able to muster enough horses from their stables—at least 600—to pursue the fleeing Israelites into the desert (*Ex* 14:7).

8. Will the real Red Sea please Rise?

Myth! Moses parted the Red Sea to escape the pursuing Egyptians.

The Hebrew text speaks of a Yam Suph, or Sea of Reeds, which, in pursuing a modern equivalent, became simply the Red Sea in later translations. Despite this etymological transformation, however, it is almost certain the Sea of Reeds was not the Red Sea

186

as we know it today. Although no one really knows whether this body of water still exists or where it was originally located, there is some speculation that it may have been the Gulf of Suez in Africa. Moses was familiar with the area and could have led his people across the Gulf at ebb tide, then watched as the water rose to its customary six and a half feet to drown the pursuing Egyptians. The crossing could have been aided by the action of a wind, the presence of which is confirmed in the Biblical account. Scientists have shown that a strong, steady wind blowing for ten to twelve hours could push water from the shoreline and expose an underwater ridge.

Another theory is that the Israelites traversed Lake Subonis, across an isthmus separating it from the Mediterranean. The area is swampy and treacherous and the isthmus itself becomes frequently submerged.

Finally, to those who believe the parting was only hypnotically suggested by Moses, a likely place would be some small branch of the Red Sea where the water was shallow enough to wade across. Certain shallow lakes and marshes north of the Gulf of Suez, which dry up at certain times of the year, and Lake Manzala farther north on the Mediterranean coast, have also been mentioned.

---

9. Repeat Performances

Myth! Moses was the only Biblical patriarch to part a body of water and cross it.

The spectacle of Moses parting the Red Sea would have been more awesome had it been unique, but it wasn't. God performed the same miracle in the river Jordan for three other prophets on separate occasions.

In the first incident, God had just given Joshua permission to lead the Israelites towards the conquest of the Promised Land. The Lord told Joshua that he would support him as he did Moses, and would demonstrate this as soon as he and the Israelites reached the Jordan. When they arrived at the river, the priests carrying the Ark of the Covenant dipped their feet in the water, whereupon the river stopped flowing and stood up in a heap, allowing the

187

Israelites to cross on dry ground (*Joshua* 3).

In the second incident, Elijah, in the company of Elisha, decided to cross the Jordan. According to 2 *Kings* 2:8, "Then Elijah took his mantle, and rolled it up, and struck the water, and the water was parted to the one side and to the other, till the two of them could go over the dry ground." After they had crossed, Elijah was taken up to heaven in a chariot of fire.

The distressed Elisha, left standing on the bank of the Jordan, "took up the mantle of Elijah that had fallen from him, and struck the water, saying, 'Where is the Lord, the God of Elijah?' And when he had struck the water, the water was parted to the one side and to the other; and Elisha went over" (2 *Kings* 2:13,14). This was the third incident.

The scientifically minded offer a natural reason for these occurrences. Quite likely, they say, the feats at the Jordan were facilitated by quakes in the Dead Sea Fault Zone, when the river's banks collapsed and briefly dammed it. Otherwise, some of the prosaic explanations given for Moses' parting of the Red Sea could be cited as well. Though these 'down-to-earth' theories augment rather than defy the Holy Book's description of the event, they nevertheless fail to impress those who would rather leave the matter entirely to faith.

10. Lost Horizons

Myth! **Moses received the Ten Commandments on a mountain in the Sinai Peninsula.**

Sinai is a well-known peninsula between the Mediterranean and the Red Sea, constituting the easternmost part of Egypt northwest of Arabia. It is generally assumed that Mount Sinai, where Moses received the Ten Commandments, is one of the mountains in this area. Pilgrims in search of the holy place are often directed to Jebel Musa, or Mount Moses, foremost of the three granite peaks of the Sinai massif. However, lacking any historical or archeological link with the Biblical landmark, Mount Moses has not been more than a symbolic shrine for the faithful. The Bible itself is not too sure about Mount Sinai, sometimes calling it Horeb, but even this odd name fails to yield any

188

significant clue to its identity. "One modern Torah commentary," says *Time* (issue of December 14, 1998), "provides a map listing eight possible locations for Mount Sinai, two of which are not even in the Sinai Peninsula."

V

A Life To Live

On the Birth of Jesus Christ

"I am not only the Queen of Heaven,
but also the Mother of Mercy."

•

Mary Mother of Jesus

1. Millennium Man

Myth! **Jesus was born in AD 1.**

If B.C. stands for "Before Christ," A.D. is the abbreviation for anno domini, or "year of our Lord." Those misled into thinking that AD means "After (the) Death (of Christ)" are quick to retract when they see that the lack of a gap between the BC and AD time frames omits almost the entire period of Jesus' earthly existence from the calendar.

The convention was established in the sixth century by the Greek monk Dionysius Exiguus, with the intention of using Year One as the pivotal point of the new calendar. Under the prior Roman system of dating, Year One was the year of Rome's founding, but Dionysius advocated a revision to conform to the Church's desire that it be the birth year of Jesus. By some anomaly, however, Dionysius' reform placed the death of Herod the Great, who Matthew says engineered the Massacre of the Innocents, at 4 BC, and this moved Jesus' birth date to somewhere between 4 BC and 20 BC. To confuse matters further, Luke describes the Nativity period as coinciding with a tax census that historians believe could only have happened in AD 6 under Dionysius' calendar.

Historically speaking, the year of Jesus' birth has remained as muddled as it was before Dionysius' time. Only a few go with Dionysius' Year One (Luke's version), and fewer still see it as AD 6 (Luke's other version). As peculiar as it may sound, 8 BC is favored by most Catholics, while other Christians consider 6 to 4 BC (Matthew's version) as the most likely.

2. Imitation of Christ

Myth! **Jesus is the only person to be announced by a star, gifted by wise men, and saved from a slaughter of innocents.**

To most people, especially Christians, the only person born under the most divine circumstances is Jesus. But there is a strange parallel in Krishna, the Hindu god born of the Goddess Devaki as an incarnation of Shiva. It is said that Krishna was announced by a star and by angelic voices; presented with gifts by shepherds and wise men; hailed as Redeemer and Sin Bearer; and fated to survive a Slaughter of the Innocents. Oddly, Krishna also met a sacrificial death, by hanging "between heaven and earth" and enriching the soil with his blood.

As awesome as these similarities are, they end there. Krishna's god-man, who was more closely related to the Greek deities of Olympus, was very erotic, with many of his adventures presenting "a classic of religious pornography." Literary interpreters like Nikos Kazantzakis dared to breathe some human failings into Jesus, but nothing comes close to the kind that characterized Krishna.

3. Home away from Home

Myth! **Joseph and Mary were in Bethlehem to participate in a Roman census when Jesus was born.**

Matthew and Luke put Jesus' birthplace in Bethlehem, but Mark and John imply that this was Nazareth, the Holy Family's' permanent hometown.

Interestingly, Matthew and Luke have different reasons for designating Bethlehem as Jesus' birthplace. Matthew says Joseph and Mary were residents of Bethlehem at the time of Jesus' delivery, and only fled afterwards with the infant to Nazareth because of the Massacre of the Innocents. Luke, on the other hand, says Jesus was born in Bethlehem when his parents went there from Nazareth, where they had been living, to participate in a Roman census. Luke's account digresses from the known fact that, while a census did occur in the area under Quirinius, this was in AD 6, some ten years after Matthew's Massacre of the Innocents. Moreover, the census was local to Roman Judaea and not, as Luke puts it, pursuant to a decree from Caesar Augustus "to all the world." The couple could not have registered at Bethlehem because Joseph as a Galilean was not under direct Roman rule and was exempt from Judaea's registration, and Mary had no legal need to leave home to accompany him.

192

Some Christian writers do not rule out the possibility that Luke may have become confused with the details and was actually referring to another census held ten years earlier under circumstances similar to those of AD 6. Nevertheless, Biblical analysts are inclined to believe Matthew and Luke's interpretations were merely to comply with the old prophecies about the coming of the Messiah. Since it had been foretold that the new Messiah would be a progeny of King David of Bethlehem, it was only natural that he should have some connection with that great monarch's hometown.

4. Astronomical Proportions

Myth! The Nativity is the earliest historical event that can be dated through a celestial phenomenon.

Scientists like Johannes Kepler and those of the Royal Astronomical Society strongly believed the Star of Bethlehem was an actual astronomical event occurring between 7 BC and AD 5. Halley's comet would have been a manifestation of this intensity, except that the recurring phenomenon was scientifically sighted in 12 BC, or 4 to 8 years earlier than the popularly accepted year of Jesus' birth.

Closer to the presumed date of the Nativity was the celestial sight reported by the Hayden Planetarium in New York. Three heavenly bodies in proximity to each other generated a single spectacularly bright light in the sky one night in 6 BC. However, this finding runs counter to Matthew's observation that the miraculous light was a single moving object.

Astronomical occurrences like Halley's comet and the Hayden appearance have often been cited to support the widely held view that the Nativity is the earliest biblical or historical episode that can be dated through a celestial phenomenon. What is not realized is that astronomy has already successfully dated a historical event nearly six centuries older than Christ. This is the war between Lydia on the west coast of Asia Minor and Media in the Iranian highland, which ancient writings say terminated in total darkness in the middle of the day in 585 BC. Scientists have correctly

193

deduced that the darkness was the result of a solar eclipse occurring on May 28 that year.

5. Goodwill Time

Myth! **The first Christmas was announced by angels singing, "Glory to God in the highest, peace on earth, goodwill toward all."**

The shepherds were out in the fields tending their flocks at night when an angel appeared to tell them about the birth of Jesus. "Suddenly a great company of the heavenly host appeared with the angel, praising God and saying, 'Glory to God in the highest, peace on earth, goodwill toward men.'" This is the standard text of Luke 2:13-14, which appears in most versions of the New Testament. The words sung by the angelic chorus have become familiar to us as the Christmas greeting that we see on cards, posters, decorations, wrappings and other items used in the Christian world to herald the season.

But traditionalists will be disappointed to learn that this popular rendition of Luke 2:14 is not what it was in the original Greek. The latter said "on earth peace to men with whom the Lord is satisfied," which Saint Jerome simplified, without changing its meaning, as "peace on earth to men of good will." "Good will" as thus used limited the persons entitled to the blessing to "those that pleased the Lord." The subsequent rephrasing in Luke and the substitution of "goodwill" for "good will" broadened the scope of the greeting, which now includes all men (and women), and increased the number of blessings from one to two.

6. Presents for the Future

Myth! **Jesus was visited in the manger by the Magi, and consecrated in Jerusalem after the Massacre of the Innocents.**

194

Most hierographic scholars veer away from the traditional view that Jesus was only a few days old when the Magi paid him a visit and gifted him with gold, frankincense and myrrh. The preferred belief is that he was already more than a year old, probably almost two, when the encounter happened, by which time Joseph and Mary had already established their home in Bethlehem. It is evident this was how long it took the Magi to find Jesus from the moment they spotted the star in the east, which was not at all remarkable given the great distances that had to be traveled on foot in those days.

The scenario drawn from Matthew's account of Jesus' birth has two rather interesting implications. First, one to two years actually passed before the First Family left Bethlehem for Egypt to escape Herod's Massacre of the Innocents. This means their visit to Jerusalem in observance of two rituals required by the faith—the consecration of Jesus to the Lord one month after his birth and Mary's "purification" forty days after giving birth (Luke 2:22-38)—was made long before the date of the Massacre and without any knowledge of Herod's murderous intentions. Second, contrary to the custom prevailing in the Christian world, the Magi were not part of the original Christmas tableau, having seen Jesus only at a much later date. Matthew mentions no one attending Jesus during his first few days on earth other than the Holy Family and the shepherds "living out in the fields nearby."

7. From May to December

Myth! Jesus was born in the month of December.

December is traditionally regarded as the month of Jesus' birth, but historically it could have been any month, with December as the unlikeliest, according to the experts. December in Judea was usually cold and rainy and would have prevented shepherds from keeping watch over their flocks in the unsheltered fields, which was what the Bible says they were doing when they first learned about Jesus' birth. May's balmy weather would have been more conducive to the fateful events that transpired during the first Christmas.

195

Clement of Alexandria (c. 200) reports that some chronologists in his day dated the birth April 19 and others May 20, although he himself settled for November 17. Members of the Eastern Orthodoxy and the Ukrainian Catholic Church still follow the old Julian calendar established by Caesar in 45 BC, which marks January 6 as Christ's birthday. December was chosen to reconcile Christ's feast day with the pagan rituals popular at that time of the year, although various dates in the month proved initially unsuccessful because of competition from the mass-based Yule of Northern Europe and the Roman Dies Natalis Invicti Solis (or Birthday of the Unconquered Sun). The 25th of the month was adopted by Bishop Liberius of Rome as the official day of Christmas beginning in 354, to counter the growing threat from Mithraism, which also set December 25 as the big day for worshipping the sun god. The idea caught on, and people started shifting to Christmas and away from the heretical celebration.

---

8. Teen Bride

Myth! **Mary was a mature married woman when she became pregnant with Jesus.**

When Matthew writes that Joseph thought of divorcing Mary upon knowing that she was pregnant (Matt 1:18), the normal inference from the statement is that the two were already married although Joseph had kept Mary a virgin.

However, a reading of the entire text (Matthew 1:18-25) makes it clear that Joseph and Mary were only engaged or 'pledged' at the time of her pregnancy following a public announcement of their intended union. Under Jewish civil law, this pre-marital bond could only be broken by death or divorce.

Luke mentions that Joseph still had not married Mary when the two registered for the census in Bethlehem (2:6) and Jesus was nearly due to be born. Matthew's own version is that they were married immediately after an angel had explained Mary's condition to Joseph (1:24).

Incidentally, while most classical artists painted the parents of the infant Jesus as relatively mature persons, Biblical researchers say Mary was barely out of her adolescence—she was

196

approximately only fifteen or sixteen years old—when she gave birth to the Savior. The artistic lapse may well be due to the paucity of Biblical information regarding Mary despite her tremendous popularity in Catholic nations. Unbelievable as it may seem, Mary as the virgin mother of Jesus also enjoys a singularly distinguished and honored position among women in the Koran and is mentioned more often in that holy book than in the entire New Testament.

9. Three Men and a Baby

Myth! **Three kings from the east paid homage to Jesus on his natal day.**

Except for Matthew's statement that "Magi from the east came to Jerusalem" (Matt 2:1), nothing is said in the Gospel about these mysterious entities, much less that they were kings or that there were three of them. "Magi" traditionally meant wise men, so the obvious reference is to learned men from various places who congregated in the east when they saw the star in that vicinity. That they were Parthian envoys visiting Jerusalem for a celebration of King Herod's new temple is probably not correct either, in light of the fact that this building had been finished since 12 BC. What seems more believable is that they were traveling astrologer-members of a priestly caste from Persia whose curiosity was aroused by the bright moving star.

The idea that there were three of these visitors arose only in the second century, at the time of the theologian Origen, who made the estimate. Origen was no doubt influenced by the mention of the three types of gifts presented to Jesus, namely, "gold, and frankincense, and myrrh." Since then, whenever the Bible story is cast into sculpture and other art forms, it has become natural to portray one wise man for each kind of gift. However, most writers tend to believe there were more than three magi with as many gifts, and in fact, St. Augustine assumed there were twelve.

In the sixth century, the three were made kings and named Gaspar, Melchior and Balthazar by the Venerable Bede before their elevation as the patron saints of the city of Cologne. There is some speculation that Bede based his kings not on the Gospel but

197

on the Old Testament song of praise to King Solomon prophesying that the Messiah would receive tribute from the kings of Tarshish, Sheba and Seba (cf. Isaiah 60:3).

10. Religious Misconception

Myth! **The Immaculate Conception is the conception of Jesus by the Virgin Mary through divine intercession.**

The Virgin Birth, referring to Mary's conception of Jesus through divine intervention—that is to say, Mary was a virgin and without sin when she conceived Jesus—is a famous hagiologic doctrine that is often confused with the Immaculate Conception. While both beliefs are integral to Catholicism and widespread in the Christian world, one has nothing to do with the other.

The Immaculate Conception does not involve Mary's conception of Jesus but her own conception by her mother St. Anne. The dogma asserts that Mary, though conceived in the normal way from the union of her mother St. Anne and her father St. Joachim, was from that moment free from original sin. Mary is thus enshrined in the Catholic faith as the only human being who has not been tainted at conception by the stigma of Adam's indiscretion in the Garden of Eden.

It is sometimes mistakenly assumed that St. Anne was herself a virgin when she conceived Mary, and that Mary derived her blessedness from this fact. Actually, as the archangel Gabriel hinted at the Annunciation, Mary's grace flowed from the future "fruit of her womb," Jesus, rather than from St. Anne, whose singular claim to sainthood is her being Mary's mother.

11. A Star is Born

Myth! **While searching for Jesus, the Magi were guided by the Star to Jerusalem.**

It is popularly believed that the Star guided the wise men to Jerusalem, but even Matthew, the only Biblical source for the story of the Magi, does not say this. Matthew recounts that the Magi first saw the Star appear in the east, and they then journeyed to Jerusalem in the west to inquire about the child Jesus. There they asked, "Where is the one who has been born king of the Jews? We saw his star in the east and have come to worship him." King Herod, his jealousy aroused, asked his chief priests and scribes what they knew of Jesus, and was told he would be born in Bethlehem because the prophet Micah had so written. Herod passed on the information to the Magi, with the request that they go and look for the child. It was only when they were about to leave Jerusalem that the Star reappeared and guided them to the resting place of the infant Jesus in Bethlehem. In the words of the New Testament, "After they had heard the king, they went on their way, and the star they had seen in the east went ahead of them until it stopped over the place where the child was. When they saw the star, they were overjoyed."

12. T'was a Bumpy Night

Myth! While the Magi rode camels in their journey to Bethlehem, the First Family fled to Egypt using only a donkey.

One of the scenes most often used in Christmas posters and cards shows the Magi sitting on camels or leading these animals as they journey under the light of the Star. Contrary to popular belief, there is nothing in the Scriptures indicating that the wise men rode on camels, or on any animal for that matter. Biblicists now consider it more likely that they walked, based on geographical and historical data for the period. These records suggest that camels were not a common sight in those days, and the Magi, like most other travelers in the area, did not use them particularly as a means of transport.

Conversely, it is probably not correct to assume that the flight to Egypt by Joseph, Mary and the infant Jesus was made on foot or, as is often depicted in art, with only the use of a donkey or ass. Medical authorities insist a trip from Bethlehem to Egypt in those days with nothing more than a small animal would have been

199

devastating for mother and child, and one without any animal at all would have been unthinkable. There must have been some means of transport even if barely adequate for the purpose, although what this is we do not know. The distance would undoubtedly have covered some of the most formidable terrain of Palestine and Israel, including the Judean Hills and parts of the Negev Desert. This is not to mention the harsh landscape that would be found within Egypt itself.

13. Stable Condition

Myth! Jesus was born in a stable.

A manger (from the Greek verb "to eat") is believed to be the court of an inn or a caravansary, which was a special place provided for the animals, such as camels and donkeys, of hotel guests. The animals were fed and rested there while their owners spent the night in the adjoining lodgings. This is different from the notion of an ordinary stable, which is used for the lodging and feeding of animals, mainly horses and cattle, and is entirely independent of human quarters.

The distinction doesn't seem to matter, however, because there is nothing in the Bible that says Jesus was born in either a stable or a manger. Luke mentions the word "manger" not to designate where Christ was born, but where he was laid after his birth. "She wrapped him in cloths and placed him in a manger, because there was no room for them in the inn" (Luke 2:7). The original Greek that translates in most Biblical versions as "manger" is *thaten*, which, when used in conjunction with a baby, means "crib." Some believe Jesus was born in a grotto or cave and was brought later to a manger. This is in consonance with early Christian tradition following the first Greek translation of Luke, which located Jesus' birthplace in a *katalemma*, or temporary shelter or cave.

VI
Superstar Bearing

On Jesus' Life

"For everyone who exalts himself will be humbled,
and he who humbles himself will be exalted."

•

Jesus Christ

1. A Face in the Crowd

Myth! Jesus was most likely a tall, white man with a handsome face, light brown hair and well-trimmed beard.

Anyone inclined to give the description of Jesus some importance must first consider that no portrayal of his exists in any authorized writing, the Gospel included. Artists tend to depict him as a member of their own particular culture, as in the case of Orientals and Africans, who have often pictured Jesus with dark or even black skin. To the Western world, Jesus' appearance as reflected in religious art (most dating back to medieval times) and traditional non-Scriptural literature has been based largely on the widely held assumption that he was a tall, white man, well-formed, pale, with blue eyes set on an angular, handsome face, his light brown hair and beard trimmed after the fashion of the Nazarite sect. This image has become even more vivid since religious illustrator Warner E. Sallman saw Jesus' Caucasian face in his mind one night in 1924 while tossing in his bed. From 1940 on, more than 500 million copies of Sallman's 'Head of Christ' have been sold, making it the most familiar portrait of Christ around the world.

Another notable reference was the Shroud of Turin, which purported to show that Jesus was 5 feet 10 1/2 inches tall. Chemical tests came up unsupportive of this relic, but hardly diminished the traditional and popular belief that the Son of Man cut an imposing figure. However, the presumption that Jesus was physically comely and charismatic (for he could not have otherwise attracted so many women as well as men) may have been changed by recent findings that reportedly enjoy some Vatican backing. In their book *The Eleven Commandments* published in Italy in 2002, two Catholic journalists—Elisabetta Broli and Roberto Beretta—endeavored to show from their research that Jesus was short and by modern standards not pleasing to look at. That he was brown-haired, blue-eyed and fair would also seem incongruous, since most Galilean men of Jesus' day were dark-complexioned, with deep black eyes and hair to match. Bolstering the view of Jesus as a peasant more than as an aristocratic holy man is an image of him generated by computers using a 2000 year-old human skull uncovered from a grave in Jerusalem.

What amounts to a Biblical description of Jesus is the overall intimation in the Gospels that he was an amiable man, but one who never laughed or smiled and who wept more often than he displayed any other emotion. As to his physical features, the prophetic words of *Isaiah* 53:2-3 (New International Version) contain a veiled reference to the Redeemer as a homely person who "had no beauty or majesty to attract us to him, nothing in his appearance that we should desire him...Like one from whom men hide their faces he was despised, and we esteemed him not."

---

2. Heavenly Creatures

Myth! **Because Joseph was only his foster father, Jesus could not have descended from King David.**

Matthew (1:1-17) and *Luke* (3:23-38) disclose Jesus' human genealogy and name King David as one of his ancestors. Experts say the intention is to prove the fulfillment of Old Testament prophecies that the true Messiah would be a descendant of David (2 *Sam* 7:12-16; *Isa* 11:1-5).

In *Matthew*, Jesus' lineage involving 46 people over a span of 2,000 years is traced all the way from Abraham in a descending order, to show that Jesus is related to all Jews. In *Luke*, the lineage goes beyond Abraham and up to Adam in an ascending order, to prove that Jesus is related to all human beings.

Significantly, very few of the names between Joseph and David are identical in the two lists. This has led scholars to conclude that there are two different genealogies, one springing from Jesus' foster father Joseph and the other from Jesus' natural mother Mary. Joseph's father is named Jacob in *Matthew* and Heli in *Luke*, an indication that the Gospellers had two different persons in mind, Heli being actually Joseph's father-in-law. This view logically separates the maternal from the foster-paternal branch of Jesus' family, and eliminates the anomaly that Jesus' bloodline started with someone who was not his true father. With the suggestion that Mary herself descended from David, Jesus'

203

kinship to the great king becomes not just legal or allegorical but real.

3. The Greatest bar None

Myth! **Christ was Jesus' second name during his lifetime.**

As was the custom in those days, everyone, including Jesus, had only one name. The New Testament seems to leave no doubt that the name of Jesus was just that—Jesus.

In Biblical times, family names, nicknames and aliases were virtually unknown and had not come into vogue until much later. Before surnames began to appear regularly in the tenth century after the Norman Conquest of England, second names usually just indicated the geographic origin of the person, as in Jesus of Nazareth. However, titles were plentiful, in some cases becoming altogether part of a person's complete name. 'Christ', for instance, was an early Hebrew title meaning 'the Anointed One'. 'Christ' is not mentioned in the New Testament because the term emerged only in early Christianity, well after the lifetime of Jesus.

Surprisingly, while scholars generally agree that Jesus had only one name, they are not certain what that name was. Many maintain it was originally not Jesus, which was a Greek name, but something much more complex, like Joshua bar-Joseph, meaning Joshua, Son of Joseph. Joshua ('Jehovah saves') was the Hebrew equivalent of Jesus, and the prefix 'bar-' was Aramaic for 'son of'. Galileans during the time of Christ spoke Aramaic and gave Hebrew names to their children. However, by the time the Gospels were written c. 60 AD, Greek had come into general use for literary purposes, and Joshua became Jesus.

4. Sect Appeal

Myth! **Jesus was called the Nazarene because he hailed from Nazareth.**

The four Gospels agree that Christ hailed from Nazareth, the town that the apostle Nathaniel derided for not speaking well of the man (*John* 1:46). Luke and Matthew refer expressly to Nazareth as Jesus' childhood home, and Mark and John imply the same thing by calling him Jesus of Nazareth.

Matthew believes Jesus was only brought to Nazareth from Egypt as an infant in fulfillment of the Old Testament prophecy that he "will be called a Nazarene" (*Matthew* 2:23). In refutation, scholars point out that there was no real prophecy about a Nazarene. Matthew could have been misled by *Isaiah* 11:1, where the term 'Nazarene' is used because of its similarity to the Hebrew word for 'branch'.

Others speculate that Nazarene meant Jesus was consecrated as a Nazarite, a member of a sect of longhaired ascetics who dedicated their lives to the service of God. This group dwelt beyond the Jordan in Peraea, rejected Temple worship, and denied the binding character of the Law. There is, of course, no direct evidence that Jesus was a Nazarite other than the fact that he acted and dressed like one. However, the sect could have influenced him after he had contact with them and learned about their ways on the annual journeys that all good Palestinian Jews made to Jerusalem for the Passover festival.

---

5. Sinking a Titanic Claim

Myth! The tomb of Jesus and his family was discovered in Jerusalem in 1980.

Titanic director James Cameron produced a widely aired documentary proposing to show that a tomb found in Jerusalem in 1980 is that of Jesus and his family, which included his mother Mary, his purported wife Mary Magdalene, and an alleged son named Judah. The conclusion of experts who have seen the presentation is that, like an "unwanted sequel to The Da Vinci Code," it uses highly speculative and questionably sourced evidence to discredit the long established religious tradition that Jesus resurrected bodily and left nothing of his material existence. Some critics have branded Cameron as an opportunistic entertainment mogul and his project "a travesty to professional archaeologists and scholars of early Judaism and Christianity, and...a disservice to the public." Israeli archaeologist Amos Kloner, who was the first to document the site in question more than 10 years ago, insists the tomb believed to contain Jesus' bones is really a regular burial chamber of a well-off family of the period and the Biblical names on it were only coincidental. He asks: "Who says that 'Mara' is Magdalena and 'Judah' is the son of Jesus? It cannot be proved. These are very popular and common names from the 1st century BC."

---

6. In God's Name

Myth! The letters IHS are the initials of the sacred Roman Catholic motto 'Iesus hominum salvator'.

IHS is a group of letters that appears regularly in Roman Catholic logos and symbols, particularly on vestments and other paraphernalia devoted to the conduct of the Holy Mass. Most often taken as an acronym of Jesus' name and title, it is also seen at various times as the initials for the Jesuit slogan *Iesus haabemus socium* ('We have Jesus as an ally'); for Constantine's rallying cry *In hoc signo vinces* ('By this sign, conquer'); for the crusaders' *In hac salus* ('Safety in this [the cross]'); and for the popular epithet *Iesus hominum salvator* ('Jesus Savior of Men'). In fact, while it may come as a surprise, it is none of the above. The H in the trio is not the seventh letter of the Latin alphabet, as is commonly thought, but a capital letter in the Greek alphabet similar to E. IHS is the Greek equivalent of the Latin IES, which is simply the abbreviation of *Iesus* in capital letters.

VII

The Third Day Prior

On Jesus' Death and Resurrection

"I am innocent of the blood of this just person;
see ye to it."

•

Pontius Pilate

1. Dark Passage

Myth! **Jesus resurrected in Galilee after three days in the tomb.**

That Jesus died on 'the third day prior' is a way of saying that he resurrected on the third day after his death. A line in the Roman Catholic credo used to read, "After three days Jesus rose again." When it was realized that the phrase 'After three days' was a chronological inaccuracy, it was changed to 'On the third day.'

None of the Gospels ever really measures in writing the time that separated Jesus' resurrection from his death. All four state that Jesus died "at the ninth hour" of Preparation Day and resurrected "very early in the morning" of "the first day of the week." It is believed that Preparation Day was the day before the Sabbath (Saturday), which means Jesus died on the afternoon of a Friday. He rose from the dead on the early morning of the following Sunday, which was the first day of the week. Hence, although Jesus remained entombed for three calendar days, the only full day he spent in that condition was the Sabbath, which was appropriately a Jewish rest day. Surprisingly, while all written references to the Resurrection in Church lore have been duly corrected, many still insist—perhaps by force of habit—that what Jesus had predicted was his rising again 'after three days'.

One question on which the Gospellers are not clearly together is whether the Resurrection happened in Galilee or in Jerusalem. In *Mark* 16:7, which is supported by *Matthew* 28:7, "a young man dressed in a white robe" appeared at the tomb of Jesus and told the two Marys and Salome, "But go, tell his disciples and Peter, 'He is going ahead of you into Galilee. There you will see him, just as he told you'." Those who define the Resurrection as the time Jesus first publicly appeared after his death take the statement of the young man (believed to be an angel) to mean that this occurred in Galilee. The theological concept, however, is that Jesus resurrected at the precise moment his dead body took on life again. In this regard, *John* 20:14, is most specific: the Resurrection happened right in the tomb—said to be a cave just outside Jerusalem—before the eyes of Mary Magdalene.

Luke 24 recounts yet another version, but agrees with John that the site of Jesus' appearance was Jerusalem and not Galilee.

According to Luke, two men at the tomb told the women that Jesus had risen. Later in the day, Jesus appeared before two believers traveling on a road near the city, and in the evening, he joined the eleven apostles in a house in Jerusalem to assure them that he had indeed risen. Though not repeated in any of the other three Gospels, this episode in Jesus' death and resurrection remains enshrined in Christian theology as the eponymic 'Road to Emmaus'.

2. Day of Wrath

Myth! Jesus died on Friday the thirteenth.

Despite its association with many unfortunate or catastrophic Biblical events, the source of the superstition that Friday the thirteenth is the unluckiest day of the month is not the Bible but Norse mythology. It is said that for some transgression committed against her peers, Frigga, the goddess of love and fertility, was banished in shame to a mountaintop and labeled a witch. In retaliation, the goddess convened a meeting every Friday of twelve witches, including her, and asked the devil to complete the gathering at thirteen. The group did nothing but plot disasters, misfortunes and trouble in general to be inflicted on humankind the coming week.

The belief that Jesus died on Friday the thirteenth actually runs counter to the Gospeller John's statement that the Crucifixion occurred on the Feast of the Passover. The Feast has always been set on the day of the full moon in March, and in AD 36, the probable year of Jesus' death, the full moon appeared on Friday the thirtieth.

Incidentally, calling this saddest and most solemn of all days in the Christian year Good Friday may seem unapt, but it isn't. The word 'good' is used in its archaic sense as a euphemism for God and a synonym for 'holy'. It is never to signify that there is anything good—in the sense of happy or pleasurable—about the tragic death of Jesus.

209

3. Last Meal and Testament

Myth! Jesus and his disciples held the Last Supper on the day of the Passover Feast.

All three synoptic Gospels say that Jesus was crucified the day after he and his disciples had arrived in Jerusalem for the traditional Passover meal (*Matt* 26:17-18; *Mark* 14:12-16; *Luke* 22:17-13). But the fourth Gospeller, John, tells us that the Crucifixion took place on the day of the Passover Feast itself, and the meal that ended up as the Last Supper was held on a non-holiday the night before (13:1).

From a comparison of the Gospels, historians deduce that John's version is the accurate one. All four evangelists accept that the Sanhedrin met the night before the Crucifixion, interrogated Jesus and adjudged him worthy of death. But according to a rabbinical treatise on the Sanhedrin, written c. 200, this body was never allowed to hold its meetings on the Passover, on the Sabbath or on any other feast day.

John is careful to note that what was held at Passover time was not the meeting of the Sanhedrin, which had finished its business the night before, but the subsequent trial before Pilate, where a prisoner was released in lieu of Jesus following a Roman custom observed only at such festival. In John's version, moreover, the Jewish contingent waited outside Pilate's residence while Pilate questioned Jesus inside. This account happens to be consistent with the practice at Passover of Jews refusing to enter the premises of a Gentile for fear of becoming unclean for the celebration.

4. Cross of Pain

Myth! Jesus most likely died of heart failure.

In some passages of the New Testament, Jesus was 'hanged from a gallows tree', causing his death. Jesus was actually crucified, the phrase 'gallows tree' being merely an old Biblical reference to the cross.

Though the Romans were probably not the first to use crucifixion as a method of execution, they were the most assiduous in applying what Cicero described as the 'most cruel and hideous of tortures' to capital offenders who were non-citizens. Death was slow and painful. Unless the victim was mercifully killed, he would linger for two or three days on the cross, totally immobile in the searing sun and the bitterly cold night air. Sometimes, even his Roman guards, taking pity, would offer him a stupefying drink, like the vinegar wine given to Christ.

The general perception is that death on the cross is caused by heart failure due to exposure, shock or dehydration, singly or in combination. Not really, medical experts opine. The more likely reason is suffocation brought on when the weight of the body pulls down on the arms while the victim is prevented from moving. As the legs weaken, increasing pressure is exerted on the diaphragm and breathing becomes extremely difficult and painful. Finally, the lung collapses and the victim dies of asphyxia.

The role of suffocation in deaths by crucifixion has long been established from records of Nazi and Japanese war camps that engaged in the practice during World War II. Lately, this was confirmed by the discovery of the skeleton of a crucifixion victim dating back to the first century. As in the case of the two robbers with Jesus, the legs were broken, obviously to hasten asphyxiation by increasing the pressure on the upper body—a technique not applied to Jesus because he had expired earlier, presumably from the same cause.

---

5. Mortal Span

Myth! Jesus was about 33 years old when he died.

The traditional view is that Jesus was 33 years old at the time of the Crucifixion, pursuant to the estimate in *Luke* 3: 2 that "Jesus himself began to be about thirty years of age" when he started his ministry. The Gospels count three Passovers during Jesus' ministry, on the third of which Jesus was executed.

211

However, the historical view holds that if Jesus was born under Herod between 7 and 4 BC, he must have been between 40 and 43 years old when he died. John the Baptist began to preach in "the fifteenth year of Tiberius' reign" (*Luke* 3:1), set at AD 29, and, according to the ancient historian Josephus, was imprisoned by Antipas, ruler of Galilee, soon after Antipas' half-brother Philip died in AD 33. The Gospel reveals that Jesus' own three-year ministry began at this time, indicating that he died in AD 36, the last year of Pilate's reign.

John 8:57 mirrors the thinking of many of the Christian elders in Asia in the mid-second century that Christ was even older than 40 or 43 on his death. A year before he was crucified, says John, Jews in Jerusalem reproved Jesus for claiming that he had seen the patriarch Abraham. Their remark, "Thou art not yet fifty years old, and hast thou seen Abraham?," is believed to imply that Jesus was nearing fifty on the penultimate year of his life. The point is shared by those historians who surmise that Jesus' ministry may have lasted up to fifteen years.

6. Damnation in two Doses

Myth! **Judas fell from where he hanged himself and his body burst open.**

There are two accounts in the Bible about Judas' fate after his betrayal of Jesus for thirty pieces of silver. In *Matthew* 27:5, Judas, overtaken by remorse, throws the silver into the temple and hangs himself. The chief priests who gave him the money retrieves it to buy a potter's field. In *Acts* 1:18, it is Judas who buys the field with the thirty pieces of silver. Later, he falls headlong and his body bursts open.

To reconcile the two accounts, traditionalists make it appear that Judas hanged himself, after which his dead body fell from its suspended position and burst open. However, this raises more questions than answers. If Judas had hanged himself in a normal way, wouldn't he have fallen feet first? And even assuming he had hanged himself upside down for some weird reason, wouldn't he have fallen headfirst and split open his noggin instead of his guts? There is also no conceivable 'hanging' place he could fall from to

212

create enough impact that would split him open. Finally, who bought the potter's field, which eventually became a burial plot for foreigners, is not fully resolved. Critics suggest that, while *Matthew* describes how Judas physically died, *Acts* shows how Judas spiritually died by falling from the grace of God. Judas' falling is actually a metaphor for sinning against God, and his body bursting open means losing all his mercy and kindness as a result of his traitorous conduct. In ancient times, the guts and not the heart was where the emotions resided.

There is a certain belief—the third version of Judas' fate—that the betrayer survived the incident at the potter's field, but was cursed to live the life of a vagabond for all eternity. This theory confuses the story of the Rebellious Apostle with the legend of the Wandering Jew, who stood by during Jesus' painful struggle along the way to Calvary and, without allowing Christ a moment's rest, taunted him to move on more quickly. For this pitiless act, he was condemned to wander the earth until Christ's second coming.

7. To Bear or not to Bear

Myth! Christ carried the whole cross all the way to Golgotha.

Emblazoned on beautifully stained glass in many churches is the Christian version of the great tragedy that occurred 2,000 years ago. Called the Way of the Cross, it is the path Christ trod to the place of his execution carrying a heavy cross on his shoulders. There, on high ground, he was crucified on the same cross and raised well above a crowd of mourners, mockers and onlookers. The Way of the Cross ended at Golgotha, or Calvary, a favorite Roman spot for executions. Except that it was sometimes called Skull Mountain possibly because of its skull-like contour or because of the skulls of those who died there, there is no indication in the Bible that this was a mountain or even a hill.

There is some ambiguity in what tradition has taught us about Jesus carrying the whole cross on the way to Golgotha. Although it was customary in Roman times for a condemned man to carry the cross on which he was to be crucified, this was generally limited to the horizontal bar called the crosspiece. The cross was

213

formed only when the crosspiece was attached to the vertical post already standing at the execution site. With the exception of John, who paints a picture of Jesus with the whole cross on his back, the Gospellers hint that Jesus may not even have carried the smaller crosspiece because he was too tired to lug anything. Mark, Matthew and Luke all state that Jesus, who had just been heavily whipped, was coming out of the temple utterly exhausted when his guards spotted Simon of Cyrene and ordered him to carry the cross to Golgotha.

---

8. Roman Indiction

Myth! The Jews were responsible for Jesus' death.

Christians in general believe the Jews instigated the Crucifixion for theological reasons. No political angle was evident, since none of Jesus' followers was arrested with him and tried under Roman law. Jesus was taken before the religious Sanhedrin, and during a brief trial of sorts was asked whether he was 'the Messiah, the Son of God'. When Jesus answered, "I am he," the Sanhedrin found him guilty of blasphemy.

Many who are convinced the real prosecutors of Jesus were the Romans express skepticism about Pilate's hand-washing routine and its implication that Jesus was a Jewish problem. It is argued that only the Jews in the Sanhedrin and the manipulated mobs that attended the trial condemned Jesus. As *Luke* observes, the Jewish masses—'the great crowds of the people'—even beat their breasts and mourned for Jesus on the way to Golgotha. Under the Roman scheme of things, moreover, the Sanhendrin conviction could not have been enforced without Roman confirmation. Blasphemy was not a capital offense under Roman law, and even if it were, only the Romans were allowed to carry out the death penalty.

Christian belief notwithstanding, the consensus among both historians and Biblicists seems to be that Jesus was indeed convicted directly by the Romans not for the assertion that he was the son of God (a religious offense punishable only under Jewish law), but for the alleged claim that he was the king of the Jews (a political offense punishable by death under Roman law). This is most convincingly demonstrated by the fact that Crucifixion as the

214

ultimate punishment reserved by the Romans for political crimes would not have been imposed on Jesus had his acts and teachings been considered politically inoffensive to Rome.

9. The Tall T

Myth! **A tall ladder was used to bring down Jesus from the cross after he died.**

Most crucifixion scenes in classic art and the cinema show the cross towering high above the heads of soldiers and onlookers. In the 1960 film *Spartacus,* a Roman road is lined with crucified rebels looking down from their crosses at the soldiers passing by on horseback. And in Paolo Veronese's *The Crucifixion*, an oil canvas done in 1575, Jesus' cross is at such a height that a tall ladder, which can be seen propped up at the back, is the only means of getting up to him.

There is some evidence that Jesus' cross may not have been so tall. A passage from John's Gospel states that when Jesus was dying, "(a) jar of wine vinegar was there, so they soaked a sponge in it, put the sponge on a stalk of the hyssop plant, and lifted it to Jesus' lips" (*John* 19:29). A Standard English dictionary defines 'hyssop' as "a bushy, medicinal herb (*Hyssopus officinalis*) of the mint family, about 2 feet high, with small clusters of blue flowers." The length of the hyssop, when added to a Roman soldier's usual height of 5'7" or 5'8", plus about two feet of that soldier's partly extended arm holding the plant, gives the distance from the ground to Jesus' head as a couple of inches below 10 feet. At such a height, using a tall ladder to get to Jesus after he died would have been unnecessary, and it was more likely that the entire cross was brought down to get Christ's body off it.

215

10. The Easter after Eastre

Myth! Easter was instituted to commemorate Jesus' resurrection.

Most people are of the impression that Easter is a word coined by the Christian churches to celebrate Christ's resurrection. In fact, Easter originally had nothing to do with Christ, and even the rabbit and the eggs are irrelevant features of the Paschal feast. Easter was an ancient Teutonic festival that paid homage to a very unchristian fertility symbol, Eastre or Ostara, the goddess of spring and offspring, about the first of April each year. Old and young rejoiced on this day with dancing, feasting, and games, with children gathering colored eggs and newly born hares for offering to the goddess to signify birth and resurrection.

Early Church fathers, noting that the pagan festival was held at the time of year Resurrection was observed, began to merge one into the other in the hope of bringing pagans into the Christian fold. With little interference with the old customs, they quietly transformed the rituals into essentially Christian ceremonies, so that even the pagan rulers never became aware that the new rites were different from what they used to follow. Eventually Resurrection, which was subsumed under the protective rubric Eastre, prevailed.

VIII
Enter The Saints

On Popes and Saints

"Therefore, rid yourself of all malice and all deceit,
hypocrisy, envy, and slander of every kind."

•

St. Peter

1. Snake Charmer

Myth! **The St. Patrick's Day parade in New York City honors the Irish saint on his birthday.**

New York City's large Irish population supports the annual St. Patrick's Day parade down Fifth Avenue, while elsewhere in the world, Irish people celebrate this saint's anniversary in several other ways. But the popular belief that St. Patrick's countrymen fete him on this day because it is his birthday is fallacious on two counts. First, it is his death, not his birth, that is commemorated, in consonance with the practice of the church to set a saint's feast day on the day of his death, as this is likely the date of his martyrdom. Also, one's real birthday, according to early Christian belief, is when he passes on to the afterlife.

Second, St. Patrick was not Irish but British, probably Welsh, and could even have been born in Scotland or France. His real name is uncertain, some saying it was Maewyn or Succat, and didn't become Patrick until shortly before he became bishop of Ireland. There is some agreement that he was born late in the fourth or early in the fifth century AD, the son of an Anglo-Roman imperial official and the grandson of a Christian priest. Kidnapped as a young boy, he was brought to Ireland by Irish marauders, where he spent nearly six years as a slave. He escaped to England and became a priest and later a bishop, after which he returned to Ireland in 435 as a missionary. His thirty years of exemplary missionary work—by the time of his death in 460, he had established the Christian Church in Ireland—became the basis for his subsequent canonization and recognition as patron saint of that country.

Patrick is honored in legend for his feat of banishing snakes from the whole of Ireland. It is said that sometime in the fifth century he stood on a hill, and, with his staff, herded the slithering multitude into the sea and total destruction. There are indeed no snakes in Ireland, unlike neighboring Scotland, which harbors quite a few. But the explanation given is scientific and finds no place in the legend. According to the Smithsonian National Zoological Park, snakes being cold-blooded animals simply aren't able to survive in areas where the ground is frozen year round. Ireland thawed out for the last time only 15,000 years ago, and

218

since then, 12 miles of icy-cold water in the Northern Channel have separated Ireland from its nearest neighbor, Scotland, which has the environment for the crawly creatures.

2. Jack of Hearts

Myth! **Valentine's Day honors a martyred bishop who eventually became a saint.**

Valentine, a bishop of Terni (or Interamna) was martyred on February 14 c. AD 270 at the hands of Claudius II. He was executed for secretly joining young men and women in the sacrament of matrimony in defiance of the emperor's order prohibiting marriage.

While this is the usual reason given for Valentine's Day, it is not really certain it is the good bishop who is so honored by the Western world. Several other Valentines, most of them saints, figure prominently in Christian tradition, and these include a priest of Rome who was imprisoned and martyred also on February 14 for succoring persecuted Christians.

Whoever the real Valentine may be, he was not always the true object of veneration on Valentine's Day, as we have been led to believe. February 14 (or February 15 in the pre-Christian period) was already significant for lovers for almost 800 years before Valentine's reputed martyrdom. The Romans dedicated an annual rite to the god Lupercus, at which adolescent men would draw from a box the names of teenage women who would be their sexual companions for a time. With the advent of Christianity, the early fathers considered the festival immoral and decided to replace it with the one honoring St. Valentine.

What caps Valentine's dubious history is the erroneous belief that he is a saint and Valentine's Day still exists. What is now true is that the Church, worried about Valentine's fame as a symbol of erotic love, had his name delisted from the book of saints and the holiday expunged from the calendar.

219

3. An Arrow Escape

Myth! St. Sebastian became the patron saint of archers for having been martyred by arrows.

St. Sebastian is honored by enthusiasts of the weapon that supposedly caused his martyrdom in AD 288 in Rome during the persecution of Christians by the emperor Diocletian.   As popularly depicted by Renaissance painters, of whom the most notable was Pietro Perugino (c. 1500), he was immolated by being bound to a tree or pillar and pierced by arrows.

Considering that he was not really killed by arrows but beaten to death, it is obvious Sebastian became the patron saint of archers for the wrong reason. He had gone to Rome and joined the army, eventually becoming a captain of the Praetorian Guard under Diocletian. When it was revealed that he was a Christian who had converted many soldiers, he was ordered to be killed by arrows. After the archers left him for dead, a Christian widow nursed him back to health, and once recovered, he went back to Diocletian, this time to beg tolerance for all Christians.   The emperor rewarded his persistence by having him beaten to death with clubs.

The true irony of Sebastian is not in the manner of his death but of his sainthood. Some hagiographers believe the saint never existed, being merely a canonized form of a Gaulish savior-god who was killed by arrows. The Church thought of converting the pagan image because of the utmost reverence it was being held by the Gauls, who had built an ancient commemorative stone temple at Knockmay in Galway in his honor. To date, however, Sebastian remains a saint on the official books of the Church.

4. In Good Shape

Myth! The Valentine symbol was modeled after the human heart.

More than the nimbus, it was the heart that finally laid claim to the Valentine tag. Some people believe the universally recognized heart symbol bears no resemblance to the real thing; obviously they don't realize that the twin lobes of the stylized version correspond roughly to the atria of the anatomical heart. This is no proof, however, that the human heart was the model used for the Valentine symbol, since other parts of the human body could have served just as well. For instance, Desmond Morris, author of *The Naked Ape* (1967), says the symbol is strangely similar to the female butt, while another sees some resemblance with the Egyptian hieroglyphic for the male testicles.

There are equally attractive possibilities that have nothing to do with the human body or sex. The ancient Greek cult of Dionysus worshipped the heart shape because this was the outline of the ivy leaf, a cluster of which Dionysus purportedly wore on his head while engaging in his famed Dionysian rites. In primitive Africa, the "heart" configuration represented animals, particularly their horns and snouts, and was expressed through ceremonial masks. The 1400s saw it being used as a suit designation on playing cards, and this we still have today.

But if the Valentine symbol was not necessarily patterned after the human heart, the reverse is also true: the human heart was not always drawn or portrayed in the shape of the symbol. In the New World particularly, the Aztecs illustrated the organ as oblong and seed-like, while other Native Americans drew it as a blob.

5. Truth of the Pater

Myth! **Only those popes after 1870 who are not considered corrupt have successfully invoked infallibility.**

The assertion of papal infallibility was first made at the Vatican Council of 1870, in reference solely to occasions when the Pope speaks *ex cathedra*, that is to say, in his role as supreme teacher of the Catholic faithful and in matters of faith and morals. The dogma has been so misunderstood that even papal pronouncements laying no formal claim to it have been regarded as infallible. Unbelievable as it may seem, no pope has ever proclaimed *ex cathedra*, and no encyclical has ever made any pretensions of infallibility. The last doctrine of faith by a pope—the Immaculate Conception in 1854—was rendered infallible only by retroactive application.

Contrary to the belief that infallibility does not operate with effect for popes before 1870 nor for those considered wicked or corrupt, the principle covers all popes, good and bad, and is retroactive all the way to St. Peter himself. The assumption is that even bad ones can be divinely inspired and thus promulgate an infallible doctrine, but popes who have been condemned for their heretical doctrines, e.g. Honorius I (625-638), are automatically excluded by the very nature of their false teachings.

Infallibility should not be confused with the concepts of indefectibility and inerrancy, the first being the infallibility of the Church as distinguished from the papacy, and the second the infallibility of the Bible as the word of God.

6. Accidental Tourists

Myth! St. Julian the Hospitaller followed St. Christopher as the patron saint of travelers.

St. Christopher, who is said to have lived in the 3rd century and died in Lycia under the Roman emperor Decius, was the giant pagan Christophorus of Syria before converting to the faith and devoting his life to carrying travelers across a river.

One of the first stories that Catholic grade-schoolers learn from their book of saints is about Christopher and a small child he was transporting on his shoulders, who became so heavy halfway across the water that the saint staggered under the burden. Complaining of the weight, he was told that he was bearing upon his back the world and Him who created it. Thus, the name Christopher (Greek for "Christ-bearing") and the iconographic representation of the saint as a huge man with the Christ child riding piggyback on him.

Many people still don't realize that Christopher was a fake whose feast is no longer obligatory after his name was dropped from the calendar in 1969. He may have been supplanted as patron saint of travelers by St. Julian the Hospitaller, but there is evidence that the latter is mythical as well, an invention of the Church to Christianize the figure of Julian the Apostate. The saint's name is in no way connected with the Knights of the Order of Malta, who

222

are called Hospitallers, but derives from a legend that Julian lived by a ford with his wife and gave shelter and assistance to travelers. It is said that he did this as penance for killing his sleeping parents by mistake, thinking they were his wife and her lover.

7. Hankering Hank

Myth! **The Pope pardoned Henry IV after he stood bareheaded and barefooted in deep snow outside the gates of Canossa.**

The so-called Investiture Conflict arose when the Holy Roman Emperor Henry IV started appointing his own men to high church offices without permission from Pope St. Gregory VII. When His Holiness proposed to negotiate the right of lay investiture (authorizing lay rulers to grant ecclesiastical officials the symbols of their authority), Henry impolitely rejected the offer and even renounced obedience to him.

The pope excommunicated the king, who became so upset that he decided to journey to the castle of Canossa, a stronghold in Central Italy to which the pope had withdrawn. It is said that the pope relented and annulled the sentence after Henry, bareheaded and barefooted, stood in deep snow outside the castle gates for three cold January days in 1077, pleading for absolution, with the castle's owner Countess Matilda and St. Hugh, abbot of Cluny, also pleading for him.

Many historians believe the Canossa incident is mainly legend, and that the real reason the pope lifted his interdiction was Henry's threat to invade the papal domain. It is also suspected that Gregory attacked lay investiture only as an excuse to get Henry to support his reform of the church, and would have ceded part of the right to the king had he gotten it.

Whatever the truth, Canossa did not finally resolve the matter. Gregory, convinced that Henry had become intransigent again, issued a second excommunication against him in 1080, and the king retaliated by besieging Rome, capturing it in 1084 and driving the pope into exile.

8. Intriguing Personality

Myth! Clement XIV, called the Protestant Pope, is the only Pope recognized by Protestants.

Though his sobriquet "Protestant Pope" conveys the notion that this pope went Protestant because of some dissatisfaction with the Catholic Church, nothing of the sort occurred. Clement XIV was a Franciscan who was trained for the priesthood by the Jesuits, and chosen pope by his predecessor Clement XIII because of his known sympathy for his mentors. The Society of Jesus was then under suppression from Bourbon absolutists, who felt the 239-year-old order was becoming far too powerful, influential and aggressive.

To the consternation of both his allies and critics, Clement, instead of protecting the Society, dissolved it in a 1773 papal brief. It was a major concession to secular power, and adherents of the faith saw it at once as a form of treason at least as condemnable as Protestantism. This earned Clement the accusation of being more Protestant than the Protestants, and the derogatory epithet "Protestant Pope."

Actually, Clement's action against the Jesuits was solely to stave off perceived threats to the solidarity of the Church. Having just ended a nine-year schism in Portugal, he feared that France and Spain, among others, were ready for one of their own unless the Jesuits were eliminated. Eventually, another pope, Pius XVII, saw that the Jesuits had always devoted themselves to the protection of the papacy against oppression by Protestants and pagans, and decided to reestablish the order in 1814.

9. The First Primates

Myth! Peter was the first pope of the Roman Catholic Church, while his brother Andrew was the first pope of the Eastern Church.

St. Peter is traditionally regarded as the first pope because of his consecration by Christ and his role in organizing the Church. But historically, the title of Pope has been accorded only to Peter's successors and not to Peter himself. The colorful and complex history of the papacy started long after the time of the apostles, even though its underlying philosophy emanates from the special relationship of Peter with Christ. According to the *Britannica*, the claim that the Church of Rome was founded by Peter, who served as its first bishop (and therefore the first pope), remains in dispute and rests on evidence that emerged only a century later.

Further compounding the problem is the allegation that Peter's brother Andrew was also a pope of sorts because he was the first to lead the Eastern Orthodoxy after the East-West Schism split up the universality of the Catholic Church. In fact, Andrew had long quit the scene when the Schism occurred, and moreover, no Western-type pope—only a patriarch—was ever allowed to take the seat at Constantinople. The Eastern Church stands on the very doctrine that there should be no official primate, whether from Constantinople or Rome, because all bishops have equal jurisdiction over their respective sees. The idea that St. Andrew was the first pope of the Eastern Church only helps to dramatize the separation of the two churches in a wrong way.

Incidentally, people tend to think there was only one set of siblings among the apostles. James and John, the two sons of Zebedee, were not only brothers, they were also fishermen like Peter and Andrew.

10. Spiked Rumor

Myth! St. Catherine, the patron saint of philosophers and scholars, died on a spiked wheel.

St. Catherine of Alexandria, the patron of philosophers and scholars, is a mythical figure and should not be confused with St. Catherine (1522-90), a real person famous for her visions of the Passion and her stigmatization. The false saint, supposedly martyred in the 4th century in Alexandria, Egypt, is described by her legend as an extremely learned young girl of noble birth who protested the persecution of Christians under the Roman emperor Maxentius and converted the latter's wife and several soldiers.

She demolished with her arguments fifty of the most eminent scholars summoned by the emperor to debate her. A bolt of lightning shattered the spiked wheel on which she was condemned to die, and she was then beheaded.

Catherine's voice was one of those Joan of Arc claimed to have heard, an anomaly that puts a cloud on the mystical nature of Joan's inspiration. Nowhere is Catherine mentioned before the 8th century, and this lack of historical references has led to the removal of her name from the Church calendar.

11. Hail, O Halo

Myth! **The yellow radiance surrounding the head or figure of a holy person is a halo.**

Strictly speaking, the radiance or aura surrounding holy people and godlike figures in paintings is not a halo but a nimbus. "Halo" first referred to the disc or luminosity of the sun or the moon particularly during an eclipse, and still properly applies to the radiant glow to be seen about any of those celestial bodies.

The nimbus began in history as a symbol for pagan gods, who were given this attribute in Hindu, Greek, and Roman art. Eventually it became an appurtenance for any figure with great spiritual power, including those thought to be evil, such as the Devil. For a Moslem holy person, the nimbus is depicted as a circle of flames rather than a glow.

Christianity, aware of the nimbus' pagan history, discouraged artists from using the device for nearly six centuries. It was only in the seventh century that the Church began to allow it as an artistic way of glorifying the image of Christ. Despite the absence of any reference in Scripture, the nimbus once started became an integral part of Christian art, and various forms emerged: triangular for the Trinity, square for living saints, but in most cases round. One version called the aureole is lemon-drop-shaped, another is round with a cross in it, while "glory" is a "generalized effusion of blessedness" used to cover up troublesome details in a painting.

12. Doubtful State

Myth! The pope is the head of the smallest state in the world.

The Vatican City is touted as the most awesome political power residing in the smallest state on earth, but this is not wholly true. The papal domain, though a state, is only the smallest political division. The smallest state is the residence of the Grand Master of the Order of the Knights of Malta, a religious military order founded in the 11th century to tend to the Christian sick and wounded from the Crusades. The order was endowed with the estates of crusaders its hospitals had once cured, and was later gifted by Charles V with the island of Malta. From there it became a strong naval power, but it was eventually ousted by Napoleon in 1798. It has since lost the prerogative of territorial rule and no longer qualifies as a political division, although it has retained its statehood within the physical boundaries of the Grand Master's residence at 68 Via Condotti, Rome, since 1834.

The Vatican City is the next smallest state on earth, which, at 108.7 acres, is smaller than the other tiny anomalous political entities of Europe, such as Andorra, Monaco, and Liechtenstein. Its location in the heart of Rome in no wise affects its sovereignty, for it is completely independent of Italy under the terms of the Lateran Treaty and Concordat of 1929. The government is headed by the pope, who has absolute executive, legislative and judicial powers within the city.

IX
Jingle Bell Time

On Christmas

"The stockings were hung by the chimney with care,
In hopes that St Nicholas soon would be there."

•

Clement C. Moore

1. X'ian Holiday

Myth! The word 'Xmas' is a vulgarism that uses the letter X as a variable with no specific meaning.

Most people put an apostrophe after the letter X in 'Xmas' and pronounce the word *èks´mes* in the belief that it is a vulgarism for Christmas and X is a variable with no specific meaning. The faithful consider 'X'mas' a sign of disrespect because "it omits Christ from Christmas," while others hesitate to end their Christmas message with the word for fear that a breach of etiquette may result.

But experts say 'Xmas', without a defacing apostrophe, is a fully rendered word and has always been one. The appearance of the term in twelfth-century manuscripts—for example, the Anglo-Saxon Chronicle—as a full Old English equivalent of Christmas belies the claim that it is a corruption begotten during the early commercial beginnings of the holiday. The Oxford English Dictionary mentions that 'Xmas', along with the longer version *Xtemmas*, obtained from the year 1551 on. It was coined by the Greeks in AD 2 or 3 to signify 'Christ's mass', and has been used in religious writing ever since. The X (the phonetic equivalent of the English K) is the transliterated *chi* and is the first letter of the Greek word *XPICTOC* (also *Xristos*, *Khristos* or *Christos*), the full literal symbol for Jesus Christ. The X may have also meant the Crucifixion, but this does not gel with the belief that Christ died on a Latin cross and not on an X-shaped Greek cross.

2. Santa's Spare Tire

Myth! Rudolph the Red-nosed Reindeer is a Scandinavian creation of the early 19ᵗʰ century.

Rudolph the Red-nosed Reindeer plays a prominent role in Yuletide folklore as the thirteenth 'deer sleigher' in the Santa Claus tableau. But unlike the others in that tableau, Rudolph did not come with the Dutch or anybody else; rather, it is a twentieth-

229

century commercial creation of a once famous American department store. In 1939, Montgomery Ward hired Robert May, an advertising copywriter, to write a Christmas poem for their Santas to give away during the holiday season. He came up with one he called 'Rollo the Red-Nosed Reindeer', about a shiny-nosed Santa's helper. Executives liked the poem but not the title, so May renamed the animal Reginald. When this also failed, his four-year old daughter suggested Rudolph.

In 1947, May's friend Johnny Marks made a musical version of the poem, and Gene Autry's rendition made it the second all-time best-selling Christmas song. It is in this format that America has been able to export Rudolph as a successful Christmas symbol, particularly to Scandinavia and Germany, the very same countries that originated Santa. The song has surpassed 'Silent Night' as the most played during the Yuletide season in many parts of the world.

3. Knickerbocker Nick

Myth! **Walt Disney invented the figure of Santa in a wagon skimming over the treetops on Christmas night.**

As children, we would look up pensively at the sky on Christmas night in the hope of seeing Santa whisk by on a wagon pulled by a team of reindeer. Most reference books trace the source of this Yuletide stereotype not to any Disney Christmas fantasy but to the poem that opens with the line, "T'was the night before Christmas," describing in vivid and exciting detail Santa's modus operandi on Christmas eve.

Some say Clement C. Moore, the recognized author of the poem, lifted his idea from the pages of Washington Irving's 1809 book *A History of New York*. Writing as Diedrich Knickerbocker, Irving had envisioned St. Nick as a jolly fellow smoking a pipe, skimming over the treetops in a wagon and dropping presents for little children down the chimneys of their homes on Christmas Eve. Irving wrote with no awareness that his was a drastic revision of the Santa Claus image introduced into the New World by German and Scandinavian immigrants. In his old Eurasian haunts, the benevolent Christmas figure had been a tall, thin man riding on a donkey to distribute gifts to children on his feast day on December 6. Critics say that, in any case, it is the appeal of Moore's poem rather than Irving's contribution to it that has made the figure of a high-flying Santa so familiar and endearing to millions of young folks around the world.

---

4. More on Moore

Myth! Clement C. Moore is the undisputed author of 'A Visit From St. Nicholas'.

Clement C. Moore, a Bible professor at New York's General Theological Seminary, has long been recognized as the composer of this 56-line one-stanza poem. His unofficial biography states that, after writing the piece in 1822 for his nine children, he had it published anonymously in the Troy Sentinel in 1823, allowing it to be reprinted without attribution over the next thirteen years in various newspapers, magazines, and almanacs. During all that time, Moore did not reveal his identity apparently for fear that the juvenile quality of the verse might affect his reputation. An 1836 reprint of 'A Visit from Saint Nicholas' finally recognized Moore, who afterwards included the verse in a volume of his own poetry published in 1844. The impeccable rhyming combined with the narrative charm made the text an immensely popular work of art, bestowing on Moore the kind of fame that he never quite imagined.

However, some very reputable sources have intimated that Moore is not really the author of 'A Visit From St. Nicholas'. For instance, according to Henry Noble MacCracken, a Shakespeare scholar and former president of Vassar College, the Livingston family has for several generations advanced the claim that their ancestor, Major Henry Livingston, Jr., and not Moore, wrote the famous poem. Following MacCracken's tack, Donald W. Foster, another scholar and expert analyst, published the book *Author Unknown: On the Trail of Anonymous* (New York: Henry Holt, 2000), confirming that Livingston, a New Yorker from Locust Grove, Poughkeepsie, and Moore's relative by affinity, indeed wrote what hitherto has been known as Moore's masterpiece.

231

Foster, who is well known for dealing with various issues of literary authorship through textual analysis, admits Moore's hand in the writing of an almost forgotten Christmas piece, 'Old Santeclaus'. But he doubts Moore composed 'A Visit From St. Nicholas', particularly in light of the revelation that Moore had disavowed authorship of the poem initially, even while, according to his accusers, he had taken false credit for other works in the past. Foster finds the anapestic rhyme scheme, meter and general phraseology of 'A Visit From St. Nicholas' more consistent with Livingston than with Moore, and its cheerful mood in accord with Livingston's style but not with Moore's, whose poems are typically dark.

5. Elves' Night

Myth! **Moore's famous poem begins with, "T'was the night before Christmas, and all through the house."**

Despite our fondest childhood memories of Clement C. Moore's legendary encounter with Santa Claus, we are still liable to miss a couple of things about the classic. First, its official title is 'A Visit from St. Nicholas', although its unauthorized title, 'The Night Before Christmas', which borrows from the poem's first line, is more popular. Second, the word 'Santa Claus' is nowhere mentioned in the poem, and his more formal name, St. Nicholas, is mentioned only once, in the title. At the time the verse was written Santa was better known by his nickname, St. Nick, and this is what appears throughout the entire text.

Also, a casual recitation of the opening line often results in a misquotation. When read quickly or when culled from memory, the line that comes out naturally is, "'T'was the night before Christmas, and (or sometimes while) all through the house." The correct wording as it appears in *The Golden Treasury of the Familiar* reads, "'T'was the night before Christmas, when all through the house..." There are other apparent misquotations, but they are actually modern variants of the original, e.g., the first part of the final line, originally written as "Happy Christmas to all," has been changed in many editions to "Merry Christmas to all," to accord with the standard Christmas greeting current in the United

States and other English speaking countries.

6. A Finite Claus

Myth! **The Santa Claus myth has always envisioned its subject as a fat, short, bearded pipe smoker.**

As far as every modern generation's young people are concerned, Santa Claus is a rotund figure, fiftyish, with a full set of white hair and beard, and dressed in a red suit and black boots with white fur trimmings. All one has to do to rekindle his memory of this beloved icon is to peek into a department store or mall at Christmas time and catch a clone in operation.

Actually, the only immutable qualities of Santa Claus are his legendary generosity and particular fondness for children. Everything else—his physical appearance especially—is a radical departure from what he was the first time he made himself felt in the American consciousness.

Santa Claus didn't always look the way he does now. The Dutch figure was thin, tall and ill dressed, although dignified. He was clean-shaven and didn't smoke. Then in America, he put on weight—literally at the stroke of a pen. In the early 1800s, Washington Irving imagined Santa as a bulky man who smoked a pipe and wore baggy pants. The famous cartoonist Thomas Nast executed this concept in a series of Christmas drawings for Harper's Weekly that spanned more than 20 years (from 1863 to 1886), and the portly bearded pipe-smoking image was born.

One interesting sidelight is the perception of Santa Claus by the author of the immortal poem 'A Visit From St. Nicholas' as a small elf-like figure riding herd on an entourage of miniature animals. To quote the relevant verse: "What to my wondering eyes should appear/ But a miniature sleigh and eight tiny reindeer/ With a little old driver, so lively and quick/ 1 knew in a moment it must be St. Nick." It is said that the small stature not only allows Santa to get in and out of chimneys, but also offers a much better sight than the preposterous dimensions of his department store counterparts.

233

7. Deer Santa

Myth! Rudolph is a male of the deer family.

Rudolph and his friends in Santa's convoy should never be mistaken for deer. They do look like deer, and because of their name, many think they are a domesticated (i.e., 'reined') type of deer. Actually, reindeer do not belong to the deer species but to the caribou family. The ones called reindeer in Northern Europe and Asia are the same species as the caribou found throughout the Western Hemisphere. The 'deer' in the name is the Old Norse *dyr*, meaning a four-footed beast. Strangely, although Santa's home has always been the North Pole, you can't expect to find Rudolph and his ilk there at any time of the year; it was discovered as early as 1925 that there are no reindeer in the polar regions of the world.

Not unlike Disney's Bambi, a young male deer who is often mistaken for a doe because of his feminine name, Rudolph is sometimes suspected to be a female reindeer hiding behind a male name. What puts Rudolph's gender in question is that, while all reindeer associated with Santa are depicted with fully grown antlers, most male reindeer in the natural world shed their antlers by early December, well before Christmas Eve, and grow them back in the spring. Cows keep their antlers all year long, which ups the chances that there are more females than males among Santa's reindeer, Rudolph included.

The idea of a female Rudolph seems far-fetched, however, since his own creator, Robert May, makes no bones about his being male. According to Rudolph's apocrypha, his father is Donner and his mother Blitzen, the last two of the eight reindeer in Santa's original team. In the beginning, their names, as appeared in the 1823 publication of 'A Visit from Saint Nicholas', were Dunder and Blixem (the Dutch words for 'thunder' and 'lightning'), but Dunder was later changed to Donder and Blixem to Blixen (to make it rhyme with Vixen, the name of the fourth reindeer). When Clement C. Moore prepared the 1823 poem for inclusion in his 1844 book of verse, he Germanized Blixen to Blitzen (German for 'lightning'), and thereafter the names Donder and Blitzen stuck. It is not clear how and when Donder became

234

Germanized as well, but Johnny Marks helped popularize the new name 'Donner' (German for 'thunder') by adapting it to the 'Rudolph the Red-Nosed Reindeer' lyrics.

---

8. Nick of Time

Myth! **The model for Santa Claus was a Teutonic pagan god.**

It is not certain whether Santa was a mythical figure lifted by the Dutch from their pagan folklore, or a real-life saint who worked miracles in ancient Turkey. Some say Nicholas, though not a documented figure, left relics in Asia Minor sufficient to flesh him out as a bishop of Myra born in Lycia, Turkey, early in the 4th century. Having lost his sainthood in the Roman Catholic Church since 1969, he is not to be confused with a ninth-century Pope also named St. Nicholas. Others deny his reality by claiming he was a false saint who evolved from Hold Nickar, the Teutonic pagan god of the sea. Possibly it is a combination of these two origins—the Turkish and the Scandinavian—that has shaped our modern image of St. Nick as a Christmas symbol.

Nicholas, however, remains a principal saint of the Eastern Orthodox Church, and in this milieu, he is dressed in bishop's garb and sports a long white beard, distributing presents to good children on his natal day, December 6. He used to be a patron saint as well of Russia, Greece, and Sicily, and later also of children. In the Netherland
s, he was Sint Nikolaas, Sinte Klaas, or Sinterclaas, the patron saint of sailors who supposedly left goodies for Dutch children in their wooden clogs on his feast day. There is reason to believe that as one or the other, the Dutch carried his cult to the New World, where the phonetics of his name lapsed into what sounded like Santa Claus and his gift giving became part of the Christmas tradition.

9. Gift Rapping

Myth! The story of the Magi was the inspiration for the Christian practice of gift giving at Christmas.

Most of the Christmas customs that we honor today were totally alien to Christmas originally. Some, like the Christmas tree, were spun off from pagan practices, myths and beliefs. Others had secular beginnings. For instance, the idea of hanging stockings on the mantel to receive small gifts started with the Turkish version of St. Nick. According to the legend, this generous but quaint old man wanted to provide dowries for the three daughters of a poor nobleman. He threw bags of money down the family's chimney and these fell into a stocking that happened to be hanging out to dry before the fire. He repeated the gesture with his other friends, and soon it became a local practice, later traveling with the image of St. Nick to the Western World.

Notwithstanding the myth about Christmas stockings, St. Nick did not originate the main tradition of Yuletide gift giving by Christians. Neither did the Magi, who visited the infant Jesus and gifted him with gold, frankincense and myrrh, although the belief that they did would in due course be assimilated into European customs and introduced into the New World. The real source of the tradition was the Romans, who practiced gift giving at the time of the winter solstice, particularly during the Saturnalia when the wealthy were obliged to share with the poor. In their relentless pursuit of Christianization, the early Church fathers found a fit between the Gospel episode of the Magi and the Roman practice, and simply merged the two for the benefit of the masses.

10. Tree of Heaven

Myth! The tradition of the Christmas tree originated with the legend of St. Boniface and the fir sapling.

To most Americans, the tradition associating the Christmas tree with the holiday began in the New World to become largely an

American institution. To others worldwide, the tree as a symbol of Christmas traces its beginnings to a period that had to do with Bethlehem, the Magi and the shepherds, and the circumstance of Christ's birth.

Neither belief is correct. In earlier times, the tree was an emblem of eternal life and magical survival to various pagan peoples, like the pre-Christian Nordics and the Romans, who revered it as an embodiment or gift of the gods. The concept of the tree as a Christmas icon began in Germany much later, but not in the eighth century, as is sometimes claimed, and it did not stem from the legend of St. Boniface. The saint, according to the story, axed an oak tree to prove to the worshipping Druids that it had no mystic powers, and in falling, it crushed every shrub and plant in its path except a small fir sapling. Because of the miracle, the saint blessed the fir as 'the tree of the Christ Child'.

The first time Christmas trees appeared as such was in the 16th century, when German families began bringing evergreens into their homes for the holidays and loading them with fruits, candles and cookies. They had been hung with apples and called 'Paradise trees' in the previous century, in reference to their use as center props in a December 24 production of a medieval mystery play about Adam and Eve. From Germany their application to a Christmas purpose spread gradually through Europe, after which German immigrants imported them as 'Christ trees' into America in the 1820s.

11. Holiday on Ice

Myth! **Christmas was the only holiday the Puritans never failed to celebrate.**

As strange as it may seem, the Puritans not only avoided the celebration of Christmas, they forbade it entirely. In 1659 the General Court of Massachusetts, voicing the views of William Bradford and Oliver Cromwell, passed a law against solemnizing the holiday, punishing "anybody who is found observing (it), by abstinence from labor, feasting, or any other way."

Thereafter, New Englanders were seen as Scrooge-like bigots who disdained Christmas because they couldn't bear to see

237

anyone, much less Catholics, rejoicing on that day. But the real reason is less an expression of anti-Catholic sentiments than of deep feelings of religiosity. The elders banned Christmas because they felt it was too holy to be celebrated in any fashion, and observing it without the utmost religious decorum was heretical and a 'pagan mockery'.

The law was repealed in 1684, but it was only with the immigration of Germans and Irish into the country two centuries later that the restrictive influence of the Puritans on the holiday was erased completely. As late as the Civil War, Christmas was very quiet and modestly observed, and there was hardly any impact on business. After the Civil War, merchants began experimenting with special Christmas sales, and it didn't take long before they discovered the commercial possibilities offered by the Yuletide season. From 1870 on, December has consistently become the single largest selling month of the year

X
Chestnuts Roasting On A Fire

11 on Mysterious Objects And Events

"Death will slay with his wings
whoever disturbs the peace of the pharaoh."

•

King Tut

1. Loch up that Beast

Myth! The Loch Ness Monster was successfully photographed in 1934.

Sir Peter Scott, a well-known naturalist, had such an unyielding faith in Nessie that he gave it a scientific name—Nessiteras rhombopteryx. The famous 1934 photo of the monster swimming in a lake purported to show the world that Nessie was well worth the esoteric name. Independently of Scott or the photo, however, Nessie is well entrenched in the public mind as a dinosaur of the species brontosaurus and/or brachiosaurus inhabiting the waters of Loch Ness.

Self-proclaimed conspirator Christian Spurling revealed more than a half century later that he helped stepfather M. A. Wetherell use a modified toy submarine to fake the "Nessie" photo. The confession remains largely uncorroborated, and by itself has not dented the popular belief that the monster exists. Based on claimed sightings, Nessie is known to haunt not only Loch Ness but also Loch Morar, Loch Awe, Loch Lomond and Lochfyne. The experience is apparently not unique to Scotland, as almost every great lake in the world is associated with a resident monster. Lake Champlain in New York has Champy, and there is a man-eater that lurks in the waters of Lake Walker in Nevada. Others have been reported in Canada, Mexico, Australia and Africa.

Several of Nessie's critics find some significance in the coincidence offered by the name Nessiterras Rhombopteryx, which happens to be an anagram of the phrase *monster hoax by Sir Peter S.* But those in the science sector who do not share Sir Peter's confidence tend to be circumspect and cite Nessie's reputed elusiveness as the more logical reason. Wondering why the creature is not seen more often, one cynic notes: "Unless 'Nessie" is presumed to be immortal, we should expect to find a breeding population of these monsters in the Loch. Such a population must consist of a sizeable number of individuals if it is to be stable... "

The same cynic points out that the chances of sighting or even catching Nessie should be high because there is no known way it could leave the Loch. "There cannot be underground channels connecting the Loch with the sea, because the Loch would drain down to sea level if there were." This fact, however, poses a

240

dilemma, as it also argues against Nessie's existence. A land-sealed lake would have no capability of sustaining a large number of huge creatures, and it would have barred Nessie's ancestors from entering in the first place.

2. A Piece of Blarney

Myth! The Blarney Stone is an Irish relic kissed by tourists who desire to become eloquent.

The attraction of the Blarney Stone to tourists and visitors lies in the legend that anyone who kisses it will be endowed with the gift of gab. "Blarney" itself means soft wheedling speech to gain an end, usually an insidious or undesirable one. Flattery, lying and cajolery are forms of blarney, and the objective may be of a political, romantic or financial nature.

The Stone's origin is set during the time of Queen Elizabeth I, when Sir George Carew, the newly appointed Lord President of Munster, required the surrender to the crown of all the castles and strongholds in the region. Cormac Macarthy, the owner of Blarney Castle in County Cork, Ireland, was unwilling to comply but did not wish to appear wholly rebellious. By using his extraordinary talent of persuasion, he succeeded in having the matter postponed from month to month and, later, almost indefinitely. The stratagem soon came to the attention of Elizabeth's ministers and the associates of the Lord President, and became such a source of amusement that they coined the word "blarney" for it after the name of the castle. To commemorate the achievement, the Blarney Stone was set up on a wall of the castle, and the myth was started.

Tourists desirous of becoming eloquent are permitted to kiss the stone, but it is not the real one. The true stone, a triangular piece with the inscription 'Cormac Macarthy *fortis me fieri fecit,* A.D. 1446', hangs some twenty feet from the top of the castle wall, and there is no safe and easy way to reach it. Naturally, this has prompted the claim that the substitute is just as good as the original when it comes to bestowing the fabled gift of articulation.

241

3. Tut-tutting a Curse

Myth! The opening of King Tut's tomb activated a curse that doomed its discoverers.

Archaeologist Howard Carter's sponsor Lord Carnarvon died a few weeks after the discovery of King Tut's tomb on November 3, 1922, evidently from the bite of a mysterious insect. Allegedly, a score of other individuals, including the British archaeologist H. E. Evelyn-White and a Professor La Fleur, were also struck down because of their involvement with the mausoleum in one way or another. The popular reaction was that a curse had been let loose by the opening of the tomb, especially since, as was later discovered in 1969, Tut had been murdered. Newspapers had published the report that carved above the entrance to the tomb in hieroglyphics were the words: "Death shall come to him who touches the tomb." This Carter denied, despite the claim of the last survivor of the excavating team, Richard Adamson, that it was Carter himself who had started the rumor to keep tourists and thieves from trying to enter the tomb.

What really happened was not quite what the legend propagated. Of the 10 principal diggers at Tut's tomb, two were still alive 40 years later and another 5 lived an average of 20 years beyond its opening. Carter himself died only 17 years later, in 1939, at the age of 67. Two other archaeologists who practically ate and slept in the tomb died at the ripe old ages of 89 and 90. A number of archaeologists and tourists who visited the tomb may have been taken ill or died soon after, but it could be argued that they were old or ill already, or that they had picked up some deadly virus from the dust and debris of the unearthed monument.

4. Ghastly Ghosties

Myth! The Amityville Horror is the true story of a haunted house in New York.

242

Jay Anson, a scriptwriter who had worked on *The Exorcist,* wrote *The Amityville Horror* based on interviews he had conducted with George Lutz and his family of four. In 1974 a man named Ronald DeFeo murdered both of his parents and all his brothers and sisters in cold blood in their house in Amityville, New York. A year later George, his wife Kathy and their three children moved into the house, but in four weeks they fled their residence because of strange occurrences they could not explain. The book became a best seller and the film that followed was a blockbuster.

Investigators from the Parapsychology Institute of America went to Amityville to check out the story, and found out that everything Anson wrote in his book was completely fabricated. The testimony of the police and a priest, as well as weather records and the general condition of the house, denied the most important assertions of the Lutzes. The conclusion of the Institute, as expressed by its director, Dr. Stephen Kaplan, was terse: "We found no evidence to support any claim of a 'haunted house'. What we did find is a couple who had purchased a house that they economically could not afford."

The lawyer for Ronald DeFeo eventually confessed that he had noted the commercial possibilities of exploiting the murders and their aftermath, and thereupon decided to enter into a conspiracy with George and Kathy Lutz. All three were beset with financial problems, and believed—quite rightly—that the idea of a haunted house would be the solution.

5. Hare Apparent

Myth! The rabbit's foot has had a long history as a good luck charm.

The rabbit's foot is probably the most universal of all lucky charms. People use it not just for good luck but also to keep away evil spirits, cure diseases, and even cast spells. Surprisingly, despite this significance, the rabbit's foot has had very little history as a talisman. Historically, it was the foot of the hare that started out as a lucky charm. There was a twelfth-century belief in Wales, and later on in other parts of Europe, that witches liked to

243

change themselves into hares. During a so-called witch-hunt, the witch would supposedly turn into a hare and sneak into a peasant home for safety, and the affair would thereafter become a hare hunt. As far back as the time of the ancient Britons, hares were considered magical creatures to be used in the rituals surrounding divination, and in books of the time it is plainly stated that the animal should not be eaten at all because of its magical qualities.

Ironically, for some ancient peoples like the Celts, the hare's foot caught on precisely because it was thought to be the rabbit's. One reason the Celts preferred the rabbit was that the animal entered the world with eyes wide open and was therefore believed to be imbued with the wisdom of a seeing fetus. Actually, it is the hare that is born with open eyes, whereas the rabbit is born blind. This mistaken identity has reversed once more in modern times, with the rabbit being mistaken for the hare and in the process becoming the more popular supplier of the lucky charm. It seems that, for one who, like Alice, needs all the luck to survive, there's little difference between the White Rabbit and the March Hare to be concerned about.

6. Horse Feathers

Myth! **The Christians of 10th-century England introduced the horseshoe as a talisman to ward off the intrusions of the devil.**

St. Dunstan was a blacksmith of the 10th century who became the Archbishop of Canterbury in AD 959. It is said that he shackled Satan to a wall on the pretense that he would fit him with the horseshoes he wanted on his cloven foot. He released the devil only after the latter made a solemn oath never to enter a house where a horseshoe was displayed above the door.

This story is believed to be the basis for the superstition that the horseshoe is a lucky charm. Since its origin in the tenth century, Christians to the present time have held the horseshoe in high esteem. In the medieval period, it was seen as a protection against witches, who rode broomsticks precisely because they were deathly afraid of horses. At first it was placed above a doorframe, and later moved down to mid door, where it served the dual

244

function of talisman and doorknocker. It was carefully positioned with points upward lest its luck drained out.

The truth, it now appears, is that the object has been prized for its magical powers long before Dustan. The Greeks introduced the horseshoe to Western culture in the fourth century and regarded it as a symbol of good fortune. The early Greeks and Romans believed in particular that its iron composition and crescent shape gave it supernatural significance.

7. E.T. v. S.P.C.A.

Myth! **Animal mutilations commonly occurring in the western US have remained unexplained.**

Published reports are not uncommon of farm animals being found with tongue, eyes, and sex organs removed. They have appeared at intervals over many years, the latest being a rash of happenings in the early 1990s in the United States. The stories, mostly involving cattle in the Western states, are often associated with contemporary reports of UFO activities in the vicinity. Revelations about abductions aboard strange spacecraft fan speculations about extraterrestrials removing animal organs for experimentation purposes. While human ghouls are not generally suspected, those inclined towards witchcraft are sometimes included in the accusations on the ground that they use the items in rituals.

It has been noted, however, that stories of mutilations are almost always offered for publication for the sake of sensationalism. Writers, particularly those required to fill newspaper space or meet a deadline, often fail to mention that the animals have been dead from normal causes for several days before the owner discovers them. In the meanwhile, animal scavengers, including wolves, coyotes and vultures, have probably attacked the carcass, eating the softest parts such as the tongue. Most if not all of the time, it is simply a case of a harried or unscrupulous editor not realizing or not caring that, for what is made to appear supernatural, a perfectly natural explanation is not only possible but likely.

8. A Ship that Passes in the Night

Myth! The Flying Dutchman was the captain of a ghost ship that plied the Cape of Good Hope.

The *Encyclopedia Britannica* describes the Flying Dutchman as a specter ship of Western folklore that haunted the waters around the Cape of Good Hope, its appearance signaling imminent disaster. Of two major versions of the legend, both equally popular, one is the basis of Richard Wagner's opera *The Flying Dutchman*, in which the main character is the shipmaster Captain Vanderdecken. In the other version, the captain is a certain Falkenberg, who must sail forever through the North Sea to play at dice for his soul with the devil. The latter is the model for Samuel Taylor Coleridge's *Rime of the Ancient Mariner* (1798) as well as Sir Walter Scott's narrative poem *Rokeby* (1813).

However, the general literature about this maritime apparition assigns the title to the captain, not the ship. While affirming that this was a Dutchman of the seventeenth century named Vanderdecken or Van Falkenberg, it puts the ship on a voyage to the Indies, where it was becalmed for so long that the captain swore he would sell his soul to the devil for a wind. A reconciliatory version says the Flying Dutchman is both the captain and the ship, although sightings that have been recorded on numerous occasions during the last 400 years are of the ship with no trace of the captain. These usually occur south of the Cape of Good Hope, especially on stormy days.

9. Loki Thirteen

Myth! The superstition about the number thirteen originated from the Biblical account of Christ's last supper.

The most popular source of the superstition involving the number 13 is the Biblical account of Christ's last supper with the twelve apostles. The true source, however, is not Christian but pagan, a Norse myth that antedates the Holy Scriptures. According to the myth, 12 spirits or gods were invited to a banquet at Valhalla, but one, Balder, was slain by a thirteenth, Loki, who was uninvited. From Scandinavia, the superstition spread throughout Europe, and by the dawn of the Christian era, it was well entrenched in countries along the Mediterranean.

Thirteen is avoided like the plague by westerners, who believe death lurks around that number. Others are not so afraid, and some even consider the number 13 lucky. Theatrical people of old, for example, tried to sign all their contracts on the thirteenth day of the month. There was also a British tradition that eating Christmas pudding in 13 different houses before January 1 would bring prosperity in the New Year. The founding fathers of America seemed intent on fighting the superstition by indulging in it. Thus, there is a surfeit of the number 13 in the patriotic symbols of this country. There were 13 original colonies, and the Great Seal of the United States contains 13 stars, 13 bars, and an eagle with 13 tail feathers holding 13 arrows and an olive branch with 13 leaves and 13 berries. "E Pluribus Unum" has 13 letters, and on the back of the US dollar bill, the incomplete pyramid has 13 steps.

10. Three on One Leaves None

Myth! The superstition about lighting three cigarettes with one match dates back to World War I.

World War I is believed to be the origin of the superstition that it is unlucky to light three cigarettes with the same match. During the conflict, there was a real danger incident to keeping a match lighted in the trenches long enough to light three cigarettes. A match continuously burning for more than a few seconds might not only attract the enemy's attention but also give him time for his aim. Their superiors constantly reminded soldiers of the danger, and the fear provoked by these warnings and reports of coincidental deaths during the war was no doubt sufficient to create the superstition.

However, an older version of the superstition dates back to the 19th century in Eastern Europe. The belief, it is said, arose in connection with the funeral service in the Russian Orthodox Church, where the ritual features the lighting of three altar candles with one taper, after which it is forbidden to repeat the act. The Russians regarded it as sacrilegious and impious to make any other lights in groups of three. The interdiction developed into the thinking that ill luck would befall anybody who lights three cigarettes with the same match, or anybody who even accepts such a light.

There are other older, though less cogent, sources of the superstition, such as the association of the number three with the Holy Trinity. This is the same notion that accounts for the belief that a drowning person surfaces three times before finally going down.

---

11. Elfin Hand

Myth! **The gremlin is an old Western folk figure with a penchant for destroying every man-made thing in sight.**

Thought to be wholly invisible, the gremlin is revealed by Hollywood in all its impish glory in the *Gremlins* film series. But shorn of lavish special effects, an earlier appearance in the 1983 *Twilight Zone-The Movie*, in which the little monster is seen hammering away at the wings of a commercial plane, is probably a more accurate representation.

Although gremlins tend to be grouped with fairies, pixies, gnomes, dwarfs, imps and other little people commonly found in Western folklore, it is doubtful they belong to the same company. Gremlins are not really as old as the many other types that boast of the same British or Irish parentage. The writer Roald Dahl claimed he invented the word during World War II, more than a decade after a reader thought he saw it occurring three times in a poem published on 10 April 1929 in the magazine The Aeroplane. According to Philip Ward, the earliest reference to "gremlin" in the files of The Oxford English Dictionary is the 7 September 1942 issue of Newsweek, which traces it to 1923.

The gremlin is in fact no older than the warplane, having arrived with it in the dogfighting days of World War I. But it did not become popular until the early stages of World War II, when British aviators began to attribute the unaccountable failures of their equipment to GE, or "gremlin effect." This bugaboo of flyers and airplane mechanics has since taken the blame for any annoying or disastrous abnormality of engine, wing, gun, propeller, flap, or other aircraft part. The gremlin is said to exist for the sole purpose of expressing nature's resentment against man's use of air machines, particularly for warfare.

XI
Wizards Of Bosh

On Nostradamus and Other Seers

"The heaven shall burn at five and forty degrees
The fire shall come near the great new city..."
•

Nostradamus

1. Man of Tomorrow

Myth! Nostradamus had an eerie talent for prophecy.

Nostradamus's universal cult following regards him as the greatest prophet in history. A more studious appraisal of his works would show him in a different light—a literary innovator, perhaps, but not a prophet. His real talent, it is said, lay in being obtuse. He hardly mentioned any names or dates, his verses were not placed in any chronological order, and his so-called prophecies were so vaguely written they could be made to apply to nearly anything.

In fact, his most famous prediction is an inconsistency. A quatrain foretold a bright future for King Henry II of France, but when Henry was killed in a jousting accident a couple of years later, another quatrain was discovered to fit the occasion and supersede the earlier one. The verse apparently foretold that a sliver from the lance of Henry's younger opponent would penetrate the king's golden helmet and pierce his eye and brain. But critics were quick to point out that the age difference between the two jousters was not really significant as the verse suggested, the king's visor was not gilded, and a tournament ground is not the same as the "field of battle" mentioned in the quatrain. Moreover, a French word Nostradamus uses in the account, *classes*, is conveniently translated as "knells, or "loppings," or "wounds", but actually means a fleet of ships.

It is suspected that many of Nostradamus' predictions were not of the distant future but of contemporary events, and that he was basically resolving those events rather than prophesying others. He worked with allegories and double-entendres so as not to upset the establishment that he served. One quatrain, for instance, obviously referred to the English queen known as Bloody Mary, who was already controversial during Nostradamus' time. Since it would not have been particularly insightful to anticipate the downfall of a ruler in those days, the prophecy was reinterpreted to predict the Great Fire of London in 1666. The verse's forecast of the fall of a lady from a high place was made to allude to St. Paul's Church, which was so ravaged by the flames that it was torn down.

The fact that many verses are written in obscure or corrupt French has helped match the predictions to real events through

251

convenient mistranslations. Thus, a verse containing the phrase "aux Itales, which is generally translated as "to Italy," was deemed applicable to Napoleon because "Itales" derives from "Aethalia," the classical name for Elba. Another verse mentions the birth "near Italy" of an emperor, "less a prince than a butcher," and is presumed to refer to either Hitler or Napoleon. But Nostradamus could have been thinking of a few other princes or would-be princes during his time who were poised to become royal butchers.

Advocates of the 16th century mystic have extended the ambit of his ambiguous prophesies to the 21st century. Shortly after the ghastly terrorist attack on the World Trade Center in New York City September 11th, 2001 the Internet and news media began circulating a supposed Nostradamus quatrain: "In the year of the new century and nine months /From the sky will come a great King of Terror.../ The sky will burn at forty-five degrees. Fire approaches the great new city.../ In the city of York there will be a great collapse, two twin brothers torn apart by chaos while the fortress falls the great leader will succumb third big war will begin when the big city is burning."

Did Nostradamus predict the bombing of the Twin Towers in New York? Not quite. The verses are actually snippets from various places in the Centuries and rephrased and reassembled to fit the horrendous event. For instance, the line, "In the year of the new century and nine months/ From the sky will come a great King of Terror," supplants the original, which reads, "In the year 1999 and seven months, from the skies shall come an alarming powerful king" (Century 10:72). There is no mention of "twin brothers" being "torn apart," as the "prophecy" actually says, "Two royal brothers shall war so much one against the other" (Century 3:97). As for collapsing in the city of York and the sky burning, this is as close as he gets: "The heaven shall burn at five and forty degrees, / The fire shall come near the great new city...when they shall make a trial of the Normans" (Century 6:97). Other variations of the fake quatrain would reshape the "terror from the sky" into a killer asteroid impacting Earth by 2012.

2. Doubling the Canon

Myth! **Nostradamus predicted the papacy of Sixtus V.**

To make Nostradamus' score sheet even more impressive, modern apologists include incidents not comprehended in any of Nostradamus' writings, although told and retold as some of the most remembered prophecies of the seer. For instance, there is the myth about the boy named Felice Peretti, who became Pope Sixtus V nineteen years later. According to the story, Nostradamus was in Italy on one of his healing missions when he encountered a party of Franciscan friars on a street in a small village. He walked up to the group, noticed a young boy named Felice, and suddenly knelt before him. When asked about his behavior, he said, "I must kneel before His Holiness."

The fake incident was one of those dramatized as fact in a TV documentary suggestively titled *The Man Who Saw Tomorrow*, with Orson Welles as narrator. The same program related another apocrypha as impressive, and as false, as the one about Pope Sixtus V. It seems that when Nostradamus died in 1566, he had secretly arranged to have a metal plaque buried with him. In 1700, when his coffin was opened in order to move his remains to a newly built tomb, the metal plaque was discovered resting on his skeleton. On it was inscribed the year 1700. Skeptics have pointed out that assuming the plaque existed, there were so many ways of knowing what it said prior to the decision to dig up the tomb.

3. Double Vision

Myth! **Jeanne Dixon had a seventy percent success rate with her predictions.**

Mrs. Dixon makes a considerable number of predictions each year, and has made some impressive hits particularly in the field of geopolitics. But her overall batting average is low despite her very broad Nostradamus-like predictions. The best seers claim up to a

70 per cent success rate, and this almost surely includes predictions so vague they can fit into any formula. Dixon's rate is placed at a modest 20 per cent. None of her ten major forecasts for 1980-2000 listed in the 1978 publication of *The People's Almanac 2* has happened or is likely to happen within the next remaining seven years. Most of her successful predictions seem to have been more analytical than psychic, and depend on her acumen for extrapolating actual developments to read into the future. This has given her celebrity status despite later commentaries that most of her "accurate" forecasts were made essentially *ex post facto*.

She claimed to have predicted John Kennedy's assassination and that of his brother Robert, in the latter case, a week before it happened while she was addressing a convention in the same hotel where it happened. The prophecy of Robert's murder would have been more spectacular than the one of John, but as far as is known, no evidence—for instance, the official records of the convention—was ever offered to support it.

4. To the Ends of the Earth

Myth! **Mother Shipton foretold the telegraph, steam engine and iron ship.**

Mother Shipton, claiming to have been born in a cave in Knaresborough, Yorkshire, in 1488, was baptized Ursula Southiel and later married one Tobias Shipton. She did not become known until after nearly two hundred years, when a tract came out in 1641 declaring that she had foretold, among others, the lives and deaths of Thomas Cromwell and Cardinal Wolsey. Another two centuries later, her reputation received a tremendous boost when it was discovered that she had devised a rhyme foretelling the telegraph, steam engines, and iron ships.

Unfortunately for her promoters, part of the same verse was the gratuitous line "The world to an end shall come, / In eighteen hundred and eighty one." When 1881 came and nothing happened, Mother Shipton's credibility took a swan dive. But even before that fateful year, many already knew Shipton was a fake and her end-of-the-world prediction nothing more than a filler to complete a rhyme. For it had been revealed by a London journal in 1873 that her prophecies were made up by Charles Hindley, a London publisher and book dealer, who in 1862 published them as a reprint of a pamphlet that he claimed had first appeared in 1684.

It is now clear that there never was any Mother Shipton and that many more of her prophecies coming to light are forgeries made up by others centuries after her "death". Her 'famous' prediction about 1881 has appeared over the years with different dates and in several countries, e.g., in the late 1970s when many news articles about Mother Shipton appeared setting the date at 1981. Yet, despite Hindley's confession and the considerable literature on the subject, Mother Shipton continues to be made a basis of comparison by writers and historians as if she were real.

5. Remembrances of Things Past

Myth! Déjà vu is a psychic manifestation of a previous life.

Déjà vú is the feeling one gets of having been in the same place before and talking to the same person about the same thing. It comes vaguely for just a second or two, and then leaves the mind in a flash. The phenomenon is often explained as a psychical experience, possibly of an occurrence that has already happened in a previous life or in another dimension, mostly the former.

The psychologists and psychiatrists in the scientific community are generally agreed that *déjà vú* is not caused by anything supernatural, extrasensory or extraterrestrial. "It is more like a mental hiccup, a brief, harmless malfunction of a basic mechanism of memory...Normally when one is in familiar surroundings, two brain functions are triggered: a concrete memory of the place and a separate abstract feeling of familiarity. In a *déjà vú* situation the familiarity sensation is triggered without a specific attendant memory." In other words, *déjà vú* is a recollection of something similar that did happen in the past—not in a previous life, as is suspected, but in one's present existence. Unlike a normal flashback, however, the recall is inadequate because there is really no memory of what happened—only a strong sense of familiarity that leaves as soon as it comes.

6. Oracular Demonstrations

Myth! **The Delphic oracle spoke in a trance induced by natural gases, and priests interpreted their mutterings in ambiguous verse.**

Legends have obscured the true character of the Delphic oracle. Herodotus claimed that the medium, usually called the Pythia, spoke in a trance induced by natural gases seeping through the rocks. Priests interpreted her mutterings, rendering them in deliberate ambiguous verse. One supposedly recorded consultation involved King Croesus of Lydia, who was told by the oracle, "Croesus will destroy a great empire." Thinking this meant Persia, he invaded the empire but was repelled. Persia then turned around and crushed Lydia in ironic fulfillment of the prophecy. Other Greek leaders who, after consulting the oracle, confronted their enemies only to suffer Croesus' fate include Pyrrhus ("I believe, Pyrrhus, that you the Romans can conquer"), an anonymous prince ("You shall go you shall return never you shall perish by the war"), and Philip of Macedon ("The ready victim crowned for death before the altar stands"). All these predictions were couched in misleading language and could be read in opposing ways, either of which would be correct depending on the actual results.

However, recent scholars have found that Herodotus erred in many respects. Most responses by the oracle were in fact straightforward commands on religious matters and, less frequently, on public or private affairs. The few that were in verse dated from the later years. A close study of all reliable evidence "reveals no chasm or vapors, no frenzy of the Pythia, no incoherent cries interpreted by priests. The Pythia spoke clearly, coherently, and directly to the consultant in response to his question."

7. What Dreams may Come

Myth! **Most prophetic dreams are psychic in nature.**

So-called prophetic dreams are another example of normal events that assume the proportions of phenomena because the perfectly ordinary results appear hard to explain. If the superstition that attaches to this human activity were cast out, the eerie coincidence between dream and reality would probably be just a function of the odds—and publicity. Psychics are quick to advertise seemingly prophetic dreams, but ignore the thousand others that have little or no relevance to their apprehension.

An important fact easily missed is that all people sleep, and millions of people sleeping mean billions of dreams. Many are prepared to believe in extraterrestrial life because of the odds offered by the billions of possible habitations in space, but just as many do not realize that one of the billions of dreams we experience each night is liable to hit foursquare on a future event. Indeed, one need not believe in fairy tales to know that not a few of the hundreds of thousands of daytime thoughts going through our heads each day are wishes that, like dreams, come true.

The most ancient beliefs about dreams were based on the assumption that they predicted future events. Now, there is no single theory of sleep and dreaming that is generally acceptable. "There is a split between those academic psychologists who believe that dreams are reflections of subconscious activity expressing our hopes and fears, and those who believe that they merely embody the 'junk' that the brain has accumulated during the day and no longer needs."

8. Water Prospectors

Myth! A dowser's ability to find water is psychic.

Dowsers are persons reputedly with mysterious powers that help them find water. This is usually done with a divining rod, which is shaped like a two-tined fork each tine being held by a hand. When the stem of the fork twitches, the presence of water in the ground is indicated.

However, scientists believe dowsing has no psychical basis. The experience of people who use the hit-and-miss method when looking for water is that they can be just as successful, or

257

unsuccessful, as well-known diviners. Subsurface water is present almost anywhere, even in deserts, provided one digs deep enough, while surface water would most likely be near vegetation, in low areas, or where land animals abound. With a little knowledge of the terrain, even the most ungifted of mediums would not find dowsing difficult.

Neither is there any scientific basis—say, electromagnetism—to link the diviner and his tool to water. The consensus thus is that some deception, however unintended, is employed. An unconscious fraud, for instance, may result from the psychological effect known as "ideomotor action," whereby conscious thought gives rise to involuntary, usually imperceptible muscle movements. A smart and experienced dowser often develops a good instinct for judging where water might be just by looking at the terrain. When he walks around prodding with his divining stick, his mind unconsciously transmits these knowledge and experience to his arm muscles, with predictable results.

9. Mind Bender

Myth! The Geller effect proves the existence of psychokinetic and ESP powers.

The young Israeli Yuri Geller was discovered performing mental acts in Israeli nightspots. Tested at the Stanford Research Institute, physicists came out convinced that he could bend metal and start broken watches by psychokinesis and perform ESP feats, such as duplicating hidden drawings. They called his strange force the Geller effect, similar to electromagnetism and seemingly present in other persons.

Since then, critics of the paranormal, including Martin Gardner, have established the strong possibility that the scientists, writers and fans of Geller have been hoodwinked and that the Geller phenomenon is based wholly on deception. Gardner comments: "If Geller has the power to bend metals, why is it necessary to bend them only under the conditions of a magic performance? If Geller possesses paranormal powers, why do they manifest themselves in such picayune ways as bending a spoon? If Geller can bend a metal bar by PK, why can't he straighten it again?"

258

Meanwhile, the Amazing Randi, an American celebrity magician, claimed he can duplicate most of Geller's effects, but in 1991, Yuri countered by filing a $15 million lawsuit against Randi for defamation of character.

Colin Wilson, the famous writer on the paranormal, is convinced that Geller is genuine, but only to an extent. "After a great deal of thought, I am still inclined to believe that Geller is an unconscious 'medium,' and that he simply produces more-or-less controlled 'poltergeist effects.'"

10. Assembly Language Problem

Myth! A worshipper who "speaks in tongues" conveys a message.

In an intensely religious moment, a worshipper enters into a trance and suddenly starts "speaking in tongues." If the language is real but unrecognized, it is called xenolalia; otherwise, it is glossolalia, meaning that the "tongue," lacking in vocabulary and syntax, is a language-type rather than a language. The occurrence is common during the rites of the Pentecostal church, which officially sanctions the phenomenon on the basis of a New Testament incident. According to *Acts* 2, the disciples were in a temple in Jerusalem celebrating the Feast of the Pentecost when, elated at the news that Christ had risen, they began shouting aloud their praise of God in all the languages of the visiting worshippers.

However, investigators have noted that since the advent of tape recorders, every single case thought to be xenolalia is actually glossolalia. Nonetheless, while the recorded information is total gibberish, no fraud is evident among the faithful, and the practice seems to be a genuine form of worship. "It uplifts the congregation and gives the speaker a sense of euphoric psychological release. But this form of communication by its very nature is emotional rather than educational, a sharing of mood rather than a conveying of information." What sometimes lends a dubious air to the proceedings is the presence in the congregation of at least one "interpreter of tongues," who speaks after the glossolalist and spontaneously gives the communication meaning. The translation into the vernacular may itself be sincere and

259

inspired, but there is almost no question that it is contrived.

Sports
&
Diversions

I

Sporting Lives

On Sports

"I get to play golf for a living. What more can you ask for—
getting paid for doing what you love."
•

Tiger Woods

1. I'd Rather have a Hole-in-two

Myth! The rarest shot in golf is a hole-in-one on a par four.

When it takes only one stroke to drive a golf ball from the tee and into the cup, it's called a hole-in-one. This 4,000-to-1 shot is honored in many record books as the rarest in the sport.

A hole-in-one is scored normally on a par-3 hole. When this happens, the shot may also be called an eagle because it scores two under par. On the other hand, a double eagle is a score of three under par, and exists almost wholly for par-5 holes. A three under par can be scored on a par-4 hole, but in that case it is actually a hole-in-one.

The double eagle, a 1.5 million to one shot, is definitely rarer than a hole-in-one, yet it is the latter that is honored. A hole-in-one can be made on a par-3 or par-4 hole (on a par-5 hole it becomes very theoretical), but the only chance that golfers have for a real double eagle is on par-5 holes, which are not too many on a regular course. Few people realize it is easier to make a par-4 hole-in-one than a par-5 double eagle because, in the former, the player hits the drive from a well-positioned tee. Guinness lists a number of par-4 holes-in-one but fails to mention double eagle achievements.

The only par-4 hole-in-one that got the better of a double eagle was the ace Norman Manley hit on September 2, 1964, on the 290-yard eighth tee at Del Valle Country Club in Saugus, California. Manley made the shot right after scoring a similar par-4 hole-in-one on the 330-yard seventh hole. There have been 16 recorded back-to-back aces, but Manley is the only one to do it on par-4s.

The odds of a golfer getting an ace in a professional tourney are 3,708 to 1, and those of four pros doing it in a 156-man field in one tourney are 332,000 to 1. The numbers in both cases are better than those of a golfer hitting a double eagle on an ordinary day. But the odds on a double eagle improve when ranged against the chances of four top pros acing it on the same day on the same hole. At the prestigious U.S. Open on June 16, 1989, four of the first 32 players to play the seventh hole hit aces with their seven irons. Doug Weaver, Mark Wiebe, Jerry Pate and Nick Price in that order made their holes-in-one within a span of less than two hours.

Experts say it's an 8,700,000-1 probability that won't happen again in 190 years.

Speaking of par, "up to par" means, in ordinary language, to operate or perform in accordance with the usual or ordinary standards—in other words, nothing special or outstanding. But in the rulebooks of golf, "par" is defined as the score that an expert golfer—not an average golfer—would be expected to make for a given hole. It means errorless play, without flukes, under ordinary weather conditions, and allowing for two strokes on the putting green. To be up to par as a golfer is to be considerably better than ordinary, although to be "above par" does not mean to be the best. The latter, yet another irony of the irons, applies the term to subnormal play, as opposed to "below par," which indicates excellent performance—quite the opposite of what it conveys in general lingo.

2. West to East to West

Myth! **Ping Pong is Chinese and Sudoku is Japanese.**

The popular table game played with paddles and a bouncy, little plastic ball is not called Ping Pong. The generic name of this game is table tennis. Ping Pong is a registered trademark used by a particular manufacturer of table tennis games. The name Ping Pong has become one of the many trademark names, such as Kleenex, that has slipped into the common language but is actually the trademark name of a specific product.

The Japanese and lately the Chinese have become dominant in table tennis, an Olympic sport since 1988, but neither played any major role in the origin and development of the game. The game originated in England as an after-dinner amusement for upper-class Victorians in the 1880s, using everyday objects as equipment, e.g., a line of books for the net, a rounded top of a champagne cork or knot of string as the ball, and a cigar box lid as the racket. The popularity of the game led manufacturers to improve the equipment and sell it commercially. The name "ping-pong", from the sound generated in play, was in wide use before English manufacturer J. Jaques & Son Ltd trademarked it in 1901, selling its rights later in the US to games manufacturing giant

264

Parker Brothers. According to Wikipedia, the defining moment for modern table tennis was in the 1950s, when the game changed dramatically with rackets that used a rubber sheet combined with an underlying sponge layer to deliver greater spin and speed. These were introduced to England by the sports goods manufacturers S.W. Hancock Ltd, and from there were picked up enthusiastically by the Japanese and later the Chinese.

Although its name Sudoku is Japanese—"su" means number and "doku" refers to the single place on the puzzle board that each number can fit into—its origins are actually European and American. According to game historians, the seed was first planted by the 18th century Swiss mathematician Leonhard Euler when he devised the concept of "Latin Squares," in which numbers in a grid appear only once, across and up and down. In the late 1970's, Howard Garnes, an American puzzle maker, produced 9 by 9 square grids following Euler's concept, and Dell Magazines, famous in the US for its puzzle books, began publishing these under the name Number Place. In the mid-1980s, Maki Kaji, president of the Japanese puzzle giant Nikoli, Inc., seeing a potential, urged his company to publish its own version of the puzzle. The Nikoli game became a huge hit in that country, but it was not until almost two decades later that *The Times* newspaper in London would take up an interest and come out with a daily puzzle. In the US, the *New York Post,* the *San Francisco Chronicle* and *USA Today* offered Sudoku puzzles to their readers by September 2005.

3. Missile on a String

Myth! **Philippine tribesmen invented the yoyo and used it as a weapon in early times.**

Legend has it that tribesmen in the Philippines invented the yo-yo and used it as a weapon as early as the 16th century, when Magellan discovered the country. The name itself sounds like a derivative from the word *tayoyo,* 'to spin', as appears in a dictionary of Filipino words first published in 1860. But experts deny this etymological claim, saying there is no such word as *tayoyo* in any Philippine dialect.

265

In fact, the only evidence of a Philippine connection for the toy is the oft-told story of how a Filipino immigrant named Pedro Flores, a sailor or busboy based in San Diego, was prevailed upon to transfer his rights to the gadget to Donald Duncan, future founder of the Duncan Yo-Yo Company. In the popular version, Duncan, after seeing Flores do tricks with the yoyo one day in the late 20s, bought the item for a few dollars from the Filipino and had it registered with the patent office. In the Duncan Company's official version, Flores himself had commercialized his invention, opening the Flores Yo-Yo Manufacturing Company in Santa Barbara, California, and by November of 1929, was operating two additional factories in Los Angeles and Hollywood, altogether producing 300,000 units daily. Duncan, recognizing the potential of the toy, purchased Flores' rights and transferred them to his new company in 1932 for an amount of more than $250,000, a fortune by depression era standards.

Flores' involvement with the genesis of the yoyo conflicts with the claim that the toy was introduced to the US in 1929 by Louis Marx, the big toymaker (1919-1978) that sold millions of its version in competition with Duncan. One may note, however, that neither Duncan nor Marx is totally inconsistent with the report that the yoyo as a concept came to America much earlier than in the 20s. Records show that the first US patent on the toy was issued to James L. Haven and Charles Hettrich in 1866 (U.S. Patent 59,745) under the name Whirligig. Flores made at least two significant contributions: one is the name Yo-Yo, which he successfully trademarked, and the other is the round shape, which was presumably patentable because it was different from the Haven-Hettrich design of two spokes joined together by an axle. These inputs seemed good enough for Duncan, who thereafter manufactured approximately eighty-five percent of all yoyos in the United States from the 1930s to the 1960s.

The yoyo has been a traditional toy of young Filipinos in Philippine barrios, and could have come down from the mountains in previous centuries or else introduced by American occupiers of the Islands in the early 1900s. Panati and others say that long before this—about 1000 BC—similar toys originated in China, the most basic of which consisted of two disks sculpted from ivory, with a silk cord wound around their connecting central peg. They eventually spread to Europe, particularly France ('bandalore') and England ('quiz'), were they were richly decorated with jewels and painted geometrical patterns to become collectible gewgaws. Thus, it may have been Chinese traders, predating the Spaniards' discovery of the Philippines, who brought the toy to the country for the first time.

The yoyo has been shown in films (e.g., the 1983 *Octopussy*) as a lethal object, which is released on a string as it is flung at a target. After inflicting its harm, the object is retracted by the action of the same string spinning around its spindle, ready to be used again. But MythBusters, the popular science television program, says it is physically unlikely that the toy has ever been used in this manner or generally as a weapon anywhere in the world. Their experiments showed that by the time the object reached the end of the string, it would not have enough momentum to do much damage, and once it struck something, it would be nearly impossible to retract. The consensus of debunkers is that the story was likely an invention of the Duncan Toy Company in the 1930s to give the yoyo a 'spin' and help promote its sale.

4. Court Jesters weave Black Magic

Myth! **New York City is the hometown of the Harlem Globetrotters.**

A style that mixes clever maneuvers with comical stunts has merited for the Harlem Globetrotters their title as the clown princes of basketball. Half of the team's name suggests a home court in a predominantly black American neighborhood, while the other half indicates a penchant for playing wherever the game attracts people.

In fact, the Globetrotters did not start in Harlem, nor were any of the team's original players from New York. Abe Saperstein founded the club in 1927 in his hometown of Chicago, where it began playing in the Savoy Ballroom until its home court was converted into a skating rink. Saperstein's team later went on the road but never played regularly in New York or any other city.

Saperstein decided to call his players the Harlem Globetrotters, Harlem "to let people know that they were black," and Globetrotters "so people would think they had been around." However, he never had any intention of establishing his

267

headquarters in the predominantly black-populated section of New York City. The team made its first appearance in Harlem only in 1969, after some 9,500 games and 42 years, and three years after Saperstein died. To date, this professional team without a home is probably the most traveled basketball group in the whole world. Ironically, while 'Globetrotters' connotes international itinerancy, it took the team 23 years after inception to live up to its name and play its first game outside the US.

At first, the Globetrotters played serious basketball, but soon they became so good they couldn't find worthy opponents. Saperstein decided he could level the field by directing his boys' special skills to a clowning style of play. This modus operandi has proved to be the Globetrotters' ticket to worldwide fame. Formed to play their foil are ragtag teams of professionals who travel with and lose to the Globetrotters in madcap exhibition games held in the US and selected places around the world. Once in a blue moon, the Globetrotters lose, too, as in a game played one night in Martin, Tennessee, against the New Jersey Reds. According to a sports bulletin: "While the Trotters go through their clowning routines, the Reds keep shooting a terrific percentage. With less than a minute left, New Jersey takes a 100-99 lead. The suddenly dead-serious Trotters have their chances but can't get a shot to fall. The upset ends a string of 2,495 consecutive Trotters wins dating back to April 1962. Included in the streak was the 1963-64 season, in which New Jersey lost 420 straight! It was the Reds' first victory in nearly 9 years."

---

5. Much Hoopla for a Dribble?

Myth! Basketball originated in the U.S.

One claim for basketball is a patriotic one—it is the only major sport played in the US that is totally American in origin. Every other sport, including baseball, the country's national pastime, was developed or copied from a game played in another country.

But basketball would be totally American in origin only if 'American' were to mean North American and not just the US. The ancient game was played in Mexico by the 16th century Aztecs, with the team that first shoots a rubber ball though a stone

268

ring on a wall winning all of the audience's clothes, and the losing team's captain getting beheaded. A Canadian named James Naismith, a gym teacher at the YMCA Training School, now Springfield College, invented the modern equivalent in 1891 in Springfield, Massachusetts. Naismith responded to his students' complaints about the boring gymnasium classes, which consisted of marching and calisthenics. After some trial and error, he devised a game with two closed-bottomed peach baskets, a soccer ball, and two 9-men teams. Dr. Naismith called it "indoor rugby" until one of the players renamed it basketball, because of the peach basket that the game used for a goal.

Naismith hurriedly printed rules in the campus newspaper, but it was only in 1893 that closed-bottom nets were used instead of baskets. Surprisingly, it was nineteen years later, or in 1912, that someone suggested using bottomless nets to increase the pace of the game.

---

6. Some don't Finish at all

Myth! American football contributed the line, "Winning isn't everything, it's the only thing."

Sometimes, losing is such sweet sorrow that the loser can't help but talk. At other times, it's winner tells all. In any case, please note that the well-said quotes on the twin arts of winning and losing are mostly from winners.

"Winning isn't everything....it's the only thing," is often attributed to Vince Lombardi, a former member and coach of the Green Bay Packers football team. Actually, it was General Douglas MacArthur, the big loser in the Pacific War, who said it. Lombardi's version was: "Winning isn't everything, but wanting to win is." The first time he said it in print was, "Winning is not the most important thing, it's everything."

"Show me a good loser and I'll show you a loser," doesn't sound like a sporting proposition. It isn't, because it's really a winning proposition that's part of a pep talk to inspire faltering players to go out and fight. Rockne supposedly said it to the Wisconsin basketball coach Walter Meanwell. But he was misheard. What Rockne really said was, "Show me a good and

269

gracious loser and I'll show you a failure."

In a more famous situation, Notre Dame Coach Rockne is asked from the deathbed of a young football player named George Gipp to "tell the boys to win one for the Gipper." Actually, Gipp's words were quoted by Rockne in a pep talk to his boys as they were about to play Army in 1928, and these were, "Rock, some day when things look real tough for Notre Dame, ask the boys to go out there and win one for me." The locker room and deathbed episodes are dramatized in the movie *Knute Rockne—All-American* (1940), in which Ronald Reagan is Gipp and Pat O'Brien is Rockne. Strangely, both scenes were long excised from the film and would only be restored when President Reagan became obsessed with the catchphrase "Win one for the Gipper." The restoration, however, did not sufficiently affirm the historical authenticity of the Rockne-Gipp conversation, which remains in doubt.

Bartlett credits Leo "the Lip" Durocher, the feisty and outspoken manager of the old Brooklyn Dodgers baseball team in the late forties, with the famous line, "Nice guys finish last." But according to Keyes, he didn't say it this way. It was July 5, 1946, and he was criticizing the New York Giants for being in seventh place at the season's midpoint while his own Dodgers team was in first in the National League. In response to a radio announcer who had asked why he couldn't be a nice guy for a change, he pointed to the Giants dugout and contemptuously said, "The nice guys are all over there. In seventh place." "For years Durocher protested to no avail that he hadn't said 'Nice guys finish last.' But his actual words...didn't have much snap. Journalists routinely ignored his protests. Eventually Durocher stopped trying to correct the record." It is not at all ironic that, by the middle of 1948, the Giants' owners fired Ott, replacing him with Durocher, who'd gotten axed in Brooklyn. Under the latter's stewardship, the Giants won two pennants and the World Series over the next eight years and never finished lower than fifth. Incidentally, Durocher's supporters claim that Rockne's famous comment about losers actually came from the Lip. He had supposedly said, "Show me a good loser in professional sports and I'll show you an idiot. Show me a sportsman and I'll show you a player I'm looking to trade."

7. Par Excellence

Myth! The Scots invented the game of golf.

The Apple Tree Gang, a group of Scots led by John G. Reid, introduced golf to America in 1888. What this means is that golf was already a sophisticate's game in Scotland before finding its way into the US. But the game apparently did not originate in Scotland. It may well have started in Holland, from where Scotland used to import her golf balls. There was an ancient and similar Dutch game called *kolven* or *kolfen*, which used a club called *kolf*, but it was played on ice. The early Flemish also played *chole*, a cross-country game in which the clubs resembled the modern version. In neither of these games, however, does the player sink balls into a hole.

It has been suggested that the Romans, who occupied Britain until A.D. 410, brought the game with them. Or else Roman soldiers, having nothing better to do, invented the game by hitting a stone over a distance with a stick or shepherd's crook in the least number of stripes. It soon developed into *paganica*, "the country game," this time played with a leather ball stuffed with feathers and a bent stick. It is said that, of all these fledgling games, it was the Scottish variant, developed into a national passion by the fifteenth century, that comes closest to the real thing.

Speaking of origins, the one of Tiger Woods, supposedly the first Afro-American and the youngest person to win the prestigious US Masters golf championship in Augusta, Georgia, is not quite true. Tiger is a real name and not some PR moniker aimed at creating a more colorful personality. It's not a combination of Thai and Nigger, as some have claimed. And Tiger is not African-American in the strictest sense, nor is he half black and half Thai, as popularly believed. His father, Earl Woods, a retired Green Beret lieutenant colonel, met his mother Kutilda in Bangkok during the Vietnam War. But Tiger is one-fourth Thai, one-fourth Chinese, one-fourth Caucasian, one-eighth American Indian and one-eighth African-American. Of the five races or nationalities he represents, the least is black.

271

8. Tenez L'oeuf, Anyone?

Myth! Tennis originated in England.

Modern tennis traces its ancestry to lawn tennis, which was invented in England in 1873. It all came about when Major Walter Clopton Wingfield, a British army officer, decided to combine the principles of court tennis, squash racquet, and badminton into one sport.

However, the real source of tennis, not to mention its name, has for some time been a matter of conjecture. There seems to be some consensus that tennis long preceded the English form. The view that once prevailed gave tennis a medieval French origin, asserting that its name came from *tenez*, the imperative of the French *tenir*, to hold. "*Tenez!*" was a cry supposedly used by French players when ready to serve, but there is no real evidence of this. The French connection was junked when experts deduced the game is much too old to have been known by a French name. Besides, what the French called the game in the 15th century, as they do now, is *la paume*, which is far detached from any form of *tenir*.

Another theory points to a fine fabric called *tissus de tinnis*, which was manufactured at Tinnis, an island at the Nile Delta. After becoming famous for this product, and also as a health resort, Tinnis sank into the sea sometime about the eleventh century. Because early tennis balls were often made of rolled fabrics, the island is said to have given the name to the game. However, whether or not tennis started in Egypt is another matter.

It seems one Lady Wentworth made a breakthrough when she claimed to have found the origin of tennis in the Arabic word *tanaz*, meaning to leap. The lady noted further Arabic variants, all with a tennis flavor, in *tenziz*, to strive against one for superiority or glory; *t'nazza*, to twang string; and *t'nazzi*, to make a thing bound. *Tenetz*, the earliest use of the word in English (about the year 1400), approximated the sound of the Arabic words. There are other tennis terms with an Arab background. Racquet, for instance, is from *ruqat* or *raqat*, a patch of cloth tied around the palm of the hand, the earliest form of the racquet. Sports historians say these and other proofs show that the game had its origins in ancient Egyptian-Arabic religious rites.

272

The idea that tennis first became popular in France lays the predicate for the claim that the zero score, 'love', came from the French *l'oeuf*, or 'the egg'. A zero looks like an egg, and is called a goose egg in many places in Europe. Nonetheless, Hugh Rawson (*Devious Derivations*, 1994) believes the French derivation is false. "More likely," Rawson says, "the love that amounts to nothing is a spin-off of a seventeenth-century expression, to play for love, to play without stakes; that is, for nothing." He thinks the phrase probably evolved from 'for love or money', which dates to before AD 1000, and is related to the biblical expression "labor of love." In all instances, "the love amounts to nothing, or zero, just as it does in tennis scoring today."

9. Golfing at their Peak

Myth! A golf ball played on a mountaintop in Argentina set the altitude record for that kind of activity.

According to Guinness, as of 1990, playing a ball off a mountain 22,834 feet high sets the record for this kind of activity. Dr. G. S. Williams, Jr. of Daytona Beach, Florida, is the golfer, and Mt. Aconcagua, Argentina, is the mountain peak. The date was January 22, 1989. However, because Williams' accomplishment does not involve a contest, Guinness has since discontinued the category.

Guinness seems to have forgotten an exceedingly greater feat accomplished in this genre that is doubly impressive because it happened almost 20 years earlier. Alan B. Shepard is only the fifth man to walk on the moon, but on that same stirring occasion on Feb 6, 1971, he became the first to tee off it. In an attempt to show how weak the gravitational pull is on that heavenly body (about 16% of the Earth's), the Apollo 14 commander hit a 6-iron shot while standing on the lunar surface. He actually hit 2 balls, shanking the second into a crater approximately 40 yards away. But Shepard claims the first ball traveled miles and miles. A sports writer says a more accurate estimate is probably several hundred yards. The same writer notes that, to this day, neither Shepard nor NASA will reveal the brand name of the golf ball used, obviously to prevent the manufacturer from using the stunt to promote its

273

product.

In any case, the true record by Alan Shepard, Jr., set at an altitude equal to the distance between the earth and the moon, cannot be exceeded or even duplicated until another astronaut with a golf club is sent to the moon.

10. When They were Kings

Myth! **Muhammad Ali is the greatest heavyweight boxer of all time.**

Most boxing aficionados would lay their bets on Muhammad Ali in a hypothetical fight against any pro living or dead. Some might go even further and agree with the British Sports Council that Ali was the greatest athlete of the twentieth century. After all, though he never said he was the smartest, he did say he was the greatest.

Ali may well be the greatest athlete, but many are not prepared to accept him as the greatest heavyweight boxer who ever lived. He lost his crown twice, first to Joe Frazier and then to Leon Spinks. He also lost to Rocky Marciano in a computer-simulated heavyweight fight enacted in the ring by the two. In 1969, the Miami promoter Murry Woroner convinced Ali and Marciano to act out the bout for the TV camera, based on a computer-written script, to show the world who might win a Super Fight between two living undefeated champions. The fight was televised in January 1970, with an estimated million fans paying $5 each for the privilege of watching it in America, and some 15 million more in England, Australia and Mexico.

Rocky Marciano was at least smarter than Ali because he knew when to retire from the game. The Brockton Bomber holds the distinction of being undefeated during his entire career despite suffering an actual knockout once by an opponent. The knockout was for a short but dramatic six seconds in the first round of his fight against Jersey Joe Walcott. He went on to win the bout and the heavyweight championship by knocking out Walcott in the thirteenth round. He successfully defended his title six times and, after whipping 49 boxers consecutively, forty-three by knockout, 26 in three rounds or less, he retired at the age of 32. He remains

274

the only undefeated heavyweight champ with a perfect record—no losses and no draws.

The Brown Bomber Joe Louis, who should have been the smartest, also retired undefeated as heavyweight champion in 1949 after defending his title 19 more times than Marciano did. He had the best record for a heavyweight, winning 68 of his 71 professional bouts, all except four by knockouts. Unfortunately, Louis went broke and tried to make a comeback, losing two fights in the process. One of them was in 1951 against Marciano, who wept after knocking out his boyhood hero.

Marciano was undefeated during his entire professional career, while Louis was an undefeated heavyweight at the time of his first retirement. The third undefeated heavyweight champion was Gene Tunney, who outfoxed the great Jack Dempsey twice. Tunney could not share Marciano's distinction because he had suffered a defeat when he was a light heavyweight. Many sports writers claim Tunney didn't have a clean record as a heavyweight either. He would have been knocked out in his second bout with Dempsey in 1927 had he not been saved by what is now known in ring annals as "the long count."

11. Climb every Mountain

Myth! Edmund Hillary set the record for the highest distance climbed.

Sir Edmund Hillary and Tenzing Norkay hold the record for the highest distance climbed. The feat was performed on the snow-covered slopes of Mt. Everest on May 29, 1953. Conventional wisdom dictates that this record can only be equaled and never broken.

Because of Hillary and Norkay's feat, it is believed those nurturing an ambition to conquer Everest can only aspire to establish new records in subcategories. Thus, Japan's Junko Tabei did not quite share in the glory when she became the first woman to climb the famous peak on May 16, 1975. What she did not know is that she actually did more than equal the Hillary-Norkay record, she broke it in much the same way that later successful climbers would break hers. This oddity results from the fact that

275

Everest is an ever-growing mountain, proof of which is that it has already grown a few feet since the previous century. In the original Indian survey of 1852, the pundits took measurements in six places—from 28,990 to 29,026 feet—and derived an average figure of 29,000 feet. Worried that the public would consider this a mere round-number estimate, they falsely reported the height as 29,002 feet. An Indian team of surveyors established Everest's height in 1954 at 29,028 ft., or 2 feet higher than its highest measurement in 1852. Snow shift on the top also constantly changes the figure.

In other words, Hillary and Norkay were the first successful climbers of Mt. Everest, but they cannot now be regarded as the climbers of the longest distance. The famous mountain already grew a few millimeters when Austrians Reinhold Messner and Peter Habeler mastered it in 1978. In the process, the couple established a new and rigorous standard by disdaining the use of supplemental oxygen, which is often necessary for the energy, health, and thinking skills of the climbers because of the thin air at Everest's high altitude. In 1991 Sherpas, who had carried the supplies for so many foreigners up Mount Everest, completed their own successful expedition to the summit. By the mid-1990s, 4000 people had attempted to climb Everest—660 successfully reached the summit while more than 140 died trying.

Incidentally, Hillary was not the leader of the expedition and regarded his accomplishment as a mere stroke of luck. He and Norkay were in a group of six climbers who followed the orders of John Hunt. Camping at 1,650 feet short of the pinnacle, Hunt dispatched two climbers to make the final, perilous journey to the top of Everest. But they quickly returned, unsuccessful and covered in ice. When the weather took a turn for the better, Hunt selected Hillary and Norkay to attempt the climb, and would have sent a third two-man team, including himself, had the Englishman and the Nepalese failed.

12. Ali Oops

Myth! "I am the greatest" and "Float like a butter-fly, sting like a bee," are original Muhammad Ali witticisms.

276

Most everyone is familiar with the phrase, "I am the greatest," the flamboyant boast of Muhammad Ali who first became World Heavyweight boxing champion in 1964. The shibboleth has become so attached to him that it even became the title of his 1977 film bio "The Greatest" starring himself. Ali admitted that he copied the slogan from a blonde longhaired, caped Las Vegas wrestler named Gorgeous George, who was preoccupied more with primping up than wrestling. This was an outright rejection of Ali biographer Thomas Hauser's claim that Ali was already using the words long before he met George. Wilfred Sheed, another biographer, speculates that the boast might have come from Ali's father.

Ali used to taunt his boxing opponents with the phrase, "Float like a butterfly, sting like a bee," and most of the time he was true to his word. But, despite his knack for colorful language, he did not devise this phrase either. It was his aide, Drew 'Bundini' Brown, who did.

As his reason for refusing induction into the Army, Ali was reported to have said, "No Viet Cong ever called me nigger." In other words, he had no quarrel with the North Vietnamese rebels as much as he had with American racists. This turns out to be wishful thinking for the liberals, who would have wanted a super celebrity like Ali to mouth what was essentially a civil rights sentiment. But Keyes quashes the thought, citing biographer Hauser, who insists he never heard Ali say it. "He would attack racism. But he wouldn't personalize it." Nobody knows where the statement came from, although it became popular in the sixties.

II

Oft-Told Baseball Tales

On America's National Pastime

"Baseball was, is and always will be to me
the best game in the world."

•

Babe Ruth

1. The Diamond Was Rounder then

Myth! Abner Doubleday invented baseball.

Organizers established the Baseball Hall of Fame in the small attractive village of Cooperstown, New York, in 1939, believing that popular Union general, sportsman and writer Abner Doubleday played the first game there according to rules he had formulated. The Special Baseball Commission of 1906-07, formed by Sporting goods magnate A.G. Spalding to inquire into the origins of baseball, had reported in the official 1908 Baseball Guide that Doubleday was the inventor of baseball and had overseen the game played in Cooperstown in 1839.

Though this was most comforting to American sportsmen, who had been disappointed to learn that the first baseball game telecast was in Tokyo and not the US, they were disappointed anew when, thirty years later, historian Robert W. Henderson from the New York Public Library debunked the Spalding claim. Henderson found that Doubleday never played a game of baseball in his life, or even watched one, or mentioned the game in his extensive writings; it seems he was not even in Cooperstown in 1839. Henderson's research confirmed that baseball used to be the British game of rounders, which originated in England and was described in *The Boy's Own Book*, first published in London in 1828. Even the word 'baseball' was not a Doubleday original, for it had appeared as early as 1798 in Jane Austen's novel *Northanger Abbey*. The only 'firsts' Doubleday achieved in his life were not in sports: he was the Civil War hero who fired the first shot at the Confederates from Fort Sumter, and the first to obtain a charter for a San Francisco cable car.

In lieu of Doubleday, the name that should have been placed in the Baseball Hall of Fame belongs to Alexander J. Cartwright, a New York City bank clerk. Actual documents show it was this unassuming sports visionary who Americanized the British game of rounders by drafting rule modifications and diagrams in 1845 and developing what would essentially become the game of baseball. Although Cartwright did not invent the sport, he formalized and structured the commonly played rounders-like game and helped establish most of its finer points through the Knickerbocker Base Ball Club. The earliest baseball game recorded was the one Cartwright organized between the New York Club and the Knickerbockers on June 19, 1846, at Elysian Fields in Hoboken, New Jersey. New York won 23-1 in four innings.

2. Once they were Giants

Myth! **Babe Ruth was the best New York Yankee player at his peak.**

Going by career achievements, Ruth is considered the best player of all time. He played at near-peak level longer than anybody else did.

In the Yankee team, Ruth is still better than Maris despite Maris' greater harvest of home runs at their respective peaks. Ruth hit a home run in every 2.5667 games and Maris in every 2.6558. In 1961, according to analysts, Maris had more opportunity than was normal to hit home runs because he was never intentionally walked. Mickey Mantle, batting behind Maris and hitting his own share of homeruns, effectively gave notice to his opponents that they could not afford to put any man on base before pitching to him. Apparently this is the same reason Maris remains the only man to hit more than 50 in one year and yet fail to attain .300 for the season, completing his campaign at a dismal .269.

There is an equally cogent argument favoring Babe Ruth over Mantle: the larger ballpark and the "deader" ball used by Ruth made it harder to hit a home run than in Mantle's time. Unfortunately for Babe's fans, the latest finding is that the ball was actually livelier in Ruth's day than it is today. According to Joe Reichler, baseball historian and member of the commissioner's staff, the Ruth years weren't called the 'live-ball era' for nothing. Reichler also maintains, along with other experts, that modern baseball parks are much larger than they were during Ruth's golden days. It has been noted that Ruth played nearly half his games at Yankee Stadium, where the distance down the right field line was only 296 feet.

The bottom line is that Ruth may have been the best of all time, but he was not the best at his peak. In this latter category, he was only second to Mickey Mantle, based on the statistics of their games and the size and skills of the athletes that played with or

280

against them in their respective milieus. Mantle was at his peak in the 1957 season, when he was slightly ahead of both Ruth and Ted Williams in hitting power and of Ruth in defense.

---

3. Trying to Make a Point

Myth! Babe Ruth called his plays at will on at least two occasions.

Babe Ruth is often mentioned as having displayed on at least two occasions an almost superhuman ability to smash home runs at will. The first of his 'calling feats' has been depicted in a popular Hollywood movie, while the second was voted by a respected poll in 1950 as one of the ten most dramatic sports events in the first half of the 20th century.

Ruth first ventured into superhero territory when he visited eleven-year-old Johnny Sylvester on learning that the boy was dying from a forehead infection caused by a horse's kick. Johnny made Ruth promise to knock not one but three homers in game four of the 1926 World Series between the Yankees and the Cardinals. That Wednesday in the designated game, the Babe fulfilled his promise by clouting exactly three home runs.

As it turns out, Ruth's visit with Johnny and his celebrated promise never happened. Upon word reaching the Yankees that Johnny wanted an autographed baseball from the great Bambino, the team sent well before game four two balls signed by their players and those of the St. Louis Cardinals, plus a get-well message from Ruth. A well-publicized visit Ruth made to the youngster in New Jersey after the Series was apparently just part of the usual gig to promote the national pastime. Johnny was not really dying, and he not only recovered but also lived into 1990. He graduated from Princeton University, served in the US Navy during World War 2, and after his discharge assumed the presidency of a packing-machinery company.

The second of Ruth's 'feats' happened in the third game of the 1932 World Series between the Yankees and the Chicago Cubs. According to the legend, Ruth did more than call the home run; he actually pointed to the spot where he intended the ball to land. It was 0-1 when Ruth stepped out of the box, gestured toward right-

281

center field, then blasted Charlie Root's pitch into the right-field seats. Some sports historians, knowing better, could only say in disbelief that baseball players make a lot of gestures with no intended meanings, and that day Ruth probably made one that he was not even aware of. In his postmortem of the event, Brandon Toropov (*50 Biggest Baseball Myths*, 1997) writes: "Most national papers did not report anything otherworldly about the home run besides its staggering distance. The exact means by which the 'shot' was 'called' often depends on who's telling the story.... Finally—and this is the clincher—Ruth did not claim credit for the 'called shot' until well after it had become established as a national myth." Despite negative comments over the years following the 1932 Series, the incident was given its dubious distinction by a 1950 Associated Press poll of leading US sports editors.

The Pride of the Yankees, a 1942 Gary Cooper film about baseball, combines in some scenes elements from two separate World Series showdowns. This American classic portrays Babe Ruth and Lou Gehrig as promising a sick young boy in his room in St. Louis that they will both hit homers for him. Babe proceeds to hit one homer and Lou two. In real life, Lou hit two homers in one of the 1928 World Series games in St. Louis, while Ruth hit not one but three home runs in game four of the 1926 Series against the Cardinals. The visit with the sick boy draws from the false encounter between Ruth and little Johnny preceding this last game.

---

4. Call me Babe, not Tootsie

Myth! The Baby Ruth candy bar was named for Babe Ruth.

Among Ruth's fabulous nicknames were the Caliph of Clout, the Wazir of Wham, the Rajah of Rap and the Wali of Wallop, but the most endearing, and enduring, was the Sultan of Swat. It was mainly an admiring media that gave the soubriquets to the great Bambino soon after he joined the New York Yankees in 1920 as a slugging outfielder. At the time, New Yorkers (including the New York Times) had seemingly acquired a fascination for Middle Eastern titles in the wake of O. Henry's christening of New York as Bagdad-on-the-Subway in his stories. The term 'Swat' may have been used figuratively for the way Babe swatted the ball, but in fact, the alliterative nickname was borrowed from a historical and literary source. There was a real state of Swat, a federal division of Pakistan, and a real Sultan (or Akhoond) who governed it. Although the state was dissolved in 1969, Swat remains a valley and a district in Pakistan's North-West Frontier Province (NWFP), with the capital at Saidu Sharif. An item published in 1878 in the London Times announcing the death of the Sultan prompted Edward Lear to write a comic verse about him and his exotic realm.

Babe Ruth, who was raised in an orphanage, was beset by rumors about his real name, none of which was true. It was claimed, for one, that his first name wasn't really George Herman but Gerhardt or Ehrhardt, suggesting some German antecedent. Certain officials of the International League alleged that his first pro baseball contract, signed with that league, bore the signature of George H. Ehrhardt.

The most amusing of the speculations about Babe Ruth's name has to do with its similarity to the Baby Ruth candy bar. Both Babe and the Baby came on the American scene at the beginning of the decade of the '20s, and despite disclaimers from all sides, the two names have since been linked together in the public mind. The association has remained so strong that, even today, people say the candy bar's name would be 'Babe Ruth' were it not for legal complications that made it impossible to call the candy by Ruth's exact name.

Originally called Kandy Kake, the candy bar was renamed in the 1920s supposedly to honor a girl named Ruth. There has been some doubt from the start as to who Ruth really was, although Otto Schnering, inventor of the confection, identified her with confidence as President Cleveland's first daughter, who was born in the White House. The press had began calling the infant Baby Ruth shortly after her birth, and thirty years later, according to Schnering, the Curtiss Candy Company, realizing the name was still popular with the American people, decided to use it to boost the market for their product.

Like many other writers, the columnist L. M. Boyd refused to buy the Schnering claim, noting that 'Baby Ruth' Cleveland died of diphtheria in 1904 and had already been gone for over fifteen years when the candy bar was invented. For Boyd, the more qualified candidate was the granddaughter of George Williamson,

283

who "developed the bar in honor of his own favorite baby, then marketed it through the Williamson Candy Company of which he was president." As expected, the issue came full circle as soon as it was revealed that "the Williamson Candy Company, producer of the 'Oh! Henry' bar, was a direct competitor of Curtiss' and would have been most unlikely to supply a product name and formula to a rival. Furthermore, the Curtiss Candy Company has never claimed this as an origin of their candy bar's name."

Babe introduced his own namesake candy bar through one of Curtiss' competitors, but Curtiss ended the venture by bringing suit against the 'Babe Ruth Home Run Bar' in 1930. Curtiss prosecuted the case successfully by first reiterating that Ruth Cleveland was the model for their brand, and then arguing that, although Babe Ruth was using his own name for his product, it still violated the 'similarity of name' rule established under the fair trade law. In subsequent years, Curtiss would be caught making two apparently false allegations in public regarding this matter, *viz.*, (1) Babe Ruth was not yet famous at the time the candy bar debuted in 1921 (when in fact he already was); and (2), Ruth Cleveland once visited the company's premises in the early 1920's (when the truth is she had been dead since 1904). Analysts say that, nonetheless, these 'lies' don't necessarily prove the Babe Ruth connection is true, and that Curtiss' 'deduced' intent, however logical, cannot be made to prevail against its 'legal' intent, which was expressed in the court decision that had earlier struck down Babe Ruth's bid for a share of the Curtiss market.

---

5. The 60ᵗʰ Parallel

5. The 60th Parallel

Myth! Babe Ruth's 60 home run total in 1927 is the official record for a 154-game season.

People continue to entertain the thought that there are two world home run records established separately by two baseball players, the first being the 60 that the great Babe Ruth hit in a 154-game season in 1927, and the second the 61 the almost forgotten Roger Maris socked in a 162-game season in 1961. The idea of co-existing home run records in the major leagues was first planted in the minds of the public by an announcement from baseball

284

commissioner Ford Frick during the 1961 season, that unless Ruth's record was broken in the first 154 games, it would remain on the books even if a new record was eventually set for 162 games in one season. Later, an urban legend probably invented by New York sportswriter Dick Young claimed that the baseball authorities affixed an asterisk to Roger Maris' home run record to distinguish it from Babe Ruth's, a practice that supposedly continued during the next three decades. It seems Frick made the ruling because of his closeness to Ruth and his (and the media's) bias against Maris as an effective hitter.

Maris failed to break 60 in 154 games (he was still two runs shy of 60 at that point), but hit 61 on October 1, 1961, the highest in the newly established 162-game season for the American League. Contrary to the common belief, no asterisk was ever used in any official record books—"Major League baseball itself had no such book"—and Frick later acknowledged that there never was any official qualification in this or any other manner for Maris' accomplishment. The October 1 homer officially ended Ruth's reign as the homerun king for one season and deprived the St. Louis Cardinals' Mark McGwire of a future honor, that of succeeding to the title when he exceeded the Babe's output in just 144 games in 1998. Significantly, the National League was still on a 154-game schedule when it recognized Maris' feat in 1961, a telling confirmation that the only official home run record currently in effect is the one set initially by Maris (but later surpassed by Mark McGuire with 70 in 1998, and more recently by the San Francisco Giants' Barry Bonds with 73 in 2001).

6. Of Shoes and Socks and Cabbages

Myth! A young baseball fan confronted 'Shoeless' Joe Jackson with the words, "Say it ain't so, Joe", after the player was accused of throwing a World Series game.

In the year 1920, baseball was at fever pitch especially on the American continent. It was a time when street urchins in major US cities like Chicago would mooch coins from passers-by to buy into bleacher seats at the local baseball stadium. While in Japan, the game's birthplace in Asia, the craving for American baseball cards

285

would augur today's craze for manga trading cards among the world's youth.

Enter 'Shoeless' Joe Jackson, an illiterate Southerner playing for the Chicago White Sox and the most versatile and arguably the best baseball player of his day (he has the third highest lifetime batting average ever and is one of only seven Major League Baseball players to ever top a .400 batting average for one season). 'Shoeless' was just coming out of the Cook County (Illinois) courthouse when "one little urchin in the crowd grabbed him by the coat sleeve and said, 'Say it ain't so, Joe'." The baseball icon had just been indicted before the grand jury with seven other teammates for throwing the 1919 World Series in favor of the Cincinnati Redlegs. The White Sox lost that series despite the fact that, having just become world champions two years earlier, they had been slated to win again on the talents of Joe and a powerhouse team.

Presumably the first to report about Joe's encounter with the urchin, sportswriter Hugh Fullerton has been credited with the ensuing conversation between the two that began with, "It ain't so, Joe, is it?" In its issue of September 29, 1920, the Chicago Herald came out with the slightly transposed "It ain't so, is it Joe?" Other phrases with essentially the same message joined the competition, with all catching the public fancy despite their nuanced differences. However, it would take 20 long years—in a 1940 history of the Associated Press, to be exact—for the phrase to metamorphose historically into the currently popular "Say it ain't so, Joe." Incidentally, the common claim for all printed versions is that one or more news reporters (most of whom have remained anonymous) were at the scene and heard the youngster's plea.

In the same versions, an anguished Joe is described as having given the penitent reply, "Yes, kid, I'm afraid it is," with a few omitting the kid's closing remark, "Well, I'd never have thought it." This apparent self-incrimination is altogether denied in the John Sayles film *Eight Men Out* (1988), where our hero, upon hearing the words "Say it ain't so, Joe," looks nonplussed and says nothing. By this token, Hollywood evidently agrees with Joe's official position on the matter, as reported in 'This Is The Truth', Sports Magazine, October 1948, which Joe explained, thus: "I guess the biggest joke of all was that story that got out about 'Say it ain't so, Joe'. Charley Owens of the Chicago Daily News was responsible for that, but there wasn't a bit of truth in it. It was supposed to have happened the day I was arrested in September of 1920, when I came out of the courtroom...It just didn't happen, that's all. Charley Owens just made up a good story and wrote it. Oh, I would have said it ain't so, all right, just like I'm saying it now." But "Say it ain't so, Joe" has persisted to this day as the signature line of a fallen sports idol.

7. The Play's the Thing

Myth! 'Shoeless' Joe admitted his guilt to the authorities after his indictment by a grand jury.

As his own wife attested, Joe denied any complicity in the Black Sox affair till his dying day. Joe was allegedly tricked into making a formal confession to the authorities, but this was never presented to the grand jury as part of the evidence. Most sports historians today regard Joe's involvement in the conspiracy as the least plausible, stating that for the World Series in question, Joe's batting average was .375, his fielding percentage was perfect, and he hit the ball a record 42 times, not to mention the only home run, during the nine games played. "Those aren't the stats of someone throwing a World Series," said Senator Tom Harkin.

It is not true that 'Shoeless' Joe was convicted, and that this caused his lifetime ban from playing baseball. Joe was acquitted in a full-fledged trial of the case to the accompaniment of cheers ("The White Sox are clean!") that reverberated nation-wide. But, seemingly influenced by the owners of the major league clubs, the recently appointed baseball commissioner, a former judge known for his racist leanings and Bible Belt moral scruples, made a turn-around by banning Joe and the rest of the Black Sox from playing baseball for life. The punishment has seemed unusually harsh and cruel, particularly in the case of Joe as the least suspected, considering that it was meted extrajudicially without a hearing and after a court acquittal. On the ground that the baseball authorities have overstepped their Constitutional limits, a national movement that started with the US Congress is seeking to have Joe reinstated in his rightful place as one of the greatest baseball players in history. While this extraordinary support for a disgraced sports hero is steadily gaining ground, Joe is still not in the Baseball Hall

287

of Fame, although he has been placed in a Virtual Hall of Fame created just for him by his supporters.

8. The Barefoot Batter from Brandon Mill

Myth! 'Shoeless' Joe Jackson was a country hick who loved to play baseball without his shoes on.

Jackson was born in Pickens County, but grew up in an industrial environment while working at an early age in a textile mill in nearby Brandon Mill. In 1900, at the age of 13, Jackson started to play for the Brandon Mill baseball team, an activity that filled up whatever free time he had and, with his job, prevented him from pursuing a formal education. Because Jackson was uneducated, he often had his wife sign his signature, which is why any thing autographed by Jackson himself brings a premium when sold.

It is said 'Shoeless' earned his nickname for playing baseball without his shoes, although most reports fail to add he did this only once, to relieve a blistered toe during the second game of a minor league double header. Some claim he was with the Brandon Mill team at the time, others that he was already playing professionally with the Greenville Spinners of the Carolina Association when it happened. In each case, Jackson suffered the blister from a new pair of cleats that was hurting him so much he had to take his shoes off before and at bat. Once Jackson was on base, a fan started yelling inappropriate and vulgar comments, including the epithet "Shoeless son of a gun." Since then, he had to bear the unwanted tag wherever he went.

9. Washing some white Socks

Myth! The Jackson affair came to be known as the Black Sox scandal thanks to media.

288

Originally called the Chicago White Stockings (not to be confused with the team's 1919 World Series adversary, the Cincinnati Redlegs, which was formerly called the Cincinnati Red Stockings), Joe's team became the Chicago White Sox in 1902 after a name change by the owner, Charles Comiskey. Following the indictment of the eight players, the newspapers started a derogatory campaign that called the affair the Black Sox scandal and the team the Chicago Black Sox. In constructing the myth around the pseudonym, print media obviously missed (or ignored) the fact that the players themselves had made the coinage long before the scandal to protest their having to perform in visibly soiled uniforms due to Comiskey's refusal to allocate cash for their laundry. According to Brandon Toropov (*op. cit.*), it was Comiskey's 'frugal ways' that practically caused the scandal, by 'forcing' the players to take bribes as the only means of augmenting their miserly pay and improving their quality of life. Comiskey (for whom the White Sox's Comiskey Park is named) was inducted into the Baseball Hall of Fame in 1939, but the White Sox would not regain its glory-day image until 2005, the year it snagged the World Series in a clean sweep over the Houston Astros.

Many critics believe the penalty on Shoeless as well as the other seven players was uncalled for, considering the very low standards of honesty in the game. Baseball's Jim Bouton, who wrote the book *Ball Four*, made an informal survey of the practices of major league players on the pitching mound, and found that a startling 87 percent of pitchers cheat some or most of the time. It is just ironic that, in the Chicago case, the cheating was to ensure a defeat and not a victory.

10. Bearly Intelligible

Myth! Yogi Bear is named for Yogi Berra.

Yogi Berra is known the world over for his Goldwynisms and his adroit use of the glove as catcher for Casey Stengel's legendary New York Yankees. Because of his name and bearish appearance, people have long suspected that he is the model for the cartoon animal Yogi Bear, star of the Hanna-Barbera animation studios

289

and a children's favorite on Saturday television.

Actually, there is no basis for the suspicion, at least not enough for anyone to bring the matter to court. When Hanna-Barbera came out with Yogi Bear, Berra threatened to sue for defamation of character, claiming that the Bear was a deliberate caricature of himself. Hanna insisted it was just a coincidence, and was able to convince Berra that the real inspiration was another television character, Art Carney's Ed Norton, the next-door neighbor in *The Honeymooners.*

III

Games Smart People Play

On Board and Table Games

"Chess is life.
All I want to do, ever, is just play chess."

•

Bobby Fischer

1. Trading on the Board

Myth! **Charles Darrow concocted the game of Monopoly and gave it its name.**

Though not as cerebral as chess or as informative as Trivial Pursuit, Monopoly has attained worldwide celebrity status as the board game that provides enjoyment and satisfaction to armchair investors and putative developers without putting real-life assets at risk. The concept has made one man rich and a corporation a giant in the genre.

We are told that Monopoly was conceived in the Depression years of the early 1930s. Charles Darrow, an unemployed engineer from Germantown, Pennsylvania, was financially and emotionally in the doldrums when he started dreaming about a board game based on the principle of real estate trading. Putting his plan into action, but unable to find a company to back him up, he had friends and relatives finance a run of 5,000 sets, which he sold through Wanamaker's department store in Philadelphia. Parker Brothers, sensing a potential winner, took over, and by 1935, the game company was selling more than 20,000 sets per week. Darrow was soon a millionaire, and Parker Brothers, an erstwhile candidate for insolvency, became one of the world's biggest manufacturers of board games.

Browsing in a toy store today, one gets to know that a board game involving business and real estate dealings does not necessarily mean Monopoly. Lining the shelves are many other versions and spin-offs, like Finance and Milton-Bradley's Easy Money. But even in its early stages, the idea of asset trading on a board using paper money, tokens, markers and dice was not unique to Monopoly. The real pioneer was not Darrow but Elizabeth Magie, who devised a pristine form called the Landlord's Game in 1904. In fact, Monopoly itself was already being played under its famous name some eight years before Darrow rediscovered it in 1933. After watching the game, and thoroughly impressed by its potentials, he had it redesigned, patented, and appropriated as his own. As an implied acknowledgment to his predecessors, Darrow left untouched some elements of the original board, which one Ruth Hoskins had

292

designed using the names and icons of Atlantic City landmarks for its squares.

According to popular lore, Parker Brothers rejected Monopoly the first time it was offered by Darrow because it had '52 fundamental errors'. This is basically true but grossly exaggerated, as there were only five flaws in the company's list. Owners George and Charles Parker actually thought the game was complicated and took too long to play, and merely mentioned the '52 errors' as an excuse in their letter of rejection. The brothers reconsidered, and Monopoly went on to become one of the two or three biggest selling board games in history. An error-filled game at the start ended up a winner!

2. Kings go Forth

Myth! **Chess originated in the East, probably Persia or India.**

It was once thought chess was a feudalistic war game born in Europe. Later, evidence surfaced placing the origins of the game in the East about AD 500. There, according to the findings, "chess had been created...centuries before the Normans heard of castles, by a people to whom elephants were no oddity."

Claims have been made for the Persians as the inventors of chess, either because these people were foremost among its early players or because evidence of the game has been found in their literature. Others say the more likely origin is India in AD 570, around the region of Hindustan, where a less evolved game called *chaturanga* (Sanskrit for 'four arms') was first played in the 6th century using references to the chariots, cavalry, infantry, elephants and other elements of large-pitched battles. It may have traveled to Persia in AD 590 only twenty years later, then brought by the Arabs into Spain in the 8th century. Later, it spread into all Europe until the 16th century, when it acquired its present form. The four 'arms' of *chaturanga* would appear to have been modified by Europeans to become gradually the bishops, knights, pawns, and rooks of modern play.

Either Persia or India as the birthplace of chess is sustained by the belief that the game could only have emerged in some location

293

with a strong mathematical history and orientation. Experts note, however, that while both nations have such a tradition, the underlying assumption that chess has a mathematical or numbers base has little validity. Chess is a game of strategy and tactics, neither of which plays any significant role in the world of numbers.

Much if not all of what historians know about the origin of chess seems to have changed with the recent discovery in the former Soviet Union of two ivory chessmen dating to ca. AD 100. This cements chess' reputation of being one of the oldest games of skill on earth today. More significantly, as this pre-empts both the Persian and Indian claims of an Asian beginning nearly five centuries later, the history of chess has come full circle with the restoration of its birthplace in Europe. Which may just as well be. An outstanding part of chess lore is the fact that the Soviet Union, mainly Russia, has produced most of the world champions (including the last two or three ones) and boasts more than 7 million registered chess players.

| 3. Playing by the Book |

Myth! Edmond Hoyle devised the rules of bridge and of many other games.

The famous expression 'according to Hoyle' is history's salute to the British writer Edmond Hoyle for his contribution to the world of games. Hoyle is given credit for systematizing the rules of whist, backgammon, chess and poker, among others. Rulebooks bearing the Hoyle name continue to be published today.

As one writer puts it, if the ghost of Edmond Hoyle were to listen to some of the heated controversies about various games of cards, and to their being settled eventually 'according to Hoyle,' "he would be the most amazed ghost that ever returned to earth." Why? It seems all Hoyle did was publish *A Short Treatise on the Game of Whist* over two centuries ago, in 1742 to be exact. Hoyle has been dead since 1769, about a century before poker, one of the games consistently credited to him, was invented. The book that he wrote was extremely popular and authoritative, settling all the arguments over whist that arose in his day and for more than a hundred years thereafter. It was so successful that dozens of writers began plagiarizing the idea if not the text, pirating even the term 'Hoyle's'. Hoyle is spoken in such reverential tones when it comes to whist that the impression given is he originated it. In fact, whist was introduced from India while its later development as contract bridge was managed in the US by the tycoon Cornelius Vanderbilt.

Incidentally, today's 'Hoyle's' rulebooks are not descendants of the original treatise but of the later 'plagiarized' versions penned by, e.g., Henry Jones ('Cavendish') in 1862 and Robert F. Foster in 1897. Foster enlarged Hoyle's work to include the rules of many other games, and since then, the book has been upgraded to accommodate even more games and their rules.

4. Another Game in Town

Myth! 'According to Cocker' is the exact British equivalent of 'according to Hoyle'.

Though similar in meaning, 'according to Hoyle' should not be confused with the British phrase 'according to Cocker'. Both are normally understood to suggest 'in a manner that is correct, accurate or reliable', but few authorities bother to mention that 'according to Cocker' could also mean 'all wrong'.

Edward Cocker was an Englishman who taught penmanship and mathematics, the latter becoming the subject of the book *Cocker's Arithmetick*, which went through 112 editions and gave rise to the proverbial phrase bearing his name. However, *Arithmetick* was first published in 1678, three years after Cocker died, leading to the suspicion that someone else designed the book to cash in on Cocker's name. The fraud was confirmed in the late 19th century, when documented proof showed that the famous book, far from being written by Cocker, was a forgery by his editor and publisher, "so poorly done that it set back rather than advanced the cause of elementary arithmetic." Augustus de Morgan, who made the exposé in his *Arithmetical Books* (1847), spitefully noted: "This same Edward Cocker must have had a great reputation, since a bad book under his name pushed out the good ones."

295

5. Raise bet, Call bluff, Show hand, Draw check

Myth! **Poker is a 19th century American invention.**

A poker aficionado's list of Hollywood films in which much of the action centers on their favorite game would surely include *The Cincinnati Kid, House of Games, California Split, The Odd Couple* and *Rounders*. A sublist titled 'Oaters that Showcase the Game of Poker' would not be far behind with such classics as *Destry Rides Again, A Big Hand for the Little Lady, Three Godfathers, Cheyenne Autumn* and *The Gunfighter*. Crime and noir movies are typically peopled by poker-playing detectives who rush out on signal to bust poker-playing gangsters. The 'smoke-filled room' is a venue traditionally assigned to politicians, but there's a lot of smoke to suggest poker players were there first, at least when smoking in close quarters was still in vogue. The preponderance of poker icons in American culture has led to the belief that poker is and has always been an American game—in fact, the country's national parlor game—and that it is of pure American vintage.

Poker awareness in the US is said to have started with a simple form of the game played in New Orleans in 1829, using a deck of 20 cards dealt to four players betting on which player's hand was the most valuable. *An Exposure of the Arts and Miseries of Gambling* (1843), by Jonathan H. Green, described the spread of the game from Louisiana to the rest of the country by Mississippi riverboats, which operated full time as floating casinos. As it traveled up the Mississippi and West during the gold rush, it is thought to have become part of the frontier pioneer ethos.

However, there is written evidence that poker existed both within and outside the US long before Louisiana and the Mississippi of the 1800s. Books about the development of the game had been published periodically since 1674, e.g., *Cotton's Complete Gamester* (1674), *Academie Universelle des Jeux* (1717) translated to English in 1750, and *Hoyle's Games - Improved by James Beaufort* (1796). Ironically, while the popularity of poker in Asia and Europe in modern times has been correctly attributed to the influence of the U.S. military, there is reason to believe the game had been played much earlier in these two continents and had in fact its beginnings in one or both of them. Part of the poker

296

legend has to do with the Chinese inventing a similar game sometime before 969 AD, when the Emperor Mu-tsung engaged his wife in a game of 'domino cards' on New Year's Eve. And because poker closely resembles the Persian *as nas*, it has been suggested that Persian sailors taught the game to French settlers in New Orleans as a prelude to its becoming a fad among Mississippi gamblers. Some familiar poker variations seem to have evolved from the Renaissance game of *primero* and the French *brelan*, which preceded the English game 'brag'. The name 'poker' was likely derived from the French *poque*, which in turn descended from the German *pochen*, both terms having been taken from the post-Chinese European versions that are believed to have influenced the development of poker as it exists today.

---

6. How to Mate in Nine...Languages

Myth! 'Mate' is an English term announcing the demise of the king in a chess game.

The word 'checkmate' literally means to check the mate of the all-powerful chess queen with permanence and thus put an end to the game. This is likely what the casual observer would infer when a player shouts the word to indicate that his opponent's main piece, the king, is being attacked and has nowhere else to go.

Actually, 'checkmate' is not a legitimate English term at all, but a corruption of the Persian expression, *shah mat*, which means 'the king is dead'. The Arabs called it *alschah-mat*, and when they took the game to Spain, the expression became *xaque mate*. In Old French it was *eschec mat* and in Russian *shahkmat*, and these in turn produced the Middle English *chek mate*, coming down to us as 'checkmate'. The Arabian *shah* means 'king', and is the earliest antecedent for the English 'check' and the British 'cheque' and for all other uses and extensions of these words (including Britain's Court of Exchequer). The French pluralized *eschec* to *esches* and made it the name of the game. When the term reached England the first syllable was dropped, like many other similar words of French origin, to produce the name by which we know the game today—chess. Hence, chess (German *Schach* and Italian *scacchi*) is just another word for 'kings', although this royal game should really have been called checkers, the name that was appropriated unadvisedly for a much simpler game better known as draughts.

Among players, 'checkmate' often yields to the shorter and more popular 'mate'. In various languages *mate* means 'to kill', and 'checkmate' announces the end for the opponent's king. But as a component of the word 'stalemate', *mate* has no such signification. 'Stalemate' refers to a situation in which the king, though not under attack, cannot move to any adjacent square without being checkmated; it ends the game by forcing a draw and not by inflicting a defeat. 'Stalemate' is also used outside the chess environment for anything that's unresolved or unyielding, like a traffic gridlock or a draw between contestants. It is sometimes suggested that 'stalemate' originated in chess usage from the belief that the inability of the king to move without being mated has placed it in a stale situation. In truth, 'stale' in the expression is from the Old French *estal*, or English 'stall', a stalled or fixed position.

7. **Marbles and Chips**

Myth! Chinese checkers is Chinese but checkers is British.

Go and Chinese checkers are widely believed to belong to the same family, but the two actually have more differences than similarities. Its name notwithstanding, Chinese checkers, a game played with colored marbles on a star-shaped board, is neither Chinese nor checkers. Although Chinese checkers is now played in China, it was only introduced there from England via the United States and Japan. Some people suspect that the name 'Chinese checkers' was derived solely from the similarity between the star-shaped playing board used in the game and the star on the national flag of China.

Chinese checkers is said to be British probably in the belief that the real game of checkers is British too. In fact, checkers came to England taking a direct path from Egypt. Chinese checkers, on the other hand, might have been originally American, although designated a Victorian British game because it attained development in England during that period. Games historian Bruce Whitehill found evidence in the early 2000s proving that it

298

"was invented between 1883 and 1884 by George Howard Monks, an American thoracic surgeon at Harvard Medical School." George's brother Robert Monks had apparently discovered the British game of Hoppity during a trip to England in 1883 or 1884 and described the game to George, who then patterned his own creation after it. According to Whitehill's research, it was Thomas Hill, a mathematician and preacher and later Harvard president, who called the game *Halma*, which is Greek for 'jump'. Halma was first patented under the name Stern-Halma in Germany in 1892, but found success only much later, when J. Pressman & Co. published the game in the US in 1928. Renamed from 'Hop Ching Checker Game' to 'Chinese Checkers', it was appropriated and the new name registered by Milton Bradley in 1941. Obviously, this latter action has not prevented the brand from becoming almost generic eventually.

---

8. Casting Luck to the Four Winds

Myth! Confucius invented the Chinese game of mahjong.

There are two fallacies concerning the addictive Chinese tile game popularly known as mahjong (sometimes spelled *mahjongg*). One has to do with its origin and the other with its name.

Explanations for mahjong's murky beginnings range from the speculative to the mystical, as, e.g., the belief that it was played on Noah's ark during the 40-day flood written about in the Bible. The most popular apocrypha is that Confucius invented the game during his peripatetic days and introduced it to the royal courts he visited. There's no written or other hard evidence of this, but enthusiasts deduce the presence of Confucius' hand from several premises: (a) the game is undoubtedly of Chinese vintage, based on its obvious features; (b) games similar to mahjong have been discovered in many of the places Confucius frequented; and (c) mahjong's dragon tiles symbolize the three Cardinal Virtues taught by Confucius—Benevolence, Sincerity, and Filial Piety. It is claimed that centuries afterwards, mahjong remained exclusively with the royal class and commoners were legally prohibited from playing under penalty of decapitation. However, around 500 A.D., the penalty was lifted, allowing the game to spread among the lower classes and to various countries around the world.

Modern historians debunk the Confucian connection as mere "mystical histories of hundreds and even thousands of years (that) have been claimed often by western tradesmen keen to impress their potential customers." They point out that the actual inventor need not have been Confucius, but only a follower who gave the dragon tiles their meanings as a sign of respect. Mahjong's link to the ancient world does appear highly unlikely absent any evidence prior to the 1880s. The earliest records were found in the provinces of Kiangsu, Anhwei and Chekiang near Shanghai on or about 1900, and its shift to the US did not occur until 1920. The popularity of the game in the West tapered off by 1929, and by 1930 it had become clear that mahjong was only a fad that catered mostly to the Jewish social set.

The name 'mahjong' or any of its variants (Mandarin: *jiàng*; Cantonese: *ma jeung*; Japanese: *mājan*; Korean: *majak*; Vietnamese: *mạt chược*) has no Chinese derivation or any particular English meaning, and would not be used anywhere until the early 1900s. When Joseph P. Babcock, an American resident of Shanghai, introduced the game to the United States in 1920, he concocted the name 'mah-jongg' and had it registered as a trademark. Prior to this, the game was called by various other names, among them *chung fa* and *ma que* ('sparrow'), the latter in reference to the ornithological significance of some of the tiles. Babcock wrote his own rules for playing the game, assigned English translations to the tiles, and imported the first few sets into the US under the trade name 'Mah-Jongg', with the hyphen and the two G's, not explaining why he thought a purely artificial word like 'mah-jongg' would sound better than an authentic Chinese one. Other entrepreneurs, authors, and companies, wanting to jump on the mahjong bandwagon, made their own sets and books but could not use Babcock's trademark, hence settled on other names, such as Ma Chong, Ma Chiang, Ma Deuck, Pung Chow, Pe-Ling, and "The Game of a Thousand Intelligences." It appears the Babcock brand eventually lapsed into the public domain through neglect or the passage of time, and it is now common to refer to the game by its generic name "mahjong" (dropping the hyphen and the double G).

9. Go in Style

Myth! The Japanese game of Go is a complex game, but less so than chess.

No matter what they say about the proven antiquity of chess as a game of strategy, Go, played with black and white disks on a wooden board etched with a grid of 19 black and 19 white lines, is still the oldest, predating chess by at least a thousand years. Popularly—but wrongly—considered a Japanese original, Go, like karate, actually had its inception in China, although when and how Go started there remains the stuff of legend. Historians aren't quite settled on whether the game was first played in the court of the Chinese emperor Yao (2337-2258 BC), or by Chinese tribal warlords and generals during the same period, or even earlier by ancient Chinese seers. Nor are they certain whether it was intended to be an educational toy or a device for tactical mapping or fortune telling. However, the Japanese clearly saw the stamp of Chinese ingenuity on the product, knew that it was good, and made it even better. Thus, after Go was introduced in Japan in the 7th century, it took no time in winning adherents at the imperial court, and by the beginning of the 13th century it had gained a foothold with the Japanese public. In the 17th century, Go had become sophisticated enough to warrant full support from the country's rulers.

The masters of Go in Japan, eager for sporting challenges from its neighbors, decided to proselytize gamers in the East Asia region. Ironically, it was the teachers who paid a price: although the most skillful players over the centuries have come from Japan, the Japanese currently lag behind Korea and China in international Go competition. The level of play in the West is less noteworthy; except for the German scientist Oscar Korschelt, who wrote the first systematic description of the game in a Western language in 1880, and some famous 1920s players (e.g., Emanuel Lasker, the world chess champion during that time, and the great Albert Einstein), knowledge of the game in America and Europe has been scant for most of its history. It was not until 2000 that a Westerner, Michael Redmond, achieved the top rank awarded by an Asian Go association, 9 dan. However, despite constant improvement through international competition and the Internet, Go in the West remains essentially an elitist game for thinkers and mathematicians like Nobel Prize winner John Forbes Nash, as seen in the Oscar best picture winner, *A Beautiful Mind* (2001).

Talking about movies, the eponymous 1999 *Go* doesn't seem to be about the game at all, as it is almost entirely about drug dealing. The title is obviously just the English verb 'go', which is totally unrelated to the name of the game. Go is the Japanese pronunciation of the Chinese characters that comprise the Chinese name Weiqi, which roughly translates as 'encirclement chess', 'board game of surrounding', or 'enclosing game'.

According to the Internet, the number of possible chess moves has been calculated at 10^{120}, give or take a few. There are thought to be only 10^{75} atoms in the entire universe, which is still a whole lot of atoms when one considers that the Milky Way galaxy alone contains billions of suns and there are billions of galaxies. The same thing has been said about Go, which means it is on par with chess in terms of complexity. Go could even be a notch higher as a tactical game, since no computer has ever beaten any of its best players. It must be remembered that IBM once launched a chess-playing automaton, RS/6000 SP, alias Deep Blue, which trounced then chess world champion Gary Kasparov in six games in May 1997.

10. A Breaker hits the Banks

Myth! Joseph Hobson Jagger, who cleaned out an entire casino in Monte Carlo in 1886, is honored in song as "The Man Who Broke the Bank at Monte Carlo."

There are several fallacies about the man for whom Fred Gilbert wrote and Charles Coborn composed the hit tune "The Man Who Broke the Bank at Monte Carlo."

First, the 'bank' that he broke in 1891 by playing the roulette table was only one table and not the entire casino. Even today, 'breaking the bank' means winning all the funds in the bank of a particular gambling table. Second, he broke the bank not once but 12 times that first day, and many more times within the next three days. Third, he was not really a gentleman gambler but a con man who raised his initial capital from gullible investors to whom he sold the idea of a fake invention. He lost all of his winnings, and

302

more, on his third sortie into Monte Carlo's gaming rooms, and was later arrested for bilking some of England's high society people of nearly $150,000.

The man was Charles Wells, although Brewer claims the real model for Gilbert's ballad was Joseph Hobson Jagger, who in 1886 won over 2,000,000 francs at Monte Carlo in eight days. Jagger was an expert on the mechanics of roulette wheels, and when one day he suspected a wheel had a faulty spindle, he watched it all week. Soon, he was able to identify the numbers that turned out with more consistency than the others, and placed his bets accordingly. Jagger, however, was not as romantic or flamboyant a figure as Wells, who had only his courage and intuition to make him win. Biographers confirm that it was indeed Wells' fantastic gambling exploits, which made headlines around the world, that inspired Fred Gilbert to introduce his tune in London's Oxford Music Hall and publish it in 1892.

Pop Images

I
Bungle In The Jungle

On Tarzan of the Apes

"How can a guy climb trees, say Me Tarzan, You Jane,
and make a million?"

•

Johnny Weismuller

1. Runts, Grunts, lying Lions and clinging Vines

Myth! The typical Tarzan movie is an accurate portrayal of life in the African jungle.

The first talkie Tarzan introduced the definitive ape-man, Johnny Weissmuller, and with him, some of the greatest fallacies Hollywood jungle movies have fallen heir to.

First, a 'pygmy tribe' is encountered consisting of dwarfs. Anthropologists tell us there is no such thing as a tribe of dwarfs in an ethnic or racial sense (except perhaps the mythical race of dwarfs Homer wrote about in the Iliad). In the modern context, the word 'pygmy' applies broadly to certain tribal peoples of equatorial Africa, the Philippines and Malaysia, whose males average less than five feet tall. However, there are usually no dwarfs in these groups, only very short persons.

Second, white hunters are shown going off in search of a fabulous elephant graveyard and actually discovering it in Africa. Underlying this idea is the misconception that elephants are driven by instinct to a specific place when they are ready to die. No real exploration has ever unearthed such a graveyard in the Dark Continent or wherever else elephants abound.

Third, lions, zebras and gnus are seen in the jungle, which is unusual for what are essentially creatures of the plains. Tarzan tries to avoid them by swinging from vine to vine. This feat is both difficult and inconvenient considering that vines in a real jungle are attached to the ground rather than to trees.

Later Tarzan movies go farther off course by letting the African jungle man fight tigers, which are Asian, and swing with orangutans, which are denizens of Borneo and Sumatra. The mythic tiger encounters, animatedly portrayed in Disney's *Tarzan* (1999), find their basis in Edgar Rice Burroughs' first magazine version of *Tarzan of the Apes*. Regarding Tarzan's ape buddies, a writer notes that, in the novels and the movies, they are "specifically neither chimpanzees nor gorillas, but some otherwise unknown apes somewhere between those two in size and strength."

2. Me and You and...

Myth! **The most famous line in the Tarzan movies is, "Me Tarzan, you Jane."**

The most famous line in all Tarzan films is properly credited to the 1932 *Tarzan the Ape Man*, but not in the form "Me Tarzan, you Jane," as is popularly imagined. The laconic "Tarzan, Jane" singsong, which has since become fodder for collectors of movie 'misquotables', is also not wholly accurate. The sequence that raised the curtain on the young Johnny Weissmuller as Tarzan and Maureen O'Sullivan as Jane begins with the jungle man confronting his new-found mate after he has shooed away a molesting she-ape, and the two groping for the right words to introduce each other. What ensues is a whole length of dialogue consisting almost entirely of the words "me," "you," "Tarzan," and "Jane." From the first "me" that Tarzan says while thumping Jane on the chest to the last "Jane" he utters in acknowledgment of her name, exactly 44 words are exchanged between them, and of these, 32 can be found in the sentence "Me Tarzan, you Jane." The legendary line is never heard as is, but in it rests the entire gist of the first ever conversation between the primal couple.

3. Starting a Family Tree

Myth! **Edgar Rice Burroughs' Tarzan is based on a historical figure.**

In 1929, the entire library system of Los Angeles County, which embraces Hollywood, removed all Tarzan books from its shelves because the two principal characters were not married. The protocol of the times dictated that if Tarzan had been real, his moral instincts would not have allowed him to live a life of 'sin' in or out of the wilds. To support this presumption, a parallel was offered from the story of William Milden, the earl of Streathem, who, it was said, was shipwrecked at age 11 off Africa in 1868, yet lived virginally with apes for 15 years before being found and returned home.

Not that it matters, but Tarzan and Jane were actually wed at the end of the first sequel, *The Return of Tarzan*, which was published more than a decade before the LA brouhaha. More significantly, the Streathem account was debunked as myth as soon as it gained public notice, and researchers have since found no evidence that Burroughs' stories were biographical to any degree. The LA attempt at censorship was, to say the least, ironic. The only Tarzan materials worth censoring have been those in his movies, particularly the nude and sexually suggestive scenes in the first two Weissmuller films and the Bo Derek fiasco, *Tarzan, the Ape Man* (1981). None of these three pictures—indeed, no Tarzan picture from any source—is completely faithful to Burroughs' concept, although the original Robert Towne screenplay for *Greystoke: The Legend of Tarzan, Lord of the Apes* (1984) is said to be the closest. Unfortunately, Towne's script was so corrupted in the filming that when it won an Oscar nomination, the respected writer agreed to take credit only under the name of his sheepdog, P. H. Vazak.

---

4. Planet Hollywood's big Apes

Myth! Elmo Lincoln was the first Hollywood actor to portray Tarzan.

Most filmographies list Elmo Lincoln as the first of seventeen Hollywood Tarzans. Playing the jungle hero in the screen debut of Edgar Rice Burroughs' classic, *Tarzan of the Apes* (1918), the actor seemed more than equal to the task. According to Mick Martin and Marsha Porter (*Video Movie Guide 2002*), Elmo actually killed the lion he fights in one of the film's exciting moments. The Hollywood beefcake may have achieved this feat of derring-do, but it isn't explained whether he did it using his bare hands or by using some weapon like an elephant gun fired from thirty meters away. Earlier sources, such as the May 1934 issue of Screen Play Magazine, reported that the lion was old and drugged and Lincoln hastily stabbed it when it appeared to threaten him. He jumped on what he thought was its carcass, but before he could give a victory yell *a la* Tarzan, the dying lion managed to bellow and scare the actor away.

Gordon Griffith preempts Lincoln as the first real Tarzan by portraying the young Lord of the Apes in the same movie, making his entrance on the screen well ahead of the star. Only ten years old at the time, Griffith presents a much better sight than his grownup counterpart, who 'looks like he is about fifty years old, with a beer belly to boot'. Lincoln is woefully miscast compared to the great athletes who have portrayed the jungle man, such as Herman Brix, Buster Crabbe, Johnny Weissmuller and Glenn Morris (Don Bragg, nicknamed Tarzan, is sometimes mentioned, but he never got the part). The four are Olympic medal winners who have done justice to scenes showing Tarzan fighting, swimming and performing feats with agility and strength. Lincoln got the job as the first *adult* Tarzan only after the magnificently built Stellan Sven Windrow (1893-1959), who was earlier chosen for the role, was drafted into World War I.

Of greater interest to movie buffs, perhaps, is Fox's 1938 *Tarzan's Revenge*, which features not one but two Olympic champions. Tarzan is 1936 decathlon king Glenn Morris, and the female lead is Eleanor Holm, the 1932 gold medalist of the 100-meter backstroke (Jane is nowhere in this film).

---

5. Swimmer to Swinger

Myth! **The American Johnny Weissmuller is the world's most popular Tarzan ever.**

To his millions of fans the world over, the literary Tarzan may be British, but his movie counterpart is indubitably American. No person has done more to Americanize the Tarzan image than actor-strongman Johnny Weissmuller. Unhappily, despite the four Olympic swimming medals that staked him to the role, Johnny's creditable screen appearances as the jungle man didn't earn him a single Hollywood award.

The shocker, however, is that Weissmuller may not even be American. At most, he may have become American only by amnesty or tolerance. No proof has ever been presented that Johnny was naturalized as a US citizen after arriving in this country from Romania. The two-time Olympic gold medalist passed himself off as an American and obtained a US passport for the Paris Olympics by forging his name on the baptismal records of his US-born younger brother Peter. He showed his birthplace as Windber, Pennsylvania, belying the fact that he was born in Friedorf, Romania, a year before his parents decided to settle in the US.

Coming as a further shock is the revelation that Weissmuller is not the most popular Tarzan, as is generally believed. The long list of Tarzan movies—98 in all—begins with the 1918 *Tarzan of the Apes*, starring the American Elmo Lincoln, and ends with the 1984 *Greystoke: The Legend of Tarzan, Lord of the Apes*, showcasing the British Christopher Lambert. In between is Weissmuller's string of twelve Hollywood movies. This is one less than the thirteen Tarzan portrayals by Indian actor Azad, all of them produced in India, the country with the largest movie-going population in the world.

6. That Chimp wasn't a Monkey's Uncle

Myth! Tarzan's pet monkey is named Cheetah.

Any zoology book should tell us the tailless Cheetah is an ape, unlike the baboons seen frolicking with him whose telltale tails indicate they are monkeys. His fans easily get confused because the talented chimp can act out the role of any kind of simian on cue.

Cheetah plays his role seamlessly in the movies, with no hint that the animal behind the name was not just one chimp but several supplied by Hollywood's talented menagerie. A chimpanzee is not the easiest animal to work with, as Cheetah's trainer and Jane's portrayer Maureen O'Sullivan have attested. Although he is most peaceable and friendly on the screen, he was notorious for biting actors and crewmembers. It is wrong to assume that Cheetah learned his tricks on the set from the studio's animal trainers; movie people long ago learned that the only practical way with animal actors is to write the tricks they already know into the script. In *Tarzan and His Mate*, for instance, Cheetah's ability to crawl on his stomach was exploited in a scene in which the ape sneaks through the tall grass to escape an attacking rhinoceros.

310

It may be mentioned, finally, that most animal actors respond only to signals coming from their handlers. Thus, "Ungawa!," the command that Tarzan is often heard to shout to Cheetah, was gibberish and had no effect on the chimp.

7. He can Ape, but can he Yodel?

Myth! Johnny Weissmuller made the best Tarzan yell among all the actors who played the role.

Of the clichés that separate Tarzan from the others in the Hollywood coterie of jungle characters, the most distinctive—yet the least visual—is his yell. The one we hear from old Tarzan reruns on midnight TV has the imprint of Johnny Weissmuller's vocal chords and was presumably recorded during his reign as Hollywood king of the jungle. We are told the yell is probably copyrighted like any original piece of music, in which case not even the real Tarzan, if he exists, can use it for any commercial purpose without proper permission.

Aficionados claim Johnny Weissmuller's signature yell, which elicits instant recognition and excitement whenever heard on any medium, is the best Tarzan call ever produced. Many can't quite believe it is not entirely the actor's own. In fact, none of the actors who played Tarzan in the movies did most of his own yell, as the studio generated this from various sound sources. In Weissmuller's case, it was a combination of several different sounds, including his own scream, a high C hit by a soprano, and a hyena's howl recorded on tape and played backward. For Johnny's imitators, three voices were put together—a bass, a baritone and a hog caller. The enhanced voice of the father of former Tarzan Buster Crabbe was sometimes used, but Tom Held, an actor who has not otherwise qualified for a Tarzan role, is reportedly the owner of the latest yell.

311

II
Out Of The Cold And Into A Dry Martini

On James Bond

"The name's Bond. James Bond."

•

Sean Connery

1. High-priced European Bonds

Myth! Sean Connery was the first actor to play James Bond.

Most of us recall our earliest screen Bond as a balding young Scot with an Irish brogue. The reverse image of that would be a Scottish-sounding Irishman, exactly what Pierce Brosnan gave us for a spell, though Bond is now back to his thoroughly English self with his new portrayer, Daniel Craig. Others who have taken on the world-famous role are suave gents who deliver their dialogues in varying English intonations while projecting equally memorable images of the quintessential British secret agent. Each has a style of bringing Fleming's character to life, but all the avid fan sees in his mind's eye is one cool, calculating voice that says, "Bond, James Bond."

The belief that Sean Connery created the James Bond screen persona when he debuted as Agent 007 in the 1962 movie Dr. No is so much wishful thinking by this actor's many partisans. Bond's visual introduction to the world was not on the big screen nor was it in the sixties, and it was not Connery who portrayed him. On October 21, 1954, American actor Barry Nelson inaugurated the fictional hero on film in a TV episode of *Climax!* entitled "Casino Royale." The feat is doubly significant because it shattered the myth that the only non-European to play James Bond is George Lazenby, an Australian. Nelson's portrayal, however, is not entirely faithful to the Fleming image, being that of an American CIA agent working on a special project with the British Secret Service.

Also wrong is the common impression that Connery and the five other European actors who have played Bond are all English. Roger Moore, Timothy Dalton and Craig hail from England, but Connery and David Niven are Scottish. The third European who is not English—Brosnan of Ireland—starred in four films as the immediate predecessor of the newest James Bond.

With the TV version and a feature film starring David Niven in 1967, 'Casino Royale' had been for a while the only James Bond story made twice for the screen. In 1983, the baton was passed to *Thunderball* (1965) when it was remade as *Never Say Never Again*, with Sean Connery reprising his original role. Now it's

313

Casino Royale holding the aces again. Its third version, a ball-crushing thriller starring Daniel Craig, came out in theaters around the world in 2006. With *Casino Royale*, Craig became the first screen Bond to have been born after the series already started, and Ian Fleming, the novels' writer, had died.

2. Gilding a Broad

Myth! **Maud Adams is the actress in the most number of Bond films.**

Maud Adams was the Swedish model that enthralled Roger Moore's James Bond in the 1974 *The Man With the Golden Gun* and the 1983 *Octopussy*. Officially, she is described as the only supporting actress to appear in more than one Bond picture. Not that it's important, but the 1974 film also features the most number of nipples anyone dared to show in a Bond scene. That's because the oddball in the picture, a villainous freak (or freaky villain) named Scaramanga, displays three pink buttons on his hairy chest in one dramatic but totally unsexy interlude.

Unofficially, Adams does not even come close to the lesser-known Lois Maxwell. Remaining fadeless after multiple exposures, the latter has established an unmatchable record of playing the same supporting role in thirteen James Bond pictures, six with Sean Connery and seven with Roger Moore. She has failed to gain notice as one of 'Bond's Broads' only because her role of M's somewhat punctilious secretary Miss Moneypenny is considered sexually unappealing. Aficionados nevertheless see some meaning in the frequent exchanges of flirtatious looks and double entendres between her and Bond, and actually consider their relationship sexier than many of Bond's casual affairs.

Nikki van der Zyl's image is never seen on screen, but her exposure in the series is probably just as frequent as Maxwell's. Nikki provided the voice for some of the Bond actresses whose vocal chords didn't match their good looks. In particular, she is the voice of all but two of the women in *Dr. No*.

But the most impressive appearance yet of a Bond moll has been that of Shirley Eaton, who claims her singular stint in

314

Goldfinger (1964) made her famous overnight. She says she owes everything to one spectacular scene showing her lying in bed dead, her naked body painted in gold from head to toe. The notion this has helped promote—that humans breathe not only through the nose and mouth but also through the skin—sounds scientific but is really bunkum. "Frogs may breathe through their skin," a critic quips, "but man never does." Still, some doctors attest that gilding the entire body can prove fatal if all the pores are effectively blocked for a length of time. The complete stoppage of perspiration will eventually ruin the body's principal means of heat regulation. The ill effects may not show themselves at once, especially in those cases where the toxic substances in the gilt, such as lead, are minimal. Thus, in Shirley's case, the gilding had to be done within a strict time limit set by studio doctors, who warned that after sixty minutes, the continued blocking of the pores by the paint could result in death from a heat stroke (not asphyxiation, as many suppose). The actress' medical handlers also insisted that a six-inch square on Shirley's midriff be left clear of paint as an added precaution. Apparently, for as long as some part of the body surface, preferably the palms, armpits and soles of the feet where a great number of sweat glands are located, is left unobstructed, an increased rate of perspiration across those places will provide relief.

---

3. Two Teas make Beer better

Myth! The best way to serve a martini is 'shaken, not stirred'.

Beginning with the 1964 Goldfinger, whenever the famous spy is asked for his drink, he invariably replies, "Martini, shaken, not stirred." The dialogue is unique to the Bond films, expressing as it does a Bond idiosyncrasy not shared by other cinematic spies. The only times Bond digresses from the usual are in some films outside the series, e.g., the 1954 'Casino Royale' (scotch) and the 1967 version of the same adventure (tea). Ditto for 007 spoofs, such as Mike Myer's *Austin Powers: The Spy Who Shagged Me*, in which the Bond-like hero eschews martini in favor of a scatological mix that's made to look like coffee.

The line, "Martini, shaken, not stirred," does not appear verbatim in any Ian Fleming book, and was apparently only induced by the films from the first 007 novel 'Casino Royale' (1953). In one of its pages, Bond orders a cocktail he has invented: one dry Martini in a deep champagne goblet, three measures of Gordon's gin, one of vodka (made from grain, not potato), half a measure of Kina Lillet, and the whole concoction shaken very well until it's ice-cold. The formula was first suggested to screen audiences when a West Indian servant in the first Bond film, *Dr. No* (1962), brings the British agent a vodka and Martini, saying, "Mixed like you said, sir, and not stirred." It is mentioned again in the same film by no less than Dr. No before Bond gets to say it for the first time in *Goldfinger*. The phrase has since become a Bond byword, although in *You Only Live Twice* (1967), what he utters is, "Perfect, cheers!," when a somewhat confused Henderson, offering him a vodka martini, comments, "That was stirred, not shaken, that was right, wasn't it?"

A dry martini shaken, not stirred, may have established James Bond's urbane sophistication and the reputation of Hugh Hefner's bar in the Playboy Mansion, but almost certainly not Ian Fleming's. The experts claim that shaking a dry martini until it is frosted turns it into a most dreadful drink. An experienced bartender might in fact suggest that it be "stirred quickly with ice in a jug." There are many ways of addressing an odd taste, but with martinis especially, Bond's method is not recommended.

4. Bonding Materials

Myth! Fleming patterned Bond after himself.

Most of James Bond's fans have been led to believe that Ian Fleming, who was once an active member of British Naval Intelligence, patterned his fabled hero after himself. The good-humored author confessed to loving the good life the way Bond does, but without 007's "sort of gallivanting about." Fleming described this lifestyle as rather unusual for a bureaucrat, because

316

it included "the best of food and wine, golf, swimming, and a hatred of office work."

Those who see Fleming as too modest to invest his creation with his own personality have come up with the names of other possible Bond models, among them that of British double agent James Morton, whose body was discovered in Shepheard's Hotel in Cairo in 1962. Apparently, Fleming failed to quell the speculation about Bond's real-life identity even with his final straightforward admission that the dashing character's fictional exploits were drawn from the true adventures of Dusko Popov, a key operative under his charge. This former German spy, who died at age 70 in France in 1981, revealed in his memoirs, 'Spy-Counterspy' (1974), that he was compromised by the British and turned into a double agent. In August 1941, the Germans had sent Popov to the US to gather information about Pearl Harbor for the Japanese. Popov alerted the British, who then told the US, but J. Edgar Hoover showed no interest and sent the double agent packing.

In 1973, John Pearson published his book 'James Bond: The Authorised Biography of 007' (London: Sidgwick and Jackson), claiming that Fleming's creation was based on a real British agent named—you got it–James Bond. Many, failing to note that Pearson's apparent coup was meant to be a spoof, thrilled at the idea of a live subject whose life and adventures paralleled those of an imagined hero. Obviously, Pearson himself was unaware that a flesh-and-blood British naturalist named James Bond had written one of Fleming's favorite books, 'Birds of the West Indies', years before the latter's death. Fleming admitted naming his character after the ornithologist to honor their friendship as neighbors in Jamaica, where both indulged in bird watching.

Contrary to Fleming's dictum that spies only live twice, the double agents he met in real life, by assuming so many identities and faking their deaths so often, must have lived many more times. At the other extreme, one of the most effective spies that ever lived died once but never lived at all! He was a World War II corpse planted by the British to fool the Nazis about the proposed Allied landings in Europe. His fascinating story may be seen on film as *The Man Who Never Was* (Ronald Neame, 1956), based on a book of the same name by Ewen Montagu.

317

5. The Spy who Nagged Me

Myth! **The real-life head of the British Secret Service is codenamed M.**

Ex-spy Ian Fleming reveals in the Bond novels that the head of the British Secret Service is a man called M, and there is a special section in the organization called Double-0. The film *GoldenEye* breaks part of the mold by showing M as a woman, albeit a very tough bureaucrat unlike any male M we have seen or read about. Bond aficionados may have been additionally chagrined by Ms. M's comment that their hero is a "sexist, misogynist dinosaur." Leonard Maltin consoles them with the observation that this may just be "a passing nod to political correctness" ('Movie and Video Guide', 1998).

Subordinates and the rest of the intelligence community once knew the flesh-and-blood head of the British Secret Service as C or CSS, apparently an abbreviation of his name. On the other hand, M, who is Admiral Sir Miles Messervy in the novels, is as imaginary as his most famous operative, James Bond. The full name of M is never mentioned in the films and only occasionally in the Fleming novels, giving rise to the highly misleading impression that in real life, the spy chief keeps his identity secret.

Bond is assigned the number 007 in the Double-0 section by virtue of his license to kill, which an agent acquires when he kills an enemy in the line of duty. Bond earned the distinction many times over, but it's as contrived as Bond's gimmick-laden weapons, cars and lifestyle. There is no such thing as a Double-0 section, and the term '007' is an apparent rip-off of '.007' (with a decimal), a number-name that Rudyard Kipling gave to a locomotive.

Ironically, the only movie in which Bond has no license to kill is the 1989 *Licence to Kill*. M does not sanction this adventure, and neither did Ian Fleming, who was already dead when his surrogate John Gardner wrote the book. The original title, *License Revoked*, was reportedly scrapped when United Artists learned that less than 20 percent of the American public knew the meaning of 'revoked'.

6. FAQ for Q

Myth! **Bond avoids gun holsters and silencers on Q's advice.**

It's not beyond Q to devise a gun that will shoot back at the shooter unless properly harnessed. Thank God he never has (or has he?). Leave that one to Matt Helm's handlers, who arms the singing operative (with tongue in cheek, of course) with a gun that fires in reverse if the trigger is not pushed forward first.

Bond is carefully dressed up so his shoulder holster will not show. Some of Fleming's compatriots deride this as pure but totally unnecessary cosmetics, noting that, with the exception of FBI operatives and American detectives, no one really wants to carry his gun in a holster. "Few people carry a gun when not 'on the job' and in action most prefer the waistband or even the trousers pocket—side, not hip." In that position, a small gun would avoid an on the spot search and give the slinger a chance of shooting himself out of trouble before he reached jail or some other destination.

In the real world, silencers are also regarded as strictly a no-no whether for heroes or for villains. An effective silencer on an auto pistol would be very ponderous and would spoil the balance of the gun. Silencing a revolver would be even more difficult because of the gas escape between the cylinder and the barrel. No wonder an assassin cannot hit Bond with a silenced gun even when both are in the same room.

7. Battling the Beasties

Myth! **None of Bond's chief adversaries are British.**

The adversaries that harass James Bond in the novels have many faces. Apparently, not one of the major ones is English. Bond's fans see their hero as a chauvinist who loves to mix it up but eschews fighting his fellow Brits. James is at his best when

319

locking horns (or limbs) with exotic racial types of either gender like Dr. No and Onatopp.

James Bond is often held up as English, but he is not. Ian Fleming's creation is the son of a Highland Scottish father and a Swiss mother, a vital stat that has allowed Sean Connery to use his brogue with good effect in the Bond films.

Fleming, who is English, might have originally wanted Bond to avoid tangling with English types. His defining novels established Bond's archenemy as the half-Polish and half-Greek Ernst Stavro Blofeld, who makes himself fearsome as the founder of SPECTRE, a technologically oriented international group bent on world domination.

Later, however, Fleming moderated the ethnic stereotype by introducing Sir Hugo Drax and Auric Goldfinger, two of the most perverse villains in the Bond repertoire who are as close to being Englishmen as James Bond is. The hideously scarred Drax, a knight of the United Kingdom, is a German whose British citizenship was acquired through naturalization. Goldfinger, probably Bond's most colorful nemesis thanks to Gert Frobe's convincing portrayal on film, is a UK citizen, having emigrated from Riga, Latvia, at the age of 20 to become the richest man in England.

The lineup of Bond villains, both Fleming and non-Fleming, discloses some English types who play minor roles in the adventures as contact men, minions, henchmen or assassins, e.g., Donald 'Red' Grant of *From Russia With Love* and Elliot Carver of *Tomorrow Never Dies*. Others, like Sir Gustav Graves of *Die Another Day* and Alec Trevelyan of *GoldenEye*, are apparently English but definitely of foreign origin.

8. Is that a Gun in his Pocket?

Myth! **The .25 caliber Beretta automatic is Bond's most durable weapon and also his favorite.**

Another mono-lettered character in Fleming's repertoire is the keeper of 007's inexhaustible supply of gadgets and devices, both lifesaving and destructive. Known to Bond as Q, Reader's Digest (December 2002) reports that he is the only one in the cast who

320

actually existed. While working at Naval Intelligence, Fleming "became fascinated by a series of ingenious devices that were helping save the lives of British secret agents, saboteurs and prisoners of war." Ranging from shaving brush handles hollowed out to hide escape maps to a miniature telescope disguised as a cigarette holder, they came out of the Ministry of Supply's Clothing Department under the responsibility of Charles Fraser-Smith. Smith, whose gizmos are currently enshrined in "Bond, James Bond," a major exhibition at the Science Museum in London, worked so deeply under cover that not even his boss knew most of what he was doing,

Fleming's treatment of James Bond's armory—from guns to gimmicks—dwelt on both the real and the imaginary. However it came out on screen, the author's allies on the one hand and critics on the other agree that it was inspired. Oddly enough, Bond's instant firepower is limited to a few ordinary weapons, some of which are no deadlier than those accessible to enterprising American schoolboys. "It really doesn't matter," we seem to hear Q arguing. "Even the CIA's reputed range of gizmos couldn't discourage men with ordinary cutters from bringing down a couple of New York skyscrapers."

Although Fleming was extremely knowledgeable about handguns, he dealt with the subject at the start in a very theoretical manner. In the early novel *Casino Royale*, Bond's favorite is a .25 caliber Beretta automatic, which, in the words of one critic, "could no more stop a man…than a peashooter could stop an elephant." Adds another: "This sort of gun is really a lady's gun, and not a really nice lady at that…The famous 'taped' butt had no advantage, and would certainly militate against accurate shooting." Later, after shifting to a Walter PPK, Fleming would learn that, in general, a revolver is better than an automatic because of the latter's tendency to jam at an awkward moment, and that high-powered, cupronickel-jacketed bullets are likely to drill rather than stop an opponent. All the same, the author failed on many occasions to apply these principles to situations in his novels where they would have counted.

III
Prometheus Unplugged

On Boris Karloff's Monsters

"Man, how ignorant art thou in thy pride of wisdom!"

•

Frankenstein

1. Beauty lands a Beast

Myth! Boris Karloff was the first actor to portray the Frankenstein monster.

When Mary Wollstonecraft, wife of the poet Percy Bysse Shelley, finished her famous horror fiction, what she had written was not a novel but a short story. She produced the manuscript in response to the challenge that she, Percy and their houseguests, the poet Lord Byron and his friend John Polidori, each write a horror piece within a few days to see who could come up with the best. Her idea proved the most interesting. Encouraged by her husband to develop the plot further, she turned it eventually into a novel with the full title *Frankenstein, or The Modern Prometheus* (1818). In some versions of Greek mythology, Prometheus was the Titan who created mankind and who, defying a wrathful Zeus, secretly took fire from heaven and gave it to man.

Hollywood hooked on to the masterpiece a century later. Contrary to popular belief, however, the movie that started the trend was not the 1931 Universal vehicle for Boris Karloff but a 1910 full-length feature with Charles Ogle as the monster and Augustus Phillips as its creator. Between these two dates, there were at least three more films: *Life Without Soul* in 1916 and the Italian production *Master of Frankenstein* in 1920. Also in 1920, Paul Wegener produced the German film classic *The Golem*, about a clay monster brought to life by a rabbi to save the persecuted Jews from a pogrom. This last one, which the 1931 *Frankenstein* closely copied both in detail and overall development, generally became an even stronger influence on the Universal film than was Mary's novel.

2. Call me Adam

Myth! Mary Shelley failed to give her monster a name.

Mary Shelley's famous creature has been called Frankenstein so often that the word is now a synonym for monster or golem.

Boris Karloff figures prominently in everyone's list of classic horror actors as the celluloid Frankenstein.

People who think they know better point out that the monster is not named Frankenstein, and that, in fact, it is not assigned a name by any of the Frankenstein films because the basic story gives it none. They are only partly correct. In one of the most chilling scenes in the Mary Shelley novel, just after the monster has been brought to life, Frankenstein impulsively calls it 'Adam'. The producers attempted to carry this part of the action into the film, but Universal decided to cut it out in many belated releases. The Studio was not prepared to disturb the myth that Karloff *was* Frankenstein.

3. Screwed-up Character

Myth! **The title character of James Whale's** *The Bride of Frankenstein* **is the mate the scientist hero creates for the monster.**

Most Frankenstein movies are faithful to Shelley's book in at least one respect—they are careful to call the monster's creator by his correct name, Victor Frankenstein. The only notable exception is the film that many consider the most definitive, the 1931 *Frankenstein*, which gives Shelley's hero a different first name: Henry. Since there was absolutely no reason for making the name change, the film is sometimes offered as a glaring example of how the smallest Hollywood whim can suborn a literary classic.

The 1931 film became popular and with it the belief that the name Frankenstein belongs to the monster. Sequels, parodies and spin-offs have chosen to ride on the early film's reputation by preserving the error implicit in the title. Thus, in James Whale's 1935 sequel, *The Bride of Frankenstein*, everybody assumes the title character is the mate created for the monster (played to perfection by Elsa Lanchester). Actually, she is the woman Henry (or Victor) Frankenstein marries (played by Valerie Hobson). Although the anomaly is of no consequence, and the movie has turned out to be an even greater classic than the original, others, carrying the misrepresentation too far, have only succeeded in bewildering their viewers. For instance, in the 1966 western-cum-horror potboiler *Jesse James Meets Frankenstein's Daughter*, the famous outlaw meets neither the offspring of the monster nor that of the pseudo-scientist, but the latter's granddaughter.

4. Monster Billing

Myth! Boris Karloff is the credited star of the 1931 film Frankenstein.

Much of the action in the 1931 *Frankenstein* revolves around Mary Shelley's frightening character, which the British actor Boris Karloff masterfully recreates. This, and the monster's commanding presence on screen, account for the general impression that Karloff is the movie's one and only accredited star.

In fact, another Briton, Colin Clive, plays the title role and has exclusive billing as the leading man. There is practically no acknowledgment to Karloff, not even as a minor support to Clive. In the opening credits, a question mark appears in lieu of the name of the actor who portrays the monster, and it is only in the closing credits that Karloff is revealed to be that actor. Karloff's many fans find it difficult to understand why he agreed to appear almost incognito in a role that was both physically demanding and artistically significant. Critics say that, by the time he was cast, he had already been an actor of note in both silent and sound films for nearly a dozen years.

Those who claim to have the answer state that Universal Pictures, sorely disappointed at the refusal of Bela Lugosi, Hollywood's iconic Dracula, to take on the role initially, thought it best to keep the casting change quiet until the last minute. Popular expectations were high that Lugosi, said to have been born for the part, would stay with the picture to the very end. Newspapers were erroneously still listing Lugosi as the performer, and some publicity, notably the 1931 'electric beam eyes' poster of the creature (before it was given its famous flat head and neck-bolt makeup), continued to credit Lugosi as the monster. Those close to Universal's management would later maintain that Karloff had been the choice all along, but was given a deliberately low profile in order to minimize his liability for the picture, which was then

325

running afoul of the censors because of its stark brutality. A portion of the film showing Karloff drowning a little girl in a stream had already been removed ostensibly to prevent the actor's genteel image from being ruined.

5. The Humor of Frankenstein

Myth! **Boris Karloff once starred in an Abbott and Costello film about Frankenstein.**

While starring in the mainstream Franknstein movies of the 40s and 50s, Boris Karloff found time to play against type in a few horror comedies. In *Abbott and Costello Meet the Killer Boris Karloff* (1949), he appears almost fleetingly as a phony mystic and not as the murderer proclaimed by the title. In *Abbott and Costello Meet Dr. Jekyll and Mr. Hyde* (1953), Karloff portrays the mild Dr. Jekyll instead of the fiendish Mr. Hyde.

Surprisingly, Karloff is not the monster in *Abbott and Costello Meet Frankenstein* (1948) and does not appear in that movie at all. The one who does the role is the giant-sized American character actor Glenn Strange, wearing the gruesome makeup that Karloff made familiar. This highest rated of the Abbot and Costello horror farces involves the comic duo with all sorts of weird characters, but never Dr. Frankenstein himself. In the latter's absence, his monster is placed under the tutelage of another bogeyman, Count Dracula. Incidentally, people will swear there are only three famous scare artists in the movie—Bela Lugosi's Dracula, Strange's Frankenstein monster, and Lon Chaney's Wolf Man. In the very last scene, however, a fourth 'appears' without being seen—the Invisible Man, announced by the booming voice of Vincent Price.

Critics find the parody of the monster in another horror comedy classic, *Young Frankenstein* (1974), more faithful to Mary Wollstonecraft's opus than are some of the serious portrayals. Mel Brooks' creature is musically inclined, romantic and intellectual, unlike the dumb brute in the standard dramas that trudges robot-like and swats people that get in the way. Brooks stumbled on the truth while attempting to distort James Whale's screen concept in

326

order to create the satire. Fortunately, he used as his model Whale's 1935 *The Bride of Frankenstein*, which, compared to the 1931 original *Frankenstein*, is popularly rated as the more authentic rendition of the Wollstonecraft novel. Particular episodes, like the one of the blind man welcoming the golem into his pathetic home, are hilarious send-ups of unforgettable scenes in the horror drama. Brooks' comic stew is flavored by spoofy bits from other Frankenstein movies, such as the wooden-armed Inspector Kemp from *The Son of Frankenstein*. But on the whole, it is the 1935 Whale classic that provides the main ingredient of Brooks' recipe.

Our final word on the Frankenstein hero concerns his hunchbacked assistant Igor, revved up to comic perfection by Martin Feldman ('EYE-gore', not 'EE-gore') in the Mel Brooks send-up. In the original 1931 film, the character, played by Dwight Frye, is named Fritz and is a hunchback who walks with the aid of a small cane. In *The Bride of Frankenstein*, Frye reprises the role as Karl, a murderer who stands upright but has a lumbering metal brace on both legs that can be heard clicking loudly with every step. It was not until *The Son of Frankenstein* that the character would finally emerge as Ygor, played by no less than Bela Lugosi. Ygor, a deranged blacksmith whose neck and back are broken and twisted due to a botched hanging, befriends the monster and later helps Dr. Frankenstein. Ygor is believed to be the first full screen image of the 'hunchbacked assistant' stereotype associated with Frankenstein in pop culture. The rub, of course, is that there is no character anywhere close to Fritz, Karl, Ygor or Igor in the Mary Shelley story.

---

6. Dr. Frankensteen, I presume?

Myth 4: **Frankenstein is a doctor who does scientific work in a Bavarian university.**

The title 'Dr. Frankenstein from Geneva' doesn't sound so impressive, but it will be remembered for as long as there are people who believe humans can be created in ways other than biological. Many are agreed Frankenstein deserves a loftier title, considering that the monster the good 'doctor' creates out of dead body parts is able to develop a soul, albeit a primitive one, before it is finally destroyed. This may not have been the intended result of the experiment, but the achievement does give Frankenstein a godly quality that should merit for him the honorific 'Lord' in lieu of plain 'Dr.'.

How our hero is to be addressed happens to be moot, considering that he is apparently titled only for Hollywood. In the book, he is not a doctor or even a medical assistant, but a teen-aged student in the University of Ingolstadt located in a Bavarian city of the same name. Having a genuine love for science, he turns to natural history and mathematics and later uses the university's facilities for creating his monster.

There really is a city of Ingolstadt in Bavaria, with a university that predates Mary Shelley's writing. Interestingly, there is also a city in Germany called Frankenstein. The locale, while not mentioned in the Frankenstein adventure, may have provided the author with the name of her tragic hero.

7. His Daddy was a Mummy

Myth! In the Mummy series of the 1930s and 1940s, Boris Karloff portrays the character Imhotep.

Boris Karloff is associated with another film monster, the Mummy, perhaps more than any other actor. Yet he played the character only once, compared to Lon Chaney, Jr., who played it three times.

The Mummy (1932), which started the series, is about an Egyptian mummy that revives after thousands of years in search of its ancient mate. The title character Karloff portrays is called Imhotep in its pre-Mummy days, and assumes the modern name Ardeth Bay in its reincarnated existence. In the four sequels that followed—*The Mummy's Hand* (1940), *The Mummy's Tomb* (1942), *The Mummy's Ghost* (1944) and *The Mummy's Curse* (1944)—the name inexplicably changes to Kharis. The monster is given a spin by Tom Tyler in *The Mummy's Hand* and by Lon Chaney, Jr., in the others. Sustained by an action-filled comedic script and end-of-the-millennium special effects, Arnold Vosloo continues the tradition in the 1999 revival of *The Mummy* by

328

director Stephen Sommers. Vosloo resuscitates his character in 2001 in Sommers' *The Mummy Returns*.

8. Whale's Brutes die Hard

Myth! **Whale's Frankenstein monster dies in the same manner as in Mary Shelley's novel.**

In the 1931 movie, Boris Karloff's character is shown perishing in the flames during the windmill scene. The monster exits differently in other films, dying in as many ways as there are sequels, versions and parodies of the original. As the definitive Frankenstein movie, Whale's masterpiece is presumed to hew closest to the literary source.

This impression is wrong. In Mary Shelley's story, Victor Frankenstein is the one who dies. The monster creation he leaves behind remains elusive and invincible as it goes on a seemingly endless journey around the world. As Mary tells it, after the monster flees from Frankenstein's laboratory, the two meet a year later on the slopes of Mont Blanc. The creature admits to an inability to identify with humans because of clumsiness, which causes unintentional injury and even death to those it tries to befriend, and not because of a lack of human sentiments. To assuage the problem, it demands that Frankenstein provide a mate that it can disappear with in the jungles of South America. Frankenstein's failure to deliver incites the monster to kill his bride on her wedding night. Frankenstein tries to escape by constant traveling, but the creature pursues him until he dies in the Arctic when the ship he is on becomes trapped in the ice. Finally, it appears treading over the ice, mourns over its creator's corpse, and then leaps from the ship vowing to destroy itself.

IV

A Trekkie's Guide To The Galaxy

On 'Star Trek' and Science Fiction

"Without freedom of choice there is no creativity.
The body dies."

•

James T. Kirk

1. Captains Courageous

Myth! The USS Enterprise was the first warp speed Federation spaceship, and Captain Kirk was its first commander.

The impression one gets from viewing the initial episodes of Star Trek on television is that Captain Kirk was the helmsman of the first Federation spaceship to experience warp speed. This assumption runs smack against the mythos in two respects: *one*, the first warp speed spaceship of the great interplanetary alliance was the USS Bonaventure under Captain Robert April, and *two*, Kirk was not, in any case, the first to take charge of the USS Enterprise.

The revelation about the USS Bonaventure may seem less than authoritative, coming as it does from the minimally animated TV version of Star Trek and not from the live action series. But the ever-loyal Trekkie who has viewed Episode 16 of the original series would doubtless agree that Kirk had at least one predecessor on the bridge of his great ship. Kirk, played by the Canadian actor William Shatner, headed the cast of characters in the TOS (The Original Series) universe from the first to the third and last season, except in the pilot episode "The Cage," starring the late Jeffrey Hunter as the original Enterprise commander Christopher Pike. For reasons of his own, Hunter declined to get on board the series after debuting on the pilot, but the latter proved so good it was mixed into the plot of the two-part 'Episode 16: The Menagerie', in which Pike is severely injured and is replaced by Kirk.

Thus, Kirk was already the third to captain a warp speed Federation ship, though it is unclear if he was also the last within the ambit of the original series. Captain William Decker took over from Kirk as commander of the Enterprise during the two and a half years the vessel was out of service while undergoing an extensive restoration and upgrade in dry-dock orbit around the Earth (*Star Trek: The Motion Picture*). But as the Enterprise was obviously lacking warp speed capability in this state, Decker could not have assumed the enviable status of captain of a warp speed vessel during his short-lived assignment. Later, Kirk came on again in his new capacity as admiral, after which the Enterprise became a training ship under the command of Spock (at last!). But again, it is doubtful if the Enterprise remained 'warp speed' ready or kept its classification as a warp speed vessel while on commission as a training ship under the Vulcan's stewardship. At any rate, it wasn't long before Spock at his own behest ceded control back to Kirk. It may look like Gene Roddenberry did not anticipate these various changes in command when he created the series, but most Trekkies insist the way Star Trek's chronology unfolds reveals a continuity that's both deliberate and well thought out

2. Going Ago-go

Myth! **It is not possible to see events as they happened in the past.**

We saw how Kirk lived the experience of time travel by stepping into what looked like an electromagnetic space frame in 'Episode 28: The City on the Edge of Forever'. This is arguably the best of the TOS episodes because of the sensitive use of romance and other elements to link the future with the past, but science-wise, it sucks. Or does it?

Much is said about the possibility of viewing the past through time travel, and there have been scientific papers and sci-fi conventions dedicated to the idea. Esoteric concepts like black holes, naked singularities, and causality violation are explored to prove that the idea is at least worth looking into in the light of Einstein's theory of relativity. Staunch realists and conventional thinkers can't seem to be convinced: "The past involves events that had a beginning and an ending…Otherwise, we would have to allow that, say, Julius Caesar, somewhere in the universe, must perpetually be having his diapers changed, cross the Rubicon again and again, and be forever stabbed by Brutus."

To those willing to consider the matter in a different though no less scientific context, 'seeing' the past is not just possible but certain. While the past is forever lost and cannot be retrieved, images of it can be seen through the vagaries of light in another time dimension such as the present. In fact, says an advocate, the question is academic "because the past can actually be viewed right now…We look out at stars many light-years distant. We see

332

them not as they are now, but as they were when the light left them. For example, a star eight light-years distant is seen as it was eight years ago. An astronomer on a planet 2000 light-years away, had he a magical telescope of superpower, might see Caesar cross the Rubicon. A mythical astronomer five billion light-years away might see the earth itself come into existence."

3. Warp Notions

Myth! **Warp speed is attainable for space travel in the future.**

With its mission of exploring a space environment many millenniums away from present reality, the USS Enterprise does argue strongly for faster-than-light travel. Given that human knowledge is not static and will progress to ever higher levels, can we expect warp speed, maybe not in the next century or two, but sometime in the future?

Warp drive is a level of power needed to boost the rate of spatial speed beyond ordinary limits. In the lingo of *Star Trek: The Original Series (TOS)*, Warp 1 is the speed of light, Warp 2 is the speed of light squared, Warp 3 is the speed of light cubed and so on. Warp speed is possible in the sci-fi world because the ship is made to operate in a hypothetical dimension of space (called hyperspace) in which the laws of nature are suspended. But in the world of scientific reality, where there is only normal space, Einstein's thesis that nothing can exceed the speed of light holds. The sound barrier may be cracked several fold—men have actually flown well past Mach 1—but the light barrier has never been exceeded and will never be even in theory.

To a TV program that is known all around to be more fiction than science, it shouldn't really matter if the script were to take some liberties with physical laws for the sake of entertainment. Nevertheless, TOS executives have insisted that "everything in Star Trek has been thoroughly researched by scientists," including warp speed, which allegedly was justified by the discovery of energy waves that travel faster than the speed of light. To reconcile hardnosed viewers to the idea, a limit was set on warp speed at Warp 10 (or 'trans warp') "because it's assumed that at

Warp 10, you were at all places in the universe simultaneously." When Trekkies became confused seeing the Enterprise traveling at speeds in excess of the limit—in fact well over Warp 14 in some episodes—production technicians recalculated warp speed to accommodate the error, using a cubic power system by which Warp 2 is 8 (2×2x2) times the speed of light, Warp 3 is 27 (3×3x3) times the speed of light, and so on. Even with the limit, however, critics wouldn't bite, saying that while scientists have *conceived* of—as opposed to *discovered*—particles that travel faster than the speed of light, these particles, called 'tachyons', remain wholly in the realm of science fantasy as much as warp speed does. Summarizing their views, one writes: "A ship won't get from Kirk's part of the universe to the nearest star in less than 5,000 to 10,000 years, and no one can ever hope to improve on this because there is no way of breaking Einstein's light barrier."

---

4. A Beam in his Eye

Myth! **One of Kirk's most frequent expressions is, "Beam me up, Scotty."**

The technology of the transporter may only be a gleam in a Trekkie's eye, but the device itself is not only common in science fiction, it has also brought about one of the genre's most popular expressions—"Beam me up, Scotty!"

In a typical episode of TOS, Captain Kirk, reconnoitering on a strange planet within 'beaming distance' of the USS Enterprise, snaps open his communicator and asks an officer to have him 'beamed' back to the space craft. Despite the frequent use of this sequence in the series, not a few have challenged the precise wording of the line. A September article in a 1993 issue of TV Guide states that Kirk almost always transmitted the request to Spock, the long-eared Vulcan, and no character in any episode ever used the words "Beam me up, Scotty!" on Chief Engineer Scott or any of his associates in the great ship. Quite likely, the most often used line was the impersonal "Enterprise, beam us up," but Ralph Keyes says "Beam us up, Mr. Scott" was also common. Trekkies who swear Shatner did say "Scotty, beam me up" once in Star Trek's fourth episode seem to have the last word.

5. No Man's Land

Myth! **The motto of the Star Trek series is, 'To boldly go where no man has gone before'.**

A phrase made famous by *Star Trek*, 'To boldly go where no man has gone before', is the last portion of the grandiloquent statement Kirk makes to open each episode of the three season series. The following trivia may help dispel some of the wrong beliefs about this cult saying:

• Because Kirk has not come on board yet, his statement is omitted in the pilot episode 'The Cage'. It is avoided as well in 'Where No Man Has Gone Before', probably to avoid repeating the episode's title.

• While touted as the motto of the series, it's actually the motto of Kirk's Enterprise beginning in the 23rd century. However, it does not appear on the ship's simple dedication plaque in any of the episodes, although it does appear on the dedication plaque of the later Enterprise-A in some of the *Star Trek* movies. It is also found engraved on the base of a non-functional decorative ship's wheel located in the ship's lounge in *Star Trek V: The Final Frontier*.

• The expression gained prominence for its flawed use of a split infinitive and the gender-leaning word 'man'.

• The phrase 'to go where no one has gone before' is believed to have been lifted from a White House publication entitled *Introduction To Outer Space* and published in 1958 to garner support for a national space program in the wake of the Sputnik flight.

• Following the events of *Star Trek VI: The Undiscovered Country*, which dealt with cross-species racism, the word 'man' was changed to the neutral 'one' by Kirk to accommodate non-human life species in the galaxy. The new version subsequently became part of the opening line of *Star Trek: The Next Generation*, though this time it was more to appease women libbers and emphasize the larger roles women play in the new series.

335

• For Trekkies, the real motto of the series is Spock's line, "Live long and prosper," accompanied by a hand gesture called the 'Vulcan salute'. The motto was not part of any *Star Trek* script but an invention by Leonard Nimoy (Mr. Spock) on the set of 'Amok Time'. Having been a devout Jew his entire life, Nimoy plucked the words "Live long and prosper" from a benediction that rabbis used to give over their congregation, while the hand gesture is a representation of the first Hebrew letter in 'Shadai', one of God's sacred names. A gem of a parody can be found in the 1999 Tim Allen movie *Galaxy Quest*.

---

6. A Philadelphia Story

Myth! Basic technology is already available for the phaser and the teletransporter.

Laser pistols were the standard weaponry of the Enterprise crew in 'The Cage', but in the series that followed, Kirk used an entirely new ray gun, the phaser. Not a few Trekkies stick to calling the shooter a 'fazer' in the belief that it's main function was to faze or disorient an adversary without lethal consequences. Most others say there should be no quarrel here; the gun deserves to be called both a fazer and a phaser because of its two major settings, or 'phases'. While the fazer setting was the weakest, there was nothing conceivably more powerful than the second, which was to disintegrate or annihilate matter.

The incarnation of the phaser as a stun gun is visible in many police armories in the US today. Undoubtedly, at the rate the technology is improving, it shouldn't take long before the phaser's full potential as a fazer is reached in the real world. However, the 'matter destroying' capability of this wonder weapon is so far out that no practical time frame for attaining it can be set. Scientists state that, applying the fundamental laws of physics, matter can't just disappear or be destroyed anywhere in the universe without leaving some trace or residue, such as gas, subatomic particles, plasma or photons, in the same or another location. Disintegration of matter by phaser should at least produce so-called 'neutrinos', which are so small they are practically invisible, and which carry no amount of electrical charge that would render them palpable.

336

But as there is no known nuclear process for the conversion of matter into neutrinos, the phaser as an alternative will probably remain a provocative fixture of science fiction for a long time yet. The still unknown principle behind the phaser may well be the same one that underlies the teletransporter, which enabled the Enterprise to move crewmembers molecule by molecule from a launching pad to a specified destination. The claim that teletransportation is realizable within the context of quantum physics and Einstein's 'unified force theory' has drummed up cult support for the infamous 1943 Philadelphia Experiment, which allegedly made a whole ship, a US Navy destroyer, invisible and capable of time travel through the use of massive coils devised by Nikola Tesla (remember him and his transporter machine in the 2006 film *The Prestige*?). As described by the proponents of that so-called experiment, the vessel 'teleported' from the Philadelphia Navy Yard to Norfolk, Virginia, and back in a matter of minutes. It is said that, were it not for the negative effects of the force field on the mental and physical health of the crew, the experiment would have been continued and would almost surely have changed the course of the war.

The US navy has denied the story, but it broke into print as William L. Moore's *The Philadelphia Experiment* in 1979. Of late, Moore has changed his tune, claiming that the real experiment was for making ships radar-proof to foil German radar-guided torpedoes. Critics say if Moore's intention was to discredit the teletransportation theory, he might have achieved just the opposite. His second version proves even more fantastic, as radar doesn't work underwater and there can be no such thing as a radar-guided torpedo. What the Germans were using in World War II were acoustic torpedoes that honed in on the sound of a ship's engines.

To give the evidence a more respectable sheen, advocates cite the more recent achievements of Professor Eugene Polzik and his team at the Niels Bohr Institute at Copenhagen University in Denmark, where huge amounts of information were successfully transmitted and processed in a way that had not been possible before. But detractors spite Professor Polzik's efforts as 'stone age' developments in the field of quantum information and computers—and thoroughly incapable of validating what has to be the 'hoax of the century'.

7. Quirky, Kinky and Kirky

Myth! TV's first interracial kiss occurred on one of the episodes of Star Trek.

In the same issue of TV Guide, William Shatner reveals that TV's first interracial kiss did not occur, as is popularly supposed, in the Star Trek episode 'Plato's Stepchildren'. Here was an opportunity for TOS, known for having boldly gone beyond the frontiers of space and sound, to break one more 'S' barrier, that of sex. If Shatner is to be believed, they muffed it.

The scene was first shot with the two actors—Michelle Nichols, a black woman playing Uhura, and Shatner playing Kirk—actually kissing on camera. When NBC executives saw the preview, they were bothered about the reception that the episode would get from television stations all over the South. Gene Roddenberry, creator and producer of the series, insisted on having the scene remain as written, but in actual production, he agreed to compromise by having it shot two ways.

In the first, there was lip contact, but in the second, the players merely simulated the kiss, turning their bodies as they embraced so that Kirk's back was to the camera long before their lips would have ever touched. It all seemed like Nichols and Shatner kissed, but only his back and her arms around his neck could be seen. Shatner says: "Sadly, the network got their way and the 'no-contact kiss' made it to the airwaves. For that reason, the widely held assumption that Star Trek features the first interracial kiss in the history of television is absolutely untrue. And if you happen across the episode, look closely and you'll see exactly what I mean." Sadly, indeed, for a breakthrough television series that endeavored to cut across time and space with an interplanetary bill of rights for all human races and for extraterrestrials as well.

In the absence of the Rodenberry version that did not air, we resorted to a DVD copy of 'Plato's Stepchildren' and compared its kissing scene with the laundered one Shatner describes. The disc shows Nichols turning her head back on the screen to prevent a full view of the actors' mouths, while Kirk presses his face close to Nichols' seemingly in preparation for a kiss. Thereafter, nothing can be discerned about their lips except the suggestion that, though

338

close together, they actually never achieve full contact. If this had aired as the version Rodenberry shot and kept under wraps, it still would have come up short of the media hype generated for 'TV's first interracial kiss' over the years.

8. Fission Vision

Myth! **Cleve Cartmill was the first to describe the atomic bomb accurately in a public writing.**

Cleve Cartmill was not a scientist nor even a science writer—and definitely not one remotely familiar with the workings of the atom bomb. Yet he did a premature, though totally innocent, write-up—according to popular perception, the first public description ever—about the super weapon in one of his short stories. Cleve gave a detailed rendition so uncannily accurate that not a few eyebrows were raised at the Manhattan Project where the bomb was undergoing development at the time. The authorities, convinced that Cartmill had no scientific knowledge of the real weapon, decided an investigation would only call attention to the highly secret project.

The original story Cartmill wrote was entitled "Deadline," and appeared in the March 1944 issue of the magazine *Astounding Science Fiction*. But others not quite impressed with Cartmill say the author most likely got his idea of the bomb from a greater name in science fiction, H. G. Wells. The British fantasist was the first to use the term 'atomic bomb', having coined it in a science fiction story entitled "The World Set Free" and published in 1914. This was in itself a feat, occurring as it did thirty years before the bomb became a reality, but Wells more than just casually mentioned the word. He described the concept in such detail that when the noted Hungarian physicist Leo Szilard read the novel, it provoked him to think about the power that could be generated by a nuclear chain reaction. The rest, of course, is history. Szilard collaborated with Enrico Fermi on a nuclear reactor that turned out to be the source of the world's first atomic bomb.

339

9. Floppy Disk

Myth! The Enterprise is shaped like a flying saucer, which is the most familiar form of a UFO.

The Enterprise of the Star Trek movies and of both TOS and TNG may look somewhat like a flying saucer, but the similarity was obviously not intended. As far as is known, there is not a single reference to 'flying saucer' in the series, and no other ship in any of the episodes comes close to being confused with a flying saucer as it was first imagined when the term was coined.

The common perception is that the famous Orson Welles 'hoax' of 1938 planted the term 'flying saucer' in our vocabulary. Actually, Welles' radio program hewed very closely to the book on which it was based—H. G. Wells' *War of the Worlds*—and did not mention saucers or saucer-like objects, as these were not in the story. What comes nearest to a description of the invaders' transport was Welles' referring to it vaguely as a meteor that was later seen to be 'a humming metal cylinder'. It was the 1953 movie version of the Wells opus that roused public awareness for flying saucers when special effects master George Pal erroneously showed the Martian space vehicles in this manner. Oddly, the movie never once spoke the phrase 'flying saucer', although this was already familiar at the time. The word 'saucer' was used as early as 1878, when John Martin saw a saucer-like aircraft over Denison, Texas, and 'flying saucers' was coined in 1947 by reporter Bill Bequette of *The East Oregonian* in reference to the sighting of UFOs by Kenneth Arnold on June 24 that year.

It was not on Halloween night in 1938, but the night before, that Orson Welles went on radio to announce that a flaming object from the sky had landed in New Jersey. Some people call Welles' performance America's most famous hoax, believing that the 23-year-old actor-impresario did the show as a Halloween joke. In fact, there was no premeditated trickery and Welles was as surprised as everyone else at the way the public reacted. He and his sponsors had even made sure to spot an announcement throughout the broadcast warning that it was all a play.

10. Alien Farce

Myth! Steven Spielberg coined the word 'extraterrestrial' and its initials 'E.T.'

The TV series *Star Trek: The Next Generation* (TNG) belongs to the rare sci-fi genre in which the concept of extraterrestrials is almost totally irrelevant. The word is used elsewhere for space beings alien to Earth, but in TNG, Captain Jean-Luc Picard's milieu is the whole universe and Earth is no longer considered a reference point for his crew, many of whom are citizens of other planets.

Hollywood and other popular writers have created the standard sci-fi bugaboo—a space alien being with monstrous qualities and a threatening attitude. With the exceptions of Steven Spielberg's cinematic creations in *E.T. The Extraterrestrial* and *Close Encounters of the Third Kind*, it's mostly hostile out there— according to the tenet that provided the *raison d'être* of the original *Star Trek* adventures. This was considerably toned down in TNG, when the Federation expanded in membership and formerly hostile beings became allies, at times even co-adventurers.

The term 'extraterrestrial' was apparently born from the perspective that anything beyond earth's atmosphere is foreboding and untrustworthy. Actually, H. G. Wells first recorded and may have invented it not in reference to life in outer space but as an adjective meaning 'outside the limits of the earth'. It was American author L. Sprague de Camp who first used 'extraterrestrial' as a noun when he described enemy beings from outer space in the May 1939 issue of *Astounding Science Fiction*. Later, Spielberg would popularize its abbreviation—the now familiar 'E.T.'—as the name of a child-like space being who endears himself to an earth family while trying to get back home.

The public is, as always, uneasy with the prospect of a close encounter with extraterrestrials, but scientists take a different view. Adjudging the Hollywood stereotype (see, e.g., M. Night Shyamalan's *Signs* [2002] and Roland Emmerich's *Independence Day* [1996], as well as TV's *The X-Files*) as unrealistic and the Spielberg mold more justifiable, they argue that any life form capable of achieving space travel at the interstellar level will not

341

have barbarian reflexes or urges to kill on sight. Alien contact, if it comes, will "more likely be one of peace and exchange of mutually beneficial knowledge...The presumption is that such sophisticated beings exploring the vastness of space will not waste time traveling fabulous distances only to destroy or enslave the human race."

11. Science Friction

Myth! Star Trek is the most realistic and predictive science fiction series shown on the screen.

In "Star Trek Realism: The Good, the Bad, and the Ugly" and "Myths: Star Trek," two internet articles at *stardestroyer.net,* Michael Wong applies cold logic and scientific insight to demolish the widespread myth propagated by Trekkie overenthusiasm that Star Trek is both scientifically realistic and predictive. He derides a host of misconceptions that he says the writers of the series have succeeded in promoting through "technobabble." For instance: "In Star Trek, it is possible to use sound waves as a weapon against a starship in the vacuum of space, cool something below absolute zero, live on an inhabitable planet which is only ten light-seconds from its star....shrink a shuttlecraft to the size of a thimble, make gravity propagate at superluminal speed...come to a meaningless 'full stop' in outer space...live without being born, fly a ship that was never built, dig up miraculously naturally-occurring alloys, vapourize something without producing any vapour...and take a drug that protects you from radiation." Wong laughs down the idea of a phaser that distinguishes between a male and a female target; of time travel creating parallel universes and alternate timelines; and of a cloaking device that can cause a ship to become invisible but not 'blind'.

Wong debunks the claim that Star Trek has predicted many developments in science and technology, e.g., cellphones, quasars, fiber optics, dark matter, black holes, and antimatter. Cellphones, he says, are miniaturized transceivers tied to a large network, and can't be the same as Star Trek communicators that transmit and receive directly with one another like walkie-talkies. Quasars and fiber optics preceded TNG, while dark matter was theorized long

342

before TOS hit the airwaves. John Mitchell's speculations on black holes two centuries ago comfortably "predate the adventures of Captain Kirk." And antimatter first became a topic of conversation among scientists and philosophers more than seventy years ago.

V

A Mild-Mannered Report On Superheroes

On Comic Book Superheroes

"I'm here to fight for truth, and justice, and the American way."

•

Superman

1. The Big Red One

Myth! **Superman is the first American fictional superhero.**

Superman is the first fictional superhero in American pop culture, but then again he is not. Using the baseline description of 'superhero' as one "with extraordinary ability or prowess dedicated to acts of derring-do in the public interest," Superman is not the earliest of the breed. Some denizens of pulp fiction and the comic strip, like Doc Savage and the Phantom, though not endowed with super powers, have physical and mental capabilities beyond the normal that help them fight crime. And they predated Superman by several years during the decade of the 30s.

Superman becomes *numero uno* only if we narrow down the definition to those superheroes that appear in a *comic book* and wear a *costume* or use an *alter ego* to protect a *secret identity*. In this sense the Man of Steel aces out the great Mandrake the Magician notwithstanding that the latter made his comic book debut four years earlier. Broadly speaking, the top-hatted and mustachioed illusionist is a superhero because, despite his lacking super traits, he has extraordinary techniques and pseudo powers, such as sleight of hand, street magic and hypnosis, which help him defeat his enemies. But for lack of a costume and a secret identity, comic book purists deny him access to the coterie to which Superman, Batman and a few others belong.

In summary, while a comic book superhero need not be super human, he must at least (1) have some *super power* or *extraordinary ability*, (2) wear a *costume* or maintain a *secret identity*, and (3) *fight lawbreakers*. There are other peculiarities common to the superhero concept, but they are not mandatory, e.g., adherence to a *moral code*; a special *motivation* to fight evil; a frailty or *weakness,* usually physical, that sometimes stops him in his tracks; a *secret headquarters* or *laboratory* with access to *advanced equipment* or *technology;* and a *bête noire* or *arch enemy* who may himself be super human. Superman as the exemplar of the genre possesses all these optional features and traits to a greater or lesser degree. Due to his extraterrestrial origin, Superman's moral and emotional make-up is almost totally incorruptible by normal human influences, but he is considerably weakened in the presence of Kryptonite. He hies to his Fortress of

Solitude to replenish his spent energy and consult its database for his next course of action. The climax of many of his adventures is a confrontation between him and the evil and cunning Lex Luthor, whose ambition to conquer the world appears to be the raison d'être for both hero and villain.

Superman may not be the first fictional superhero, generally speaking, but he is the best known of all time. His post-World War II popularity has transcended the comic book and the Man of Steel is now common fare in practically all media, including radio, television, movies and digital disks. Three movies in the 70s and 80s and one in 2006 have generated considerable box office success and helped boost Superman's image as an American culture icon even more.

2. American Splendor

Myth! Action Comics No. 1 is the most valuable comic book because it's the most rare.

Considered the first true superhero comic book for featuring the original appearance of Jerry Siegel and Joe Shuster's Superman, Action Comics No. 1 continues to be the most popular and the most marketable of all such media. Though not among the most rare—a little less than 100 copies are known to exist—it is the most expensive bar none. In 1996, NY-based Metropolis Comics sold two high-grade copies for $150,000 each. Lower grade copies have gone for less—one was sold for $100,000 in 1997, while another quoted at $250,000 went for a mere $40,101 on eBay recently. As of September 2007, Action Comics #1 is the most valuable comic for a given condition, based partly on the report that in 2003 Stephen A. Geppi, owner of Diamond Comic Distributors, offered to buy a near mint (CGC grade 9.4) copy for $1,000,000 at the First Annual Las Vegas Comic-Con. This distinction has been garnished many times over by an announcement from *yahoo.com* that in November 2011, a copy of Action Comics #1 was sold at auction for an awesome $2.16 million—from a starting bid of $1!

346

For now, however, the most rare comic book is still Motion Picture Funnies Weekly # 1, an unpublished, 36-page, black-and-white American series created in 1939. Designed to be a promotional giveaway in movie theaters, the issue was aborted after only a handful of sample copies were printed. Seven, plus one without a cover, surfaced in 1974 among the assets of the deceased publisher, with no indication that there may be more elsewhere. This collectors' item is known for introducing the Marvel Comics character Namor the Sub-Mariner, the god-prince of the sea, which writer-artist Bill Everett created. However, being rare is obviously no guarantee of a high price; in 2005, Motion Picture Funnies Weekly # 1 emerged as a 'pay copy' carrying a pre-auction estimate of $100,000, but fetched only $43,125. Oddly, the more accessible Marvel Comics # 1 featuring the color debut of Namor the Sub-Mariner sold for a whopping $161,000 in the same auction.

---

3. This Red Cheese got Spoiled

Myth! Superman's unrivaled popularity caused the demise of Captain Marvel.

There is no truth to the hype that Superman was hugely more popular than Captain Marvel, or that this was the reason the latter bowed out of the Golden Age of comics.

There was a time not far from the recollection of forty-niners when Superman was running a poor second to Captain Marvel in popular acceptance. The Big Red Cheese, as Captain Marvel was fondly called, is no longer around, but on memory lane, he will always be the Fred MacMurray look-alike that appeared in a flash of lightning whenever young Billy Batson shouted the acronym 'SHAZAM'. Billed as 'the World's Mightiest Mortal', he came out eighteen months after Superman's introduction in 1938, and by 1943 his Captain Marvel Adventures was selling about a million copies per issue. In 1946 the figure approached a million and a half, a level that has not been equaled by any other comic book to this date.

347

Captain Marvel would have gone on to establish more records had he not been stopped in his tracks by the courts. DC Comics brought a case in 1941 against Fawcett Publications for infringement of copyright, alleging that Captain Marvel stole many features from Superman, including his super powers (flight, super-strength, super-speed and invincibility), his general costuming and his secret identity. Fawcett argued back that, although Superman came on the scene earlier than Captain Marvel, there were enough differences in essential plot and concept elements to overcome their similarities. In addition, certain superhero features that debuted with Captain Marvel but not with Superman—e.g., an alter-ego in lieu of a secret identity and powers that are magic-based as opposed to science-based—were Fawcett properties in their own right and did not constitute infringement.

Twelve years after the case was filed, the courtroom battle between the red titans ended when a highly respected American magistrate, Justice Learned Hand of the US Court of Appeals for the Second Circuit, unexpectedly ruled in favor of DC Comics. Critics lauded Justice Hand's erudition but insisted the decision dealt a blow to freedom of competition by snuffing out a budding icon of popular culture in one stroke of the pen. Among the matters that, in their opinion, should have reversed the outcome but were glossed over or totally ignored were:

• Superman could not have claimed exclusive rights to super-strength, super-speed, flight and invulnerability, as these were generic traits of most fantasy creations and would in fact become common standards to many superheroes after the Golden Age.

• Captain Marvel was a mortal with extraordinary powers, whereas Superman was an extraterrestrial with ordinary powers in the context of his home planet.

• Captain Marvel did not pilfer his costume from Superman's wardrobe. The first to use a skintight costume with briefs worn over it was an earlier superhero, the Phantom, implying that both Captain Marvel and Superman borrowed their costumes from that source. But unlike Superman, Captain Marvel had at least the decency to leave off the briefs.

Learned Hand's decision effectively put an end to the Fawcett stalwart as well as to Captain Marvel, Jr., Mary Marvel and the rest of the Marvel family of superheroes. In 1980, DC bought the rights to the Fawcett characters outright, and in 1987 relaunched

348

Captain Marvel in a miniseries entitled 'Shazam!: The New Beginning'. But it was a case of too late the hero. DC could no longer capitalize on the name Captain Marvel, as a competitor, Marvel Comics, had succeeded in registering the comic book's title during the years Fawcett was out of the market. DC had to promote the new adventures under the name Shazam, in reference to the mysterious old wizard that gave Captain Marvel his powers, but the move confused most readers into thinking the superhero's name was Shazam. Though the miniseries was moderately successful, DC has never been able to recapture the post-war fame of the Big Red Cheese under the Fawcett brand.

4. This Old Steel gets Polished

Myth! **Krypton is named after a real chemical element discovered in 1898.**

Those feeling stiff towards some aspects of American pop culture are bound to question the logic of the entire Superman universe. Could there be anything more ludicrous than the image of a man wearing briefs over tight pants who is "faster than a speeding bullet, more powerful than a locomotive, and able to leap tall buildings in a single bound?" In the never-ending effort to expand the superhero's market appeal, inconsistencies, fallacies and other sources of confusion have been made to pile up season after season. DC Comics as owner of the franchise has endeavored to catch up with the problem through revisions and corrections, at times to give the character and his macrocosm some needed tensile strength and at other times their rationality. According to the critics, it's like taking two steps backward for every step forward all the way.

• DC introduced the *deus ex machina* of the 'multiverse within the same fictional universe', which allowed characters published in the 1940s to exist alongside updated counterparts published in the 1960s. The justification offered to the reader was the notion that twin sets of characters inhabited parallel Earths. The ploy allowed Superman to become a member of both the 1940s Justice Society of America and the 1960s Justice League of America.

349

• There were attempts to rein in the superpowers of the hero to make him more credibly human, but there were as many attempts to bring him back to his original superhuman self. Thus, the 1990s saw Superman killed by the villain Doomsday, only to see his character resurrected as strong as ever not too long after. In 2006 Superman was stripped of his powers, but later these were restored within a fictional year. In the 1980s his space flights were limited by how long he could hold his breath; apparently he couldn't hold it long enough because within the decade he was again seen surviving in the vacuum of outer space without oxygen.

• Just before Krypton explodes, the baby Kal-El (Superman's real identity, as opposed to Clark Kent, which is his secret earth identity) is placed in an earthbound capsule by one of his parents—his father, according to the 1978 movie *Superman*, or his mother, if we go by the 1980 sequel. Later editions of the comic book as well as the movie adaptations show that the Man of Steel can fly and wield superpowers deep in outer space, raising the question why his fellow Kryptonians did not think of using the same abilities to save themselves from the planet's destruction. The answer usually given is that, like Superman, they could only rise to the level of super beings when they were no longer breathing Kryptonian air or touching Kryptonian soil. From the comics' own writers comes a second explanation: Kryptonians, whose native star Rao had been red, possessed superpowers only under the light of a yellow sun like Earth's. Both premises have also been used to explain why Superman weakens in the presence of Kryptonite and why his X-ray vision can melt anything except matter indigenous to Krypton.

• The little known fact is that Kryptonite was introduced to the public in 1943 for a more practical reason, i.e., as a plot device to allow the radio serial voice actor, Bud Collyer, to take some time off. Only later, in 1949, did the comic book writers begin to incorporate it into their stories as both a convenient danger and weakness for Superman. Kryptonite is a fictional piece off Superman's home planet Krypton and has nothing to do with the chemical element Krypton, which Nobel Prize winner Sir William Ramsay and Morris Travers discovered in Great Britain in 1898 from residue left after evaporating nearly all components of liquid air. Apparently, Siegel and Shuster adopted the name Krypton because it sounded out of this world, an apparent misconception

350

on their part considering that the real Krypton is a noble gas that has never escaped the earth's atmosphere since its formation.

• Superman's eye vision is yet another anomaly that needs some explanation. It is claimed that Clark's glasses were fashioned out of the windshield of the space capsule that brought him to earth in order to avoid melting them when he uses his eyes for x-ray purposes. This seems both unnecessary and illogical, since Clark can always regulate his vision so as not to melt anything, or else he only has to remove his glasses if he wants to use his vision for melting. When Clark Kent tried to enlist in the US Army in World War II, he was declared 4-F, meaning unfit to serve, because he had accidentally pierced a wall with his x-ray vision, read the wrong eye chart in the other room, and consequently flunked the test. This may have forced Clark to remain a civilian, but it was no reason for Superman to be absent from the war. If the idea was to keep Superman out of the conflict, as it no doubt was, he could just have filed an application and waited for the draft board to reject it based on his alien status as a Kryptonian.

5. One Dark Knight

Myth! Bob Kane originated the name and persona of Batman.

The origin of Batman is revealed in two pages of Detective Comics # 33, relating how the young Bruce Wayne witnesses the sidewalk slaying of both his parents by a hold-upper. The boy vows on the spot to "avenge their deaths by spending the rest of his life warring on all criminals."

Detective Comics #33 is available as part of a 20-issue Batman archive from Amazon at less than $10 for the whole batch. Yet its story on Batman's origin is reprinted as the main feature in Batman #1, which can only be bought at auction for thousands of dollars. Such are the vagaries of the comic book trade. As pricey an asset as this story would be, it was made to suffer some degradation when it was rescripted for the movie screen. Flub collectors have noted that in the 1989 *Batman*, the Joker—played to the hilt by Jack Nicholson—admits to the masked crusader that

351

he (Batman) was "just a kid" when he (the Joker) killed Bruce Wayne's parents. Bob Kane, author of the comic book source and reportedly a consultant on the script of the movie, evidently missed this odd piece of dialogue. Quite clearly, Nicholson's line is premised on the idea that the Joker knows Bruce Wayne is the man in the iron-like mask, an assumption totally forbidden in the comic book.

Kane's omission is unusual for one who has always been regarded as the sole creator of the Batman character. But it becomes perfectly understandable once it's made clear that the Batman idea and its early development were not by Kane alone. Although Bill Finger's name never once appeared on the feature, it was this writer who did the early stories under the influence of his hero The Shadow, and Kane only drew them. On the other hand, another Kane teammate, Gardner Fox, and not Finger or Kane, authored the tale of Batman's origin. Kane's original vision of Batman, whom he called Birdman, was of a figure in a domino mask clad in a flamboyant red and blue outfit, fighting insipid criminal elements in urban ghettos. Finger changed the character's basic appearance and renamed him Batman. He also invented Batman's sidekick Robin, and gave names to things Kane hadn't bothered to put a tag on, such as the Batmobile, Bruce Wayne, Gotham City and the Batcave. Kane had little to do even with Gotham City's villains, who were designed over the years by other imaginative ghost artists, such as Jerry Robinson, creator of the irrepressible Joker and one of the first to draw for the strip.

6. Web Site

Myth! **Stan Lee created the concept of Spider-Man.**

Bitten by a radioactive spider at a science exhibit, Peter Parker gains superhuman strength and agility and the ability to cling to any surface. He becomes Spider-Man, the amazing superhero that everyone assumes is the brainchild of Stan Lee, writer and editor of the Spider-Man magazines. According to Lee, he came up with the project because he wanted "a strip that would actually feature a teenager as a star" and "in which the main character would lose as often as he'd win." The name Spider-Man was in homage to one of his favorite pulp magazine heroes, a stalwart named the Spider.

But artist Jack Kirby insists Spidey was his idea, not Lee's. "It was the last thing Joe Simon and I had discussed. So the idea was already there when I talked to Stan." Simon is yet another claimant, who says he and a writer named Jack Oleck started the whole thing in the mid-1950s. Working with artist C.C. Beck, they created a character first called Spiderman and then the Silver Spider. Later in the 1950s, Simon and Kirby turned the Silver Spider material into The Fly and sold it to the Archie Comics group. Simon admits that none of these concepts ever became the final version of Spider-Man, as artist Steve Ditko, who favored his own interpretation when he drew the stories in 'Amazing Fantasy', junked every one of them. Who among the six is Spidey's real father has not been resolved—and probably need not be, since the question of multiple progeny should ensure a long life for this humorously bizarre character.

---

7. Shadow of his former Self

Myth! **Before gaining the power of invisibility, Lamont Cranston wore a mask as The Shadow.**

The Shadow has been a comic strip character since the 1940s, and in comic books since 1964, but he was an even greater fantasy figure in his own pulp fiction magazine and on his own radio show in the 1930s. This multi-media development has given rise to many inconsistencies, the most notable of which concerns The Shadow's identity. During the 1930s he was Lamont Cranston, millionaire playboy, but towards the end of the decade, it was discovered that the name was just another alias lent to him by a friend, the real Lamont Cranston, and that he was really the well-known aviator Kent Allard. Later in the comic books, he resumed being Lamont Cranston.

The Shadow's power of making himself invisible is yet another anomaly. It was revealed that many years before, he had picked up the knack of clouding men's minds so they could not see him. However, he did not have this power during his pulp magazine

353

days, having acquired it only when he passed on to radio and later to comics. His real talent was in assuming various disguises, e.g., as Fritz the janitor at police headquarters.

When Orson Welles was playing him on radio in the 1930s, the typical promo material for the series was a photo of The Shadow before a radio microphone, dressed in black and wearing a mask. His fans were made to believe this was the costume he wore, although he was never so described on the programs. The stories and the comic books, while just as vague, omit the mask and refer only to a slouch hat and a cape, obviously the only accouterments for a hero who prefers to stay in the shadows.

VI
Don't Forget The Duck!

On Mickey Mouse and his Friends

"Animation can explain whatever
the mind of man can conceive."

•

Walt Disney

1. Give Mickey a big Hand

Myth! Cartoon humans like Bart Simpson have five fingers, while cartoon animals like Louie the Orangutan have only four.

According to a Disney biography, the idea actually came from Mickey's artist Ub Iwerks, and the principal reason was aesthetic. Mickey had big hands, which were made even bigger by the white minstrel gloves that were given him to provide color contrast to his black body. Walt agreed with Iwerks that five fingers were one too many.

For the characters after Mickey, the bigger reason was economic. Animation used to be drawn one frame at a time, and eliminating one finger from a figure made the chore so much easier to do. Consistency was also a reason—the four-fingered Mickey would have looked odd in the company of five-fingered characters. However, it was obviously not a strong reason, since consistency has not always been a hallowed point in Mickey's world. Pluto has paws while his two-legged cousin, Goofy, has fingers (people who maintain that Goofy is really a horse are not bothered that he was once called Dippy Dawg). Goofy talks and Pluto barks (except that in one cartoon short, the latter utters the line "Kiss me!" in a very clear voice).

If there is anything to be gleaned from Disney's art, observers say it is that a human being's right to a full set of five fingers is assured but animals are cursed with four. Still, this is not a hard and fast rule. In *The Jungle Book* (1967), King Louie the Orangutan is drawn with five fingers, obviously to fulfill in part the jazzy ape's wish "to be like a man." In non-Disney art, the rule has been compromised as well. Witness the two-dimensional human Bart Simpson, who has only four fingers.

2. Mad about the Mouse

Myth! Mickey Mouse is the most popular Disney character ever.

Shirley Temple's monthly average of 60,000 letters in 1936 is the largest number of fan mail received in one year by a movie star—that is to say, a movie star with the requisite five fingers on each hand. In 1933-34, Mickey Mouse, a screen star in his own right, received an average 66,000 letters a month, every single one of which was addressed to Mickey directly. Multiplied a thousand fold, this wouldn't even get close to the kind of popularity Mickey must be enjoying in this age of email and cell phones.

While there are arguments for Mickey as the most popular personality to grace the silver screen, he is only the second most popular Disney character ever created. Donald Duck has appeared in more film footage than any other Disney character, and his comic books have outsold Mickey's since decades ago. After World War II, Mickey's popularity has shifted from the artistic to the commercial, and is now largely built outside films and the comics. He has not appeared in cartoons in ages, but he has kept his image fully alive on TV's Disney Channel and by working as the Disney Studio's mascot. In this latter capacity, he shows up regularly in Disneyland, organizes membership clubs, participates actively in TV specials, and advertises and promotes products.

Although Walt drew neither Donald nor Mickey, he managed Mickey's development into stardom. Donald's patron, on the other hand, was his own artist, Carl Barks, who fleshed out the duck from being a minor character in cartoon shorts to a superstar of comic books. Carl rehabilitated Donald and his nephews and created Uncle Scrooge, a contribution that the Disney Organization publicly acknowledged after Walt died in 1966.

3. Dwarf Stars

Myth! **The first full-length cartoon feature was** *Snow White and the Seven Dwarfs.*

Disney's *Snow White and the Seven Dwarfs* is one of the most successful movie productions in history. But when it came out in 1937, critics proclaimed that the public was not ready for its innovations and called it 'Disney's Folly'. Most now agree that it is the best of Disney's animated features, superior even to many of those blessed by the magic of modern technology.

Disney's masterpiece is proudly listed in many video books as "the world's first feature-length animated movie." This is false. Two from Argentina preceded it by decades—one, the 1917 *El Apostol*, rightfully holds the record, and the other, the 1931 *Peludopolis*, is the first full-length cartoon talkie. *Snow White* is only the first full-length cartoon with both sound *and* color.

It is said that Snow White was the first and last animated heroine Disney drew himself. This is fascinating trivia, but extremely doubtful. If Walt hired others to draw Mickey Mouse or Donald Duck at a time when he could barely afford the cost, why, it is asked, would he have eschewed professional help for the more technically difficult *Snow White* when he was perfectly capable of paying for it? What seems more likely is that Disney crystallized the idea of Snow White in his mind and presented it to his artists, who then produced the film images that he later edited. Quite likely, this is also what he did for Cinderella, Alice and Sleeping Beauty, all of whom Disney created conceptually before they were fully executed by professional animators hired for the purpose.

4. It's not Cricket to Lie

Myth! In the story of Pinocchio, a whale swallows Geppetto and Jiminy is the cricket's name.

Jiminy is a cricket in Walt Disney's 1940 *Pinocchio*, about a puppet who becomes a boy, while Bambi is the title character in Disney's 1942 *Bambi*, about a fawn undergoing the travails of forest life. Despite animals that talk and the appearance of a fairy, neither fantasy can be called a fairy tale. *Pinocchio* is based on a story published in 1883 by the Italian author G. Lorenzini, whose pen name was Collodi, and *Bambi* is adapted from a1929 book written in German by Felix Salten.

Disney, as was his wont, deviated noticeably from the originals in producing both classics. In *Pinocchio*, the cricket uses a name that predates the film and has nothing to do with insects; Jiminy Cricket is believed to be an expression that originated in the American colonies as a roundabout way of invoking Jesus Christ.

358

Collodi's book gives no name to his character, which appears early on only to be smashed with a hammer by Pinocchio. The cricket's ghost appears later to offer the puppet guidance as he goes on his journeys. Pinocchio is completely turned into a donkey, sold in the market and forced to perform in a circus, and near the end rescues Geppetto from the belly of a shark, not a whale. He does not immediately turn into a boy after this deed, but still has to work for five months before his wish is granted.

In Disney's version, Bambi, who is often mistaken for a doe because of his name, is implied to be a denizen of North America, but in Salten's book, the story is set in the Black Forest of southern Germany. The excitement of the stag fight and the forest fire that highlight the movie is based on the book's descriptions, but the winning charm of the scene-stealing rabbit named Thumper can only come from the genius of Disney's art.

5. Four-finger Exercise

Myth! **Walt Disney was the first to draw Mickey Mouse.**

A persistent myth about Mickey is that Disney himself first drew him. In fact, the maestro never laid a hand on the Mouse—not in his first short cartoon or any later animated films, nor in any other medium. Disney may have originated the idea of Mickey and developed his world-renowned image—even supplying his squeaky voice in the first few cartoons—but someone else's artistry made the character visual. When Disney realized he would have trouble sketching the Mouse, he had asked his old friend from Kansas City, the relatively unknown Ubbe Ert Iwerks, to do the drawing. Ub Iwerks did the other characters as well, and became Disney's chief animator in the early days of the studio. Iwerks also started Mickey in the comics, but entrusted him later to his assistants.

6. Suspended Animation

Myth! Walt Disney's body was placed in deep freeze pursuant to his final wish.

No less than 40 people, members of the American Cryonics Society, have had their bodies frozen after death, and many more have committed themselves to this form of post-mortem disposition in hopes that they would someday be revived from their frozen state and restored to health. The science to support these hopes, called cryonics (or sometimes cryogenics), is still in the experimental stage, but its adherents stand by it on the ground that no cost is too big for the privilege of living life anew in the future.

There is a persistent rumor that Disney, who was known to have been preoccupied with death and whose funeral services were held in secret, availed of cryonics. An elaboration of the rumor insists that not only was Walt placed on ice, his body was deposited in some niche below the Pirates of the Caribbean exhibition at Disneyland. The truth, of course, is that Walt, who died of cancer of the left lung, was cremated on December 17, 1966, two days after his death. His ashes are kept at a site in the Forest Lawn cemetery's Court of Freedom section. How long Disney could have held out in deep freeze is anybody's guess, but many of the 40 in cryonic suspension, some of them millionaires, have already been thawed because their estates have run out of money

7. Sweet Sign of Success

Myth! The principal element in the Disney Studios logo is Walt's signature.

Alexander Korda, Samuel Goldwyn and Walt Disney are some of the movie moguls who have chosen to express their individualities through company logos brandishing their signatures. But in Disney's case at least, the evidence is misleading. While a casual observer might see the logo as a distinctive signature, closer analysis reveals it is actually fashioned from a standard script. Will Eisner, creator of The Spirit, a comic book superhero, signs his name on his work in much the same style, with the letters in common with those in Walt Disney— particularly the 'W'— being completely identical.

Some official sources have alleged that the Disney logo is a "stylization of its founder's signature" and is "a formulated version of it." Still, the Disney organization has not disclaimed (and most likely never will) that Disney had a signature totally different from the Disney logo appearing on all his products. "Ironically," says one source, "a number of people have thrown away authentically signed books and records (of Disney) under the impression that the autographs were fake." We don't know to what extent this statement is true, but logic strongly dictates that, for security and privacy reasons, Disney maintained a personal signature apart from the one that supported his public identity.

8. The Last Tycoon

Myth! **Darryl Zanuck was the last of Hollywood's big moguls.**

The last of Hollywood's big moguls wasn't any of the great studio chiefs who dominated movie filmdom's Golden Age. Rather, it was Walt Disney, who quietly headed one of the largest and most powerful entertainment conglomerates in the world until his death in 1966. The likes of David Selznick, Sam Goldwyn and Louie Mayer had quit the Hollywood scene long before Walt himself passed on, leaving the legacy of his vast enterprise to his brother Roy and some close associates. Ironically, the man is remembered not as a businessman but as the greatest cartoonist who ever lived. The witty style of most of his animations, and of Disney art in general, has given the impression that Walt built his fame and fortune on his artistic ability. The truth, according to Richard Schickel in *The Disney Version*, is that Disney couldn't draw anything, and had to rely completely on his stable of animators for his productions. Disney was better known for his

361

business savvy and the overall management of his varied enterprises, from movies and toys to amusement parks.

9. Toons of Glory

Myth! Mickey Mouse appeared in his first film *Steamboat Willie* after debuting in a comic strip.

Forget the thought that Mickey Mouse, like most other cartoon characters of the 20s and 30s, was born in a comic strip. The world's most popular rodent started in a black-and-white film, as did Felix the Cat, Donald Duck and Betty Boop. Although it is no longer uncommon for animation figures to get freeze-framed in comic books or strips after debuting in films, the trick during Mickey's salad days was how to get into print first. Print, which was more technically advanced than film, was the preferred medium of artists.

To set matters right, Mickey's hallowed career was not launched in the 1928 cartoon short *Steamboat Willie*, as is commonly believed. His initial appearance was in another short, *Plane Crazy*, which was made in 1927 but exhibited only in 1928 in the heels of *Steamboat Willie*. Having proved to Disney that sound, particularly music, could fit well into the animation, *Steamboat Willie* was released ahead of the silent *Plane Crazy*.

□□□

362

LIST OF TOPICS IN THIS VOLUME

ICONS & SYMBOLS

Wheeling And Dealing
Have Wheels, can't Travel
The Cart before the Horse
Walking for a Camel
Where There's a Wheel
Spin Story

Pyramid Schemes
Battle of the Pyramids
Old, Cold and Balled
Mister Sandman
Shape of Things Past
Time Sentinel
Forever Amber?
A Belabored Point

Japanned in Usa
Lacquered up and Ready to Go
Low-breed Hybrid
Chopsticks in four Hands
Does Karate Rate as Art?
Mighty Mites
On the Papyrus Trail
Chowhound's Delight
Messages from the Cookie Factory
Chinese Noodling at Work
Familiar Words in an Inscrutable Language

Key Noting An Event
Composed amid the Turmoil
Enemy Soil in Friendly Waters
They didn't Play it, Sam
Flagging Interests in Peacetime

364

Key Words of an Old Tune
All Through the Night
Double Standard
Rally Round the Flag, Boys
It didn't Fly
A Seamstress's Tale
Mourning Stripes
Connecting the Stars
Image Exposure
Burning Questions

Rebel Manifesto
Born on the 2nd of July
In Pursuit of Paul Revere
Signs of the Times
The Virginia in Sam's Past
The Deed is Gone
The Young Philadelphians
The Declarers were Trumped

Let Freedom Ring
For Whom the Bell Tolled
Cracked Symbol
Vying for the Lady's Favors
Lighting the Way Home
Belle de France
His own Sons call him Uncle
Flagg Waving the Draft
Elephant Man in Donkey Skin

The Objects Of Our Affection
Olympian Medical Staff
Wave Lengths and Band Widths
Cross of Iron
Veiled Prophet
Healing Mantra
All that Glitters
The Holy Grail of Sailors?
Flight in the Piazza
Phallic Symbols?
Names from the X-Files

365

Tools of a Clandestine Trade?
Club Europa
Jailhouse Rock
After the Flood
From both Sides Now
A Colossal Mistake
Sign of the Pagan
Roman Thumbers
Reformed Bastion

INSTITUTIONS

Invasion Of The Body Snatchers
Equal but Separate
Southern Comfort
Captive Resources
Unlocking the Cabin
A Dred-ful Decision
Better Nixed than Mixed
Under the Spanish Whip
Cry Freedom
African-American History X

Clash Of Colors
The Dreams of King
Black Man's Burden
Days of the Locust?
Scared Crow
Sub Rosa in Alabama
Crossing the Bar
Reversal of Fortunes

Strangers In Their Own Land
Don't ask How, just say How
Most Chiefs have Hatchet Men
Return of the Natives
Wampum Talk
Smoke Gets in your I's and U's
Um's the Word

Cardboard Indians
Scalping causes Permanent Hair Loss
The two Sides of Genocide
Give and Take in the Old West
Como Sabe 'Kemo Sabe'?
Tippling in the Tepees
How to Program a Pogrom
All Wet and Hot Air
Shout before you Chute
Forrest's Little Tree
The One with the Funny Haircut
Imitations of History
Squaw Guide for Explorers
Losing the Tent and Getting the Sack
The Crazies get the Monuments

Way Out West
West Point
City Slickers or Country Slackers?
Years of the Horse
Ride, Vaquero!
Not Suitable for a Pinhead
Bronco Bluster
Range of Colors
The Hip Shooter was a Deadwood
The Front in Frontier
Phony Express
Defense Circle
The Horseman called Death
New Kid on the Block

Invitation To A Beheading
Killed by his own Device
Cutting a Ridiculous Figure
Just a Pain in the Neck
Death in Small Pieces
Little but Lethal
Not a Capital Idea
Fry and Fry Again

BELIEFS & TRADITIONS

Brother, Can You Spare A Rib?
Madame, I'm Adam
Therein lies a Tail
Look, Ma, there's a Hole in my Tummy
Apple Polisher
Hey, Doc, there's a Lump in my Throat
A Tree grows in Eden
Curses!
Garden Variety
The Banishing Truth
Noah Connection
His son Seth
The Mark of Sorrow
Population Postulation
Abel is able but Cain can't

According To The Book
Solar Standoff
Blast from the Past
Soup Sale
Onan the Barbarian
Man for all Seasons
What is Truth
Technicolor Dream Coat
Game of Patience
He ain't Heavy, he's our Brother
A Lot of Salt
Stairway to Heaven
Old Boy
Gay City
Mountain Suspense
We're no Angels

Might And Mane
The Long and Short of Ancient Hairdos
The Hair is human, the Strength divine
That Philistine Woman

Shearing her Love
The Nagging Truth
Neither Hide nor Hair
Heir Head
The Seventh Veil
Harlot Times
The Bigger they Come

Moses With The Mostes'
The Burning Truth
Tribal Travel
Manna Matters
Grandpa Moses
Lambkill
Trinity is my Name
Plague with Doubts
Will the real Red Sea please Rise?
Repeat Performances
Lost Horizons

A Life To Live
Millennium Man
Imitation of Christ
Home away from Home
Astronomical Proportions
Goodwill Time
Presents for the Future
From May to December
Teen Bride
Three Men and a Baby
Religious Misconception
A Star is Born
T'was a Bumpy Night
Stable Condition

Superstar Bearing
A Face in the Crowd
Heavenly Creatures
The Greatest bar None
Sect Appeal
Sinking a Titanic Claim

In God's Name

The Third Day Prior
Dark Passage
Day of Wrath
Last Meal and Testament
Cross of Pain
Mortal Span
Damnation in two Doses
To Bear or not to Bear
Roman Indiction
The Tall T
The Easter after Eastre

Enter The Saints
Snake Charmer
Jack of Hearts
An Arrow Escape
In Good Shape
Truth of the Pater
Accidental Tourists
Hankering Hank
Intriguing Personality
The First Primates
Spiked Rumor
Hail, O Halo
Doubtful State

Jingle Bell Time
X'ian Holiday
Santa's Spare Tire
Knickerbocker Nick
More on Moore
Elves' Night
A Finite Claus
Deer Santa
Nick of Time
Gift Rapping
Tree of Heaven
Holiday on Ice

Chestnuts Roasting On A Fire
Loch up that Beast
A Piece of Blarney
Tut-tutting a Curse
Ghastly Ghosties
Hare Apparent
Horse Feathers
E.T. v. S.P.C.A.
A Ship that Passes in the Night
Loki Thirteen
Three on One Leaves None
Elfin Hand

Wizards Of Bosh
Man of Tomorrow
Doubling the Canon
Imperfect Vision
To the Ends of the Earth
Remembrances of Things Past
Oracular Demonstrations
What Dreams may Come
Water Prospectors
Mind Bender
Assembly Language Problem

SPORTS & DIVERSIONS

Sporting Lives
I'd Rather have a Hole-in-two
West to East to West
Missile on a String
Court Jesters weave Black Magic
Much Hoopla for a Dribble?
Some don't Finish at all
Par Excellence
Tenez L'oeuf, Anyone?
Golfing at their Peak
When They were Kings
Climb every Mountain
Ali Oops

371

Oft-Told Baseball Tales
The Diamond was Rounder then
Once they were Giants
Trying to Make a Point
Call me Babe, not Tootsie
The 60th Parallel
Of Shoes and Socks and Cabbages
The Play's the Thing
The Barefoot Batter from Brandon Mill
Washing some white Socks
Bearly Intelligible

Games Smart People Play
Trading on the Board
Kings go Forth
Playing by the Book
Another Game in Town
Raise, bet, Call bluff, Show hand, Draw check
How to Mate in Nine...Languages
Marbles and Chips
Casting Luck to the Four Winds
Go in Style
A Breaker hits the Banks

POP IMAGES

Bungle In The Jungle
Runts, Grunts, lying Lions and clinging Vines
Me and You and...
Starting a Family Tree
Planet Hollywood's big Apes
Swimmer to Swinger
That Chimp wasn't a Monkey's Uncle
He can Ape, but can he Yodel?

Out Of The Cold And Into A Dry Martini
High-priced European Bonds
Gilding a Broad
Two Teas make Beer better

Bonding Materials
The Spy who Nagged Me
FAQ for Q
Battling the Beasties
Is that a Gun in his Pocket?

Prometheus Unplugged
Beauty lands a Beast
Call me Adam
Screwed-up Character
Monster Billing
The Humor of Frankenstein
Dr. Frankensteen, I presume?
His Daddy was a Mummy
Whale's Brutes die Hard

A Trekkie's Guide To The Galaxy
Captains Courageous
Going Ago-go
Warp Notions
A Beam in his Eye
No Man's Land
A Philadelphia Story
Quirky, Kinky and Kirky
Fission Vision
Floppy Disk
Alien Farce
Science Friction

A Mild-Mannered Report On Superheroes
The Big Red One
American Splendor
This Red Cheese got Spoiled
This Old Steel gets Polished
One Dark Knight
Web Site
Shadow of his former Self

Don't Forget The Duck!
Give Mickey a big Hand
Mad about the Mouse

Dwarf Stars
It's not Cricket to Lie
Four-finger Exercise
Suspended Animation
Sweet Sign of Success
The Last Tycoon
Toons of Glory

SELECTED READINGS

Adams, Cecil, *The Straight Dope*, New York: Ballantine Books, 1986

Adams, Cecil, *More on the Straight Dope*, New York: Ballantine Books, 1988

Agel, Jerome and Glanze, Walter D., *Cleopatra's Nose, The Twinkie Defense, & 1500 Other Verbal Shortcuts in Popular Parlance*, New York: Prentice Hall Press, 1990

Alterman, Eric, *When Presidents Lie*, London: Penguin Books, 2004

Aron, Paul, *Unsolved Mysteries of History*, New York: Barnes & Noble Books, 2000

Aron, Paul, *More Unsolved Mysteries of History*, New York: Barnes & Noble, 2004

Aron, Paul, *Did Babe Ruth Call His Shot?*, New Jersey: John Wiley & Sons, 2005

Barham, Andrea, *The Pedant's Return*, New York: Bantam Books, 2006

Barthel, Manfred (translated by Howson, Mark), *What the Bible Really Says*, New York: Wings Books, 1992

Battle, Kemp P., *Great American Folklore*, New York: Barnes and Noble, 1992

Boardman, Barrington, *Flappers, Bootleggers, "Typhoid Mary" & the Bomb*, New York: Harper & Row, 1968

Boller, Jr., Paul F., *Presidential Anecdotes*, New York: Penguin Books, 1981

Boller, Jr., Paul F. and Davis, Ronald L., *Hollywood Anecdotes*, New York: William Morrow, 1987

Boller, Jr., Paul F. and George, John, *They Never Said It*, New York: Oxford University Press, 1990

Boller, Jr., Paul F., *Not So!*, New York: Oxford University Press, 1995

Boorstin, Daniel J., *The Discoverers*, New York: Random House, 1983

Boorstin, Daniel J., *The Creators*, New York: Random House, 1992

Breuer, William B., *Daring Missions of World War II*, New Jersey: Castle Books, 2001

Breuer, William B., *Deceptions of World War II*, New Jersey: Castle Books, 2001

Brokaw, Tom, *The Greatest Generation*, New York: Random House, 1998

Brown, Anthony Cave, *Bodyguard of Lies*, London: W. H. Allen & Co. Ltd., 1977

Brown, Peter H. and Pinkston, Jim, *Oscar Dearest*, New York: Harper & Row, 1987

Botting, Douglas & the Editors of Time-Life Books, *The Pirates*, Virginia: Time-Life Books, 1978

Bullis, Don, *The Old West Trivia Book*, California: Gem Guides Book Company, 1993

Carnes, Mark C. (ed.), *Past Imperfect,* New York: Henry Holt and Company, 1996

Cole, Sylvia & Lass, Abraham H., *The Dictionary of 20th-Century Allusions*, New York: Ballantine Books, 1991

Cowley, Robert (ed.), *What Ifs? Of American History,* New York: G.P. Putnam's Sons, 2003

Craughwell, Thomas J., *Urban Legends,* New York: Barnes & Noble, 2000

Crofton, Ian, *Brewer's Cabinet Of Curiosities,* London: Weidenfeld & Nicolson, 2006

Davis, Kenneth C., *Don't Know Much About History*, New York: Avon Books, 1992

Davis, Kenneth C., *Don't Know Much About Geography*, New York: Avon Books, 1993

Davis, Kenneth C., *Don't Know Much About Mythology*, New York: Harper, 2005

Davis, Kenneth C., *Don't Know Much About World Myths,* New York: HarperCollins, 2005

Davis, Kenneth C., *Don't Know Much About Anything,* New York: Harper, 2007

Del Re, Gerard & Patricia, *History's Last Stand*, New York: Avon Books, 1993

Dickson, Paul & Goulden, Joseph C., *Myth-Informed*, New York: Putnam Publishing, 1993

Diefendorf, David, *Amazing...But False!,* New York: Sterling, 2007

Donald, David Herbert, *Lincoln*, London: Jonathan Cape, 1995

Durant, Will, *Caesar and Christ*, New York: Simon and Schuster, 1944

Durant, Will, *The Age of Faith*, New York: Simon and Schuster, 1950

Durschmied, Erik, *How Chance And Stupidity Have Changed History,* New York: MJF Books, 1999

Eastman, John, *Retakes*, New York: Ballantine Books, 1989

Editors of Time-Life Books, The, *Visions and Prophecies*, Virginia: Time-Life Books, 1988

Editors of Time-Life Books, The, *Feats and Wisdom of the Ancients*, Virginia: Time-Life Books, 1990

Evans, Harold, *They Made America*, New York: Back Bay Books, 2004

Evans, Ivor H., *Brewer's Dictionary of Phrase and Fable*, New York: HarperCollins, 1991

Farquhar, Michael, *A Treasury of Deception,* New York: Penguin, 2005

Farquhar, Michael, *A Treasury Of Foolishly Forgotten Americans,* New York: Penguin, 2008

Feldman, David, *Why Do Pirates Love Parrots*, New York: Collins, 2007

Filler, Louis, *The Muckrakers*, Chicago: Henry Regnery Company, 1968

Flexner, Stuart Berg, *Listening to America*, New York: Simon & Schuster, 1982

Flexner, Stuart and Doris, *The Pessimist's Guide to History*, New York: HarperCollins, 2000

Fox, Robin Lane, *The Unauthorized Version*, New York: Vintage Books, 1993

Funk, Charles Earle, *Thereby Hangs A Tale*, New York: Harper & Row, 1985

Gardner, Martin, *The Magic Numbers of Dr. Matrix*, New York: Dorset Press, 1990

Gardner, Martin, *Science Good, Bad and Bogus*, Buffalo: Prometheus Books, 1989

Garrison, Webb, *Behind the Headlines*, Harrisburg: Stackpole Books, 1983

Garrison, Webb, *A Treasury of White House Tales*, Nashville: Rutledge Hill Press, 1996

Gentry, Curt, *J. Edgar Hoover*, New York: W.W. Norton & Co., 1991

Goldberg, M. Hirsch, *The Book of Lies*, New York: Quill / William Morrow, 1990

Gore, Chris, *The 50 Greatest Movies Never Made*, New York: St. Martin's Griffin, 1999

Gottlieb, Agnes Hooper et al., *1000 Years, 1000 People,* New York: Barnes & Noble, 199

Graham, Lloyd M., *Deceptions and Myths of the Bible*, New York: Citadel Press, 1975

Greenberg, Gary, *101 Myths of the Bible,* New York: Barnes & Noble, 2000

Greig, Charlotte, *Conspiracy,* New York: Barnes & Noble, 2003

Gribbin, John, *The Scientists,* New York: Random House, 2002

Griffin, Lynne & McCann, Kelly, *The Book of Women*, Maine: Bob Adams, 1992

Haining, Peter, ed., *A Sherlock Holmes Companion*, New York: Barnes & Noble, 1994

Hamilton, Edith , *Mythology*, Boston: Little, Brown and Co., 1942

Handford, S.A. (transl.), *The Fables of Aesop*, London: Penguin Books, 1964

Hardwick, Michael, *The Complete Guide to Sherlock Holmes*, New York: St. Martin's Press, 1986

Hay, Peter, *Movie Anecdotes*, New York: Oxford University Press, 1990

Haycraft, Howard (ed.), *The Art of the Mystery Story*, New York: Grosset & Dunlap, 1946

Haycraft, Howard, *Murder for Pleasure*, New York: Carroll & Graf Publishers: 1984

Hayward, James, *Myths & Legends of the Second World War*, Stroud,

Sutton Publishing, 2003

Hendrickson, Robert, *World Literary Anecdotes*, New York: Facts on File, 1990

Hendrickson, Robert, *American Literary Anecdotes*, New York: Facts on File, 1990

Hendrickson, Robert, *British Literary Anecdotes*, New York: Facts on File, 1990

Herbert, A. P., *Uncommon Law*, London: Methuen & Co., 1964

Hersch, Hank and Bechtel, Mark, *Classic Rivalries*, New York: Sports Illustrated Books, 2003

Holden, Anthony, *Behind the Oscar*, New York: Plume, 1993

Holland, Barbara, *Hail to the Chiefs*, New York: Ballantine Books, 1990

Holt, Patricia Lee, *George Washington Had No Middle Name*, New Jersey: Citadel Press, 1988

Innes, Brian, *Fakes & Forgeries*, New York: Reader's Digest, 2005

Isaacson, Walter, *Pro & Con*, New York: G. P. Putnam's Sons: 1983

Jackson, Robert, *Unexplained Mysteries of World War II*, New York: Gallery Books, 1991

Jeffers, H. Paul, *History's Greatest Conspiracies*, New York: Barnes & Noble, 2004

Jennings, Peter & Brewster, Todd, *In Search of America*, New York: Hyperion, 2002

Johnsen, Ferris, *The Encyclopedia of Popular Misconceptions*, New York: Carol Publishing, 1994

Johnson, Paul, *Modern Times*, New York: Harper Collins, 1991

Jones, Judy and Wilson, William, *An Incomplete Education*, New York: Ballantine Books, 1987

Kahn, David, *The Code-Breakers*, London: Weidenfeld and Nicolson, 1967

Kerr, Philip, ed., *The Penguin Book of Lies*, London: Viking Press, 1990

Keyes, Ralph, *"Nice Guys Finish Seventh,"* New York: Harper Perennial, 1993

Kick, Russ, *You Are Being Lied To*, New York: MJF Books, 2001

Kick, Russ, *Everything You Know Is Wrong*, New York: Barnes & Noble Books, 2002

Lane, Sheldon, ed., *For Bond Lovers Only*, New York: Dell Publishing, 1965

Lass, Abraham H., Kiremidjian, David & Goldstein, Ruth M., *Dictionary of Classical, Biblical, & Literary Allusions*, New York: Ballantine Books, 1988

Leighton, Isabel, ed., *The Aspirin Age*, 1919-1941, New York: Simon and Schuster, 1965

Lindskoog, Kathryn, *Fakes, Frauds & Other Malarkey*, Grand Rapids: Zondervan Publishing House, 1993

Llewellyn, Sam, *Small Parts In History*, New York: Barnes & Noble,

1992

Lloyd, John & Mitchinson, John, *The Book Of General Ignorance,* New York: Harmony Books, 2006

Loewen, James, *Lies My Teacher Told Me*, New York: Simon & Schuster, 1995

Loewen, James, *Lies Across America*, New York: Touchstone, 1999

Lorie, Peter, *Superstitions,* New York: Simon & Schuster, 1992

Macrone, Michael, *By Jove!,* New York: HarperCollins, 1992

Macrone, Michael, *Brush Up Your Shakespeare!,* New York: Harper Collins, 1990

Magee, Bryan, *The Story Of Philosophy,* New York: Barnes & Noble, 2006

Manser, Martin, *Melba Toast, Bowie's Knife & Caesar's Wife*, New York: Avon Books, 1990

Matthews, John, *Pirates*, London: Carlton Books, 2006

McCullough, David, *Truman*, New York: Simon & Schuster, 1992

Montagu, Ashley and Darling, Edward, *The Prevalence of Nonsense*, New York: Dell, 1969

Moore, Laurence, *Lightning Never Strikes Twice*, New York: Avon Books, 1994

Morrow, Ed, *The Grim Reaper's Book of Days*, New York: Carol Publishing Group, 1992

Most, Glenn W. and Stowe, William W. (eds.), *The Poetics of Murder*, New York: Harcourt Brace, 1983

Nash, J. Robert, *Darkest Hours*, New York: Simon & Schuster, 1977

National Insecurity Council, The, *It's A Conspiracy!*, Berkeley: Earth Works Press, 1992

Opie, Iona & Peter, *Classic Fairy Tales*, New York: Oxford University Press, 1980

Page, Michael & Ingpen, Robert, *The Time-Life Encyclopedia of Things That Never Were*, Virginia: Time-Life Books, 1988

Panati, Charles, *Panati's Extraordinary Origins of Everyday Things*, New York: Harper & Row, 1989

Panati, Charles, *Sacred Origins Of Profound Things,* New York: Penguin, 1996

Pappas, Theoni, *The Joy of Mathematics*, California: Wide World Publishing / Tetra, 1989

Pappas, Theoni, *Mathematical Scandals*, California: Wide World Publishing/Tetra, 1997

Pearson, John, *James Bond*, London: Colins Publishing, 1986

Perkes, Dan, *Eyewitness to Disaster*, New York: Gallery Books, 1985

Platnick, Kenneth B., *Great Mysteries of History*, New York: Dorset Press, 1987

Poirier, René (transl. by Crosland, Margaret), *Engineering Wonders of the World*, New York: Barnes & Noble, 1993

Poundstone, William, *Big Secrets*, New York: Quill, 1983

Poundstone, William, *Bigger Secrets*, Boston: Houghton Mifflin Company, 1986

Poundstone, William, *Biggest Secrets*, New York: William Morrow & Co,. 1993

Powell, Michael, *Forbidden Knowledge*, Massachusetts: Adams Media, 2007

Randi, James, *Flim-Flam!*, New York: Prometheus, 1982

Rawson, Hugh, *Devious Derivations*, New York: Crown Publishers, 1994

Reader's Digest, The, *Great Cases of Interpol*, Hong Kong: Reader's Digest, 1982

Reader's Digest, The, *Facts & Fallacies*, New York: The Reader's Digest Association, 1988

Rees, Nigel, *The Nigel Rees Book of Slogans & Catchphrases*, London, Unwin Paperbacks, 1984

Rees, Nigel, *A Word in your Shell-like, London: Trafalgar Square, 2007*

Roberts, Andrew (ed.), *What Might Have Been*, London: Phoenix, 2005

Robertson, Patrick, *The Guinness Book of Movie Facts & Feats*, New York: Abbeville Press, 1991

Rogers, Tom, *Insultingly Stupid Movie Physics*, Naperville: Sourcebooks Hysteria, 2007

Rosenbaum, Ron, *Travels with Dr. Death*, New York: Penguin Books, 1991

Rosenberg, Bernard & White, David Manning, eds., *Mass Culture: The Popular Arts in America*, London: Collier-Macmillan, 1964

Rowan, Richard Wilmer, *33 Centuries of Espionage*, New York: Hawthorn Books, 1967

Rowse, A. L., *William Shakespeare*, New York: Harper & Row, 1963

Sanders, Dennis & Lovallo, Len, *The Agatha Christie Companion*, New York: Berkley Books, 1989

Sanello, Frank, *Reel v. Real*, New York: Taylor Trade Publishing, 2003

Shenkman, Richard & Reiger, Kurt, *One-Night Stands with American History*, New York: Quill, 1982

Shenkman, Richard, *Legends, Lies & Cherished Myths of American History*, New York: Harper & Row, 1988

Shenkman, Richard, *Legends, Lies & Cherished Myths of World History*, New York: Harper Collins, 1993

Shirer, William L., *The Rise and Fall of the Third Reich*, New York: Exeter Books, 1987

Stewart, Desmond and the Time-Life Editors, *Early Islam*, New York: Time-Life Books, 1972

Tamarkin, Bob, *Rumor Has It*, New York: Prentice Hall, 1993

Thornton, Willis, *History: Fact & Fable*, New York: Dorset Press, 1992

Tiballs, Geof, *The Olympics' Strangest Moments*, London: Robson

Books, 2004

Tuleja, Tad, *Fabulous Fallacies*, New York: Harmony Books, 1982

Vankin, Jonathan and Whalen, John, *Based On A True Story*, Chicago: Chicago Review Press, 2005

Walker, Barbara G., *Woman's Encyclopedia of Myths and Secrets*, San Francisco: Harper & Row, 1983

Wallace, Robert and the Editors of Time-Life Books, *World of Leonardo*, New York: Time, 1966

Wallace, Robert and the Editors of Time-Life Books, *World of Rembrandt*, New York: Time, 1968

Ward, Philip, *Panama Hats, Crocodile Tears and Other Common Fallacies*, New York: Barnes & Noble, 1993

Wecter, Dixon, *The Hero in America*, Michigan: The University of Michigan Press, 1963

Weir, Stephen, *History's Worst Decisions*, New York: Metro Books, 2009

West, Nigel, *A Thread of Deceit*, New York: Random House, 1985

Whitehouse, Arch, *Espionage and Counterespionage*, New York: Doubleday, 1964

Wiley, Mason and Bona, Damien, *Inside Oscar*, New York: Ballantine Books, 1988

Williams, Hywel, *Days That Changed The World*, London: Quercus, 2006

Wills, Gary, *What Jesus Meant*, New York: Penguin Books, 2007

Winter, Gordon and Kochman, Wendy, *Secrets of the Royals*, New York: St. Martin's Press: 1990

Wise, David and Ross, Thomas B., *The Invisible Government*, New York: Bantam Book, 1964

Wright, Mike, *What They Didn't Teach You About The 60s*, California: Presidio, 2001

Zich, Arthur, and the Time-Life eds., *The Rising Sun* (World War II), Alexandria: Time-Life Books, 1978

———*Mysteries of Mind, Space & Time*, Westport, Conn: H. S. Stuttman Inc., 1992

———*The New Encyclopedia Britannica*, 15th Ed., Chicago: Encyclopedia Britannica, 1994

———*The Truth About History*, New York: Barnes & Noble, 2